A DIRECTORY OF
EDINBURGH
—— IN ——
1752

A DIRECTORY OF EDINBURGH
—— IN ——
1752

COMPILED BY
J. GILHOOLEY

EDINBURGH UNIVERSITY PRESS

© James Gilhooley 1988
Edinburgh University Press
22 George Square, Edinburgh

Set in CRTronic Times Roman
by Polyprint, Edinburgh and
printed in Great Britain by
Redwood Burn Limited
Trowbridge, Wilts

British Library Cataloguing
  in Publication Data
Gilhooley, James
A Directory of Edinburgh in 1752.
1. Edinburgh, 1727-1760
I. Title
941.3'4072
ISBN 0 85224 595 5

CONTENTS

Introduction	vii
a. Public Servants	xi
b. Population Statistics	xiv
The Directory	1
a. A-Z	3
b. Residents: Close by Close	57
Trade Directory	83
a. A-Z	85
b. Apprentices and Masters	102
Street Guide and Maps	107

INTRODUCTION

(a) Public Servants
(b) Population Statistics

INTRODUCTION

PLANS for the urban growth of Edinburgh beyond the stifling confines of the city's Flodden Wall had been the subject of much debate and speculation long before Daniel Defoe gave voice to the city's location and potential in 1727. From his book "A Tour through the Whole Island of Great Britain":-

... "By this means the City suffers infinite disadvantages, and lies under such scandalous inconveniences as are, by its enemies, made a subject of scorn and reproach; as if the people were not as willing to live sweet and clean as other Nations, but delighted in Stench and Nastiness, whereas, were any other People to live under the same management. I mean as well of a rocky and mountainous Situation, throng'd Buildings, from seven to ten or twelve Storey high, a Scarcity of Water, and that little they have difficult to be had, and to the uppermost Lodgings, far to fetch; we should have a London or a Bristol as dirty as Edinburgh, and, perhaps, less able to make their Dwelling tolerable, at least in so narrow a Compass; for, tho' many Cities have more people in them, yet, I believe, this may be said with Truth, that in no City in the World live in so little Room as at Edinburgh.

"On the North Side of the City, as is said above, is a spacious, rich and pleasant Plain, extending from the Lough, which (as above) joins the City, to the river of Leith, at the Mouth of which is the town of Leith, at the Distance of a long Scots Mile from the City: and even here, were not the North Side of the Hill, which the City stands on, so exceeding steep, as hardly, (at least to the Westward of their Fleshmarket) to be clamber'd up on Foot, much less to be made passable for Carriages. But, I say, were it not so steep, and were the Lough fill'd up, as it might easily be, the City might have been extended upon the Plain below, and fine beautiful Streets would, no doubt, have been built there; nay, I question much whether in Time, the high Streets would not have been forsaken, and the City, as we might say, run all out of its Gates to the North".

This was less a prophecy than a statement of what common sense would have dictated were the citizens of Edinburgh not instinctively disinclined to abandon the security of the Old Town's situation and its surrounding wall. Hundreds of years and generations of clinging to the city's natural defences in the face of enemies, sporadically real and constantly imagined, had created a genetic strain that was not about to respond to any outsider's common sense suggestions — and an Englishman at that! The absurdity of the situation became manifestly apparent in September 1745 when the city's defences and wall were put to their first real test with the approach of Bonnie Prince Charlie's Jacobite Army. Despite the most frenzied efforts of the University's professor of Mathematics, Colin MacLaurin, it became very evident that the city's defensive capacity was simply not matched to the demands of modern siege warfare or frontal attack. Citizens' views vis-a-vis their huddled defensive situation and the obviously disgusting living conditions that this created were, post 1745, ready for change. Daniel Defoe's views began to make sense after all, and, after a period of re-assembling the political wreckage of the Jacobite upheavals, plans were set afoot to expand the City beyond the malodorous limits of the Old Town. On completion of the first project, building of the "Royal Exchange" [today's City Chambers] — an obscure priority which never gained any popularity with the merchants it was built to serve — work commenced on removing the two obstacles to Defoe's vision of the expanded city. — Draining the Nor' Loch and building a negotiable connection between the Old Town and the site of the New: the North Bridge.

These plans were finalised in 1752, set in motion during the following year and continued virtually unabated for more than a century. A Directory of Edinburgh for the year 1752 is not, therefore, a random selection, it was the year when the city decided to shrug off what were essentially medieval social conditions and habits to encompass a whole new spectrum of values and ideas. — It is not without significance that the period marks the emergence of Scotland as a centre of brilliance in every branch of the arts and sciences during the 18th Century Enlightenment.

Edinburgh's improvement programme, however much welcomed and however desperately needed, also served to demonstrate some fundamental weaknesses of social engineering which persist to the present day. This programme, while solving, for some, the problems of overcrowding and inadequate housing also served to destroy a socio-ecological balance which, as a result of enforced propinquity, found the landed gentry sharing common stair or entry with the labourer. In short, Edinburgh's Old Town was a community where people knew their places in the social order but where social barriers were virtually unknown. Drink also had a lot to do with it.

The sense of community in Old Town Edinburgh is well conveyed in the following report from the Scots Magazine of February 1771. Twenty years removed from the date of the Directory it nevertheless reflects with great accuracy some aspects of eighteenth-century Edinburgh life — social order within the tenements, selfless co-operation from almost every segment of the community, the sophistication of early communications (a fire-engine from Leith!), and that the Edinburgh criminal element has remained unremittingly soulless for centuries. The populace was responding to Edinburgh's perennial source of communal fear — fire. There was no disaster, natural or otherwise, that could inspire so much panic in the breasts of Edinburgh as the prospect of furnace-like infernos rushing through the narrow vennels and closes of the town's usually inaccessible back-lands. Fortunately, this one was in the Lawnmarket what is now George IV Bridge facing Bank Street (in the Directory at 'A' on page 78).

"On Saturday, Jan. 26. between five and six o'clock at night, a fire broke out in the garret-storey of Buchanan's tenement, on the fourth side of the Lawnmarket, at the head of the Old-Bank close, Edinburgh. It was discovered by the flames bursting through the roof, and at first seemed to threaten destruction to all that quarter of the city. Notwithstanding every attempt to check its progress, it soon communicated to the storey below, and burnt with great violence. Here it baffled the efforts of three fire engines, which played incessantly upon it both in front and towards the back part, besides the most active exertions of a number of workmen, wrights, smiths, masons, soldiers, etc many of whom resolutely, or rather rashly, exposed themselves in tearing down the linings, and most combustible parts of the houses, which were thrown over the windows; but all proved ineffectual to stop the conflagration. It descended with great rapidity from storey to storey, till it reached the shops; and even there it was not entirely quenched till Sunday morning about eight o'clock. Providentially the wind blew from the west, which circumstance proved the means of preserving a large front timber tenement to the westward of the fire. The danger appeared so great, and the prospect, from the raging of the flames, so dismal, that it was for a long time doubtful where it might stop; which induced most of the inhabitants of the adjacent buildings to remove their furniture and effects; by which many sustained a great loss. The fire was, however, luckily confined within the walls of the tenement where it began. The city-engines being not in good repair, the defect was happily supplied by the timely arrival of one from Leith, which did great execution. The brewers were of great service, who voluntarily sent their servants and horses with carts loaded with casks of water for the engines. — The houses that suffered on this melancholy occasion, were possessed as follows, viz. the shops by Messrs. Dalgleish and Henderson, grocers, and Mr Ronaldson, baker; the first storey, by General Lockhart of Carnwath, the second storey, by Mrs Porterfield; the third, by Mr Ilay Campbell, advocate; the fourth, by Mr John Bell writer to the Signet; the fifth, by John Hume, Esq; of Ninewells; and the garret, where the fire began, by Gen. Lockhart's servants, to whose carelessness this catastrophe is imputed.

"One Robertson, a cadie, and Mitchel, a house-carpenter, who had exerted themselves very strenuously, perished in the flames. Their bodies were found the next day, and on Monday the funeral was attended by the magistrates and a number of the inhabitants. Many others were greatly bruised and scorched, of whom the magistrates had ordered particular care to be taken.

"The New Church and Weigh-house were opened during the fire, for the reception of goods and furniture belonging to the sufferers, and to the inhabitants of the adjacent buildings which were kept under a guard till Tuesday, and then delivered to the owners at sight of a magistrate; yet it is said great loss has been sustained by pilfering on this occasion.

"On the discovery of the fire which was observed from the parade in the castle, forty soldiers of the 22nd regiment dressed themselves in short jackets and caps, and voluntarily offered to assist extinguishing the flames: their generous offer was accepted, and also a guard of sixty men under arms. Most of the officers of that regiment likewise gave their attendance; and Mr Wemyss, Lieutenant-Governor, ordered the workmen to be supplied with axes, shovels, taken from the stores in the castle. — In short, a general spirit of emulation prevailed among all ranks to assist the unhappy sufferers, and such as appeared, from the situation, to be in danger; of which a noble example was set by the magistrates.

"The loss of the houses and furniture, it is computed, will amount to upwards of five thousand pounds; two thousand of which was insured in the Edinburgh Friendly Insurance-office; and we are told, that this office has paid in to the magistrates twenty guineas, to be distributed with the town's bounty, to the brewers' servants, firemen, military, &tc. &tc. who exerted themselves in extinguishing the flames; we likewise hear, that the workmen belonging to the Leith fire-engine (which was chiefly instrumental in preventing the fire from spreading), will be rewarded as they deserve. — The Old Bank has also generously rewarded those who contributed their assistance in removing the Bank-effects to their vaults, which are fire-proof.

"The greatest sufferer, with regard to the loss of furniture, appears to have been Mr Hume of Ninewells, his house being more immediately exposed to the first ravage of the flames. Happily, however, he recovered a trunk, or strong box, containing some very valuable papers".

(Scots Magazine February 1771 pages 108-109)

The Political Scene
Universal suffrage was unknown and, to those in charge, unthinkable in eighteenth-century Edinburgh. The city, its institutions, churches, the University and the Infirmary were all under the control of the City Council, and the City Council was elected exclusively from the ranks of the merchant and trade burgesses and guild-brothers. These totalled on average 1200 persons — 500 merchants and 700 tradesmen whose numbers were controlled by the council, primarily by monitoring the numbers of apprentices who could be indentured each year and the number allowed to practice in the city upon completion of the apprenticeship. Thus, in 1746, when Edinburgh had no city government after the Jacobite occupation, no apprentices were indentured.

By modern standards of suffrage, the 1200 members of Edinburgh's "electorate" represented less than ten per cent of the total poll and given the opportunities for advancement, patronage and nepotism that this system offered, the privileges of membership were very closely guarded indeed. Out of 33 council members, 17 were from the merchants' ranks and were usually selected by the preceding or out-going council. The trade councillors, Council Deacons and extraordinary Deacons although theoretically freely elected to represent the interests of their various trade guilds were restricted to a short list of three candidates each of whom had to have the approval of the sitting council. Power in the city was almost absolute, and in the hands of a very small number of very highly privileged people.

Edinburgh's member of Parliament was elected solely by the City Council whose 33 members were taken to be representative of the views of the whole 1200 electorate. It was customary almost automatically to elect the Lord

Provost to this position which, in the life of the existing 1752 Parliament would have seen Lord Provost George Drummond as the incumbent after election in 1747. He was unanimously rejected for the post on the grounds of being neither a merchant nor a resident of Edinburgh (circumstances which should also have excluded him from the Lord Provost's ermine). His place was taken by William Keir, Trades Convener and Deacon of the Baxters.

Meantime, the disenfranchised had little or no recourse to democratic expression of their wishes and would take to the streets over any issue of public concern that was not receiving appropriate attention from the City fathers. Rioting was a finely-honed instrument of public protest and it was a rare year that passed without some issue, from meal prices to grave robbing, giving rise to wild public disorder. However, the transition from the Julian to the Gregorian calendar which removed 11 days from September 1752 passed without incident despite the disquiet and rioting that took place in England.

Population Statistics
The population statistics for Edinburgh within the city wall have been mathematically derived from the Bills of Mortality which were published monthly between 1740 and 1756 in the Scots Magazine. These statistics provide details of deaths in the City by age and cause and, apart from the inaccuracies surrounding the horrendous level of infant mortality, demonstrate remarkable consistency over the sixteen-year period.

For the whole city, including the West Kirk Parish, the derived population for 1752 is 31,430 (Rev Alexander Webster's estimate in 1755 was 31,120) and for the area within the wall, 23,568. Approximately 75 per cent of this population is represented by the households listed in this Directory.

Not included in either this Directory or the available statistics is any figure for the great number of vagrants and itinerants who were a a constant source of irritation to the city authorities. Attempts to licence beggars in the early 1740s had been only temporarily successful and the city was constantly plagued by small bands of professional beggars coming in from their dens to the south and east.

The only reliable source of information on the city poor is contained in the annual report of the Charity Workhouse which however, catered only for the "deserving poor" and at the Paul's Wark annex in Leith Wynd for those under some kind of detention. It is interesting to note that whereas a City Council of 33 members was deemed sufficient to govern Edinburgh, it took a 92-member board of managers to oversee the activities of the Charity Workhouse.

Window Tax and Annuity Tax Rolls
The greater part of this Directory has been drawn from the records held in Register House and the Edinburgh City Archives of tax rolls for Window and Annuity taxes respectively. These provide not only the names and addresses of householders, they allow a certain level of analysis into the social standing of people and areas within the city.

Window tax was charged on a sliding scale:-

0-9	windows	no charge
10-14	windows	6d /annum/window
15-19	windows	9d /annum/window
20+	windows	1/- /annum/window

By window is meant "lights" or panes of glass which allowed natural light into a habitable area. First introduced in the late 1740s this system of taxation (or rate collection) persisted until 1795 when Old Town overcrowding had reversed the fundamental principle of windows per family to one of families per window.

Window tax was levied on the property owner who need not necessarily have been the occupant or householder.

Annuity tax was levied on all householders — with exceptions for those already paid from the public purse, such as Ministers, some city employees and pensioners, according to the size of the household and very often according to their means. The Annuity Roll is peppered with the assessors' comments on the straitened circumstances of particular households which although not exempt were clearly not expected to pay.

Armed with this information on the background to both the Annuity and Window taxes, it is possible to make some approximate judgements on the status of the householder or property owner.

1 Any person appearing on both Window Tax and Annuity Tax Rolls is generally both the owner of the property and the occupier. i.e. Owner/occupier of property with more than 10 windows.

2 Any person appearing only on the Window Tax Roll is generally a property owner who lives elsewhere (or is exempt from the Annuity Tax). i.e. Owner of property with more than 10 windows.

3 Any person appearing only on the Annuity Tax Roll is a householder who is either the owner/occupier or a tenant. i.e. Owner/occupier or tenant of a property with fewer than 10 windows.

These divisions have been marked in the geographic guide to the closes and their occupants as follows:

1	(11)	Mrs Frances Grant
	(10)	Wm McGhie, Writer
2	(13)	Archibald Murray
	(13)	Archibald Campbell, W.S.
3		Wm Govan, Glazier
		David Grahame, Barber
		Thos Mitchell, Jeweller
		Jas Linday, Tobacconist
		Angus Sinclair, Ale Seller
		John Scotland, Bookbinder

The bracketed numbers indicate the number of taxed windows and serve to indicate the size of the property involved.

Acknowledgements
This Directory could not have been completed without the co-operation and frequently patient assistance of many people in various places throughout Edinburgh — too many to mention all by name but my heartfelt thanks go out to my friends at the Scottish Records and Office at Register House, the City Archivist at the Edinburgh City Chambers, all of the staff in the Edinburgh Room at the Central Library, George IV Bridge, Edinburgh.

(a) PUBLIC SERVANTS

i. EDINBURGH CITY COUNCIL 1751-1752

Office	Elected September 1751	Elected September 1752
LORD PROVOST:	GEORGE DRUMMOND	WILLIAM ALEXANDER
BAILLIES:	John Brown Alexander Scot* Robert Fleming Patrick Lindsay	Robert Montgomery James Grant Alexander Grant James Rochead
DEAN OF GUILD: TREASURER:	James Stuart William Sands	David Flint Adam Fairholm
OLD PROVOST: OLD BAILLIES:	William Alexander Alexander Kincaid Andrew Wardrop William Tod jr. John Carmichael	George Drummond John Brown James Milroy Robert Fleming Patrick Lindsay
OLD DEAN OF GUILD: OLD TREASURER:	David Flint Adam Fairholm	James Stuart William Sands
MERCHANT COUNCILLORS:	George Lind Robert Cleugh James Rochead	Gilbert Laurie John Walker Alexander Donaldson
TRADE COUNCILLORS:	Robert Gordon William Dempster	James Ker James Mitchelson
COUNCIL DEACONS:	James Ker (Convener) George Cunningham William Keir Patrick Lawson James McDouall William Dickson	James Russell Alexander Cleugh Thomas Simpson John Moubray Patrick Jameson William Keir
EXTRAORDINARY COUNCIL DEACONS:	Alexander Cleugh John Fairholm Thomas Simpson John Moubray Patrick Jameson Robert Brown James Williamson Archibald Gibson	William Gilchrist George Pringle William Sibbald James Williamson Stephen Ronaldson Patrick Fairlie John Millar Robert Wight

* Retired through ill-health 6/11/51
  replaced by James Milroy.

ii. CITY OFFICIALS 1752-1753

Sheriff's Officers	Patrick Burns	Keeper of Tolbooth	James Rob
	William Johnstone	Clapman	Robert Ramsay
	James Scott	Letter Carrier	William Hill
Hangman	John Dalgleish		

Constables elected April 29 1752

David Somervail	Merchant	Andrew McArra	Merchant
Adam Murray	Baxter	Andrew Hardie	Baxter
Robert Williamson	Merchant	Alexander Burton	Glazier
Patrick Drummond	Merchant	Angus McPherson	Taylor
Francis Jaffrey	Wigmaker	Peter Walter	Taylor
Archibald McCoull	Merchant	James Wotherspoon	Weaver
James Robertson	Merchant	William Smith	Merchant
George Dunsmuir	Merchant	Walter Scott	Baxter
Alexander Dickson	Glazier	James Dalgleish	Merchant
David Paterson	Merchant	John Barclay	Merchant
Robert Russell	Merchant	Robert Dewar	Glazier
John Ronaldson	Merchant	James White	Wigmaker
John Bell	Baxter	William Lauder	Staymaker
William Fettes	Merchant	William Murray	Merchant

iii. NEW TOWN DIRECTORS

A. APPOINTED AUGUST 1752

1. The Lords of Session:
The Rt. Hon. the Lord President
The Hon. the Lord Minto
The Hon. the Lord Drummore

2. The Barons of Exchequer:
The Rt. Hon. the Lord Chief Baron
The Hon. Baron Maule

3. The Faculty of Advocates:
Robert Dundas; Dean of Faculty
Alexander Boswall
Gilbert Elliot

4. Clerks to the Signet:
Alexander McMillan; Keeper of Signet
Hew Crawford
John McKenzie

5. The Town Council of Edinburgh:

	For the time being
The Lord Provost:	George Drummond
Baillie:	John Brown
Dean of Guild:	James Stuart
Old Dean of Guild:	David Flint
Old Baillie:	Alexander Kincaid
Convener:	James Ker
Baxters' Deacon:	William Keir
Merchant:	Alexander Sharp
Old Provost:	William Alexander
Treasurer:	William Sands
Late Baillie:	Gavin Hamilton
Surgeons' Deacon:	George Cunningham

B. 10 Directors chosen by the SUBSCRIBERS: APPOINTED NOVEMBER 1752

Duke of Hamilton	Lord Milton
Duke of Argylle	The Lord Justice Clerk (Charles Erskine)
Marquis of Tweeddale	Sir Alex. Dick of Prestonfield
Earl of Morton	James Dewar of Vogrie
Earl of Hopetoun	John Forrest, Merchant in Edinburgh

iv. CHARITY WORKHOUSE

ANNUAL GENERAL MEETING 28 JULY 1752

Managers for the year 1752-53

For the City
LORD PROVOST: George Drummond
BAILLIES: John Brown
James Milroy
Robert Fleming
Patrick Lindsay
DEAN OF GUILD: James Stuart
TREASURER: William Sands
OLD PROVOST: William Alexander
OLD BAILIES: Alexander Kincaid
OLD DEAN OF GUILD: David Flint
OLD TREASURER: Adam Fairholm
DEACONS: James Ker
George Cunningham
William Keir
Patrick Lawson
James McDowal
William Dickson

For the particular sessions
TOLBOOTH: Alex. Noble
John Welsh
OLD GREYFRIARS: John Sword
Andrew Petrie
LADY YESTERS: Baillie John Wilson
James Yourstone
NEW GREYFRIARS: Baillie Robert Forrester
Andrew Ranken
COLLEDGE KIRK: Robert Walker
Walter Jollie
OLD KIRK: Hugh Hamilton
Patrick Tod
TRON KIRK: George Wishart
William Wight
NEW KIRK: Thomas Donald
Andrew Mouat
NORTH NEW KIRK: George Gray
Francis Jeffries (Jaffrey)

From the Lords of Session
Lord Tynwald: Lord Justice Clerk
Lord Milton
Lord Drummore
Lord Elchies
Lord Kilkerran

From the Faculty of Advocates
Robert Dundas
Kenneth McKenzie
James Balfour
Thomas Hay
Robert Pringle
Joseph Williamson

From the Writers to the Signet
Robert Wallace
George Chalmers
James Armour
Archibald Campbell
James Haliburton
James Graham

From the Colledge of Physicians
Dr W. Porterfield
Dr John Boswall

From the Colledge
Mr Colin Drummond

Merchants
ex-Provost John Osborne — Charles Butter
Robert Anderson — William Baillie
Ralph Dundas — Oliver Tod
James Allan — William Scott
William Mercer — Alex. Hepburn
George Rigg — George Dunsmuir
Allan Beg — Claud Inglis
Alexander Hunter — Robert Greenlees
John Mossman — John Cleland

Incorporations
SURGEONS: Adam Austen
FURRIERS: Thomas Jamieson
GOLDSMITHS: Thomas Mitchel
HAMMERMEN: William Armstrong
SKINNERS: John Callender
MASONS: Samuel Neilsen
WRIGHTS: James Norie
WEAVERS: James Brown
TAILORS: Thomas Hunter
WAULKERS: Peter Duncan
BAXTERS: George Home
BONNETMAKERS: Charles Brandon
FLESHERS: Thomas Robertson
BARBERS: James Stuart
CORDINERS: Stephen Ronaldson
CANDLEMAKERS: William Gairdner

From the Conveenry
Charles Mack
John Mathie

TREASURER'S REPORT

Number of the family upon 30th June 1752 was:

94 men	
282 women	
73 boys	
94 girls	543
The Mistress, Chaplain Clerk and other servants	6
Lunaticks in Bedlam	18
Criminals in the house of Correction	9
Beggars Confined	5
Quarterly Pensioners	78
Weekly Pensioners	31
Orphans at Nurse by Church Treasurer	26
Total	716

That there have been bound 8 boy apprentices and 11 girls all gone to service from 1st July 1751 to 1st July 1752

That there have been given out to Poor People 120 Coffins which with those to people who in the house 119 in all 239 Coffins.

(b) POPULATION STATISTICS

POPULATION OF EDINBURGH OLD TOWN 1752

Age Ranges	Mortality	Estimated Population	Cumulative
0-1	461	942	942
1-2		750	1'692
2-5	126	1269	2'961
5-10	68	2118	5'079
10-20	58	3391	8'470
20-30	87	4395	12'865
30-40	107	3720	16'585
40-50	97	2820	19'405
50-60	74	1995	21'400
60-60	56	1245	22'645
70-80	30	645	23'290
80-90	16	233	23'523
90-100	7	45	23'568

Estimated Total: 23,568

RECORDED DEATHS AND CAUSES 1752

Aged	. 87	Consumption	.198	Jaundice	. 1	Smallpox	.147
Ague	. 14	Convulsion	. 74	Meagrim	. 81	Sore Throat	. 2
Apoplexy	. 19	Cramp	. 1	Measles	.81	Stillborn	. 18
Asthma	. 15	Dropsy	. 8	Mortification	. 1	Suddenly	. 48
Childbed	. 18	Fever	.241	Palsy	. 8	Sweating	. 2
Chincough	.102	Fistula	. 1	Pleurisy	. 7	Tympany	. 3
Colic	. 4	Flux	. 11	Rheumatism	. 5	Water in head	. 1

EXECUTED 5

THE DIRECTORY

(a) A-Z
(b) RESIDENTS: Close by Close

THE DIRECTORY

(a) A-Z

		OCCUPATION		ADDRESS
Abercrombie,	Mrs		Abercrombie's	Bess Wynd
Abernethy,	Mrs		Wight's	Forrester's Wynd, West
Adam,	John		Inglis's	West Bow, South
Adams,	John	Architect	Adams's	Kinloch's Cl. Foot
Adamson,	George	Druggist	Hastie's	Cowgate South
Adamson,	Mr		Sinclair's	Blackfriars Wynd
Adamson,	Thomas	Taylor	Hastie's	Borthwick's Close
Aikman,	Isobel	Milliner/Ale Seller	Telfer's	Luckenbooths
Aikman,	Margt.	Milliner/Ale Seller	Nicol's	Luckenbooths
Aikman,	Mistress	Milliner	Garbiston's	Clamshell Turnpike High Street South
Aikman,	William	Merchant	Magdalen's	High St. above Tron
Ainslie,	Mrs		Ainslie's	Bell's Wynd Head
Ainslie,	Walter	Shipping Agent		Covenant Close
Aitchison,	Alex.	Jeweller	Mitchel's	Luckenbooths
Aitchison,	Alex.	Ale Seller	Chirnside's	New Stairs, Parliament Cl.
Aitchison,	James	Stabler	Jamieson's	Covenant Close
Aitchison,	James	Merchant	Sandiland's	Forrester's Wynd East
Aitken,	George	Smith	Aitken's	Cowgate South
Aitken,	John	Stationer	Brown's	Fleshmarket Close
Aitken,	John	Wigmaker	Bavelaw's	President's/Scott's, Cowgate South
Aitken,	Mrs	Ale Seller	Hay's	Back of Cross, High Street South
Aitken,	William	Wright	Riddel's	Con's Close
Aitkenhead,	David	Surgeon	His Own	Dickson's Close
Aitkenhead,	James	Merchant	Stewart's	Trunk Close
Aitkenhead,	James	Cordiner	Carnegie's	Dickson's Close
Aiton,	Walter	Glover/Perfumer	McCulloch's	Mary King's Close
Aiton,	William	Merchant	Gray's	Grassmarket East
Aiton,	William	Goldsmith	Maxwell's	Writer's Court
Aiton,	William	Writer		Writer's Court
Alexander	Christopher	Vintner	Baillie's	Bull's Close
Alexander,	James	Dyer	Bull's	Cowgate South
Alexander,	John	Limner	Finlay's	Barringer's Close
Alexander,	Keith			Custom House Stairs, Parliament Close
Alexander,	Mr	Merchant	Moffat's	Trunk Close
Alexander,	Mrs	Widow		New Stairs Passage, Parliament Close
Alexander,	William	Merchant		Royston's Close
Alison,	Alexander	Merchant	Wight's	Cowgate Head, South
Alison,	Andrew	Merchant		
Alison,	Colin	Wright	His Own	Covenant Close
Alison,	Mrs		Hellistob's	Cowgate South
Allan,	Andrew	Merchant	Forrest's	Kennedy's Close
Allan,	James	Painter	"Queen's Head"	Libberton's Wynd Head
Allan,	James	Ale Seller	Foulis's	Castlehill South
Allan,	James	Wright	Smith's	Skinner's Close
Allan,	James	Merchant	Stonehouse's	Con's Close
Allan,	James	Merchant	Forrest's	Luckenbooths
Allan,	John	Baxter	Veitch's	Cowgate Head North
Allan,	Mrs		Allan's	Forrester's/Libberton's Lawnmarket South
Allan,	Robert	Baxter	Mylne's	Castlehill, South East
Allan,	Robert	Baxter	Baxter's	Under Baxter's Close
Allan,	Thomas	Merchant		
Allison,	James	Hammerman	Clerk's	Castlehill South
Alston,	Charles	Professor of Botany		University
Alstone,	David	Glazier	Douglas's	Forrester's Wynd, West

NAME		OCCUPATION	ADDRESS	
Alstone,	James	Stabler	Hamilton's	Grassmarket, North West
Alstone,	Mr	Gauger	Hamilton's	Grassmarket, North East
Alstone,	William	W.S.		James Court
Alves,	Andrew	W.S.		James Court
Alves,	David		Good Town's	Candlemaker Row
Anchorfield,	Lady		Hutton's	Gosford's Close
Anderson,	Adam	Wigmaker	Scheill's	Chamber's Close
Anderson,	Adam	Hammerman	Auchenleck's	Trunk Close
Anderson,	Adam	Candlemaker	Herring's	Grassmarket Mid.
Anderson,	Alexander	Coppersmith	Anderson's	Grassmarket Mid.
Anderson,	Alex.	Coppersmith	Anderson's	West Bow, Cowgate North
Anderson,	Andrew	Merchant	Kinneir's	Cullen's/Royston's Lawnmarket South
Anderson,	Christian			
Anderson,	David	Waulker		Carruber's Close
Anderson,	David	W.S.	West Scale Strs.	Old Assembly Close
Anderson,	Helen,	Roomsetter	Forbes'	Anchor Close
Anderson,	Hendry	Cordiner	Elliot's	Upper Baxter's Close
Anderson,	James	Goldsmith	Carnegie's	Trunk Close
Anderson,	James	Manservant	Scott's	Brown's Land, Opposite Tolbooth
Anderson,	John	Grocer	Hutton's	Blackfriar's Wynd
Anderson,	Mr	Writer	Tod's	Advocate's Close
Anderson,	Mr	Teacher	Rae's	Peebles Wynd
Anderson,	Mrs		Lothian's	Lady Stair's Close
Anderson,	Mrs		Wallace's	Borthwick's Close
Anderson,	Mrs		Fyfe's	Lady Stair's Close
Anderson,	Robert	Taylor	Wight's	Cant's/Dickson's Cowgate North
Anderson,	Robert	Merchant	Martin's	Cowgate Head North
Anderson,	Thomas	Saddler	Stewart's	Candlemaker Row
Anderson,	Widow		Davidson's	Upper Baxter's Close
Anderson,	Widow		Geddes's	West Bow/ Lawnmarket
Anderson,	William			Baillie Fyfe's Close
Anderson,	William	Ale Seller	Newland's	Milne Square
Andrew,	Robert		MacLeod's	Halkerston Wynd
Andrew,	Robert			Kinloch's Close
Andrews,	Mrs			Craig's Close
Angus,	Archibald	Merchant	Swinton's	Roxburgh's Close
Angus,	Archibald	Merchant	New Stairs	Parliament Close
Angus,	David	Merchant	Angus's	
Angus,	James	Wright	Fouler's	Cant's Close Foot
Angus,	Mary	Merchant	Angus's	Advocate's Close
Angus,	Peter	Ale Seller	Buchan's	Murdoch's Close
Anna,	Robert	Merchant		High Street South at Clamshell Turnpike
Annicus,	Mrs		Kerr's	Fleshmarket Close
Anthonius,	John	Wright	Monteith's Close	
Anthonius,	Mrs		Paterson's	Blackfriar's Wynd
Arbuthnot & Scot		Merchants	Monro's	Geddes Close
Arbuthnot,	Alex.	Merchant	His Own	Milne Square
Arbuthnot,	George	Merchant	Brownhill's	Cowgate North
Arbuthnot,	Robert	Silk Merchant	"Golden Fleece"	High Street
Arbuthnot,	Robert	Merchant	Carmichael's	Bull's Close
Armour,	James	W.S.		Bank/Cullen's, Lawnmarket South
Armstrong,	Mrs		Tod's	Horse Wynd West
Armstrong,	Mrs			Murdoch's Close
Armstrong,	William	Coppersmith	Veitch's	West Bow Foot
Arnistone,	William	Bookbinder	Duncan's	Argylle Square
Arnot,	James	Manservant to Earl of Loudon		

NAME		OCCUPATION	ADDRESS	
Arnprier,	Lady		Kerr's	Jackson's Close
Arthur,	Patrick	Tavern Keeper	British Coffee House	Mary King's Close
Arundale,	Widow		Walker's	Milne's Back Court
Auchenbowie,	Lady		Learmonth's	Skinner's Close
Auchenleck,	David	Vintner	Ramsay's	Bull's Close
Auchinleck,	David			Kennedy's Close
Auchinleck,	Gilbert	Cutler	Gray's	Bull's Close
Auchinleck,	James	Hammerman	Auchenleck's	Trunk Close
Auchinleck,	Mrs	Milliner	Aikman's	Peebles Wynd
Auchterfardel,	Lady		Syme's	Barringer's Land
Auld,	Robert		Good Town's	Candlemaker Row
Auld,	William	Wright	Butter's	Carruber's Close
Austin,	Adam	Surgeon		Forrester's/Libberton's Lawnmarket South
Bailey,	George of Hamilton			Carruber's Close
Baillie, Seton & Houston		Merchants	Reid's	Lawnmarket North
Baillie,	David	Writer (*Home*)	Symes'	Monteith's Close
		(*Office*)	Royal Bank	New Bank Close
Baillie,	George of Bagbie		His Own	Carruber's Close
Baillie,	James	Merchant	Seton's	Warriston Close
Baillie,	James	Merchant	Wardrop's	Libberton's Wynd
Baillie,	John	Coppersmith	Halyburton's	Grassmarket East
Baillie,	John	Bookbinder	Miln's	Mealmarket
Baillie,	John	Bookseller	Ross's	Anchor Close
Baillie,	Lady		Home's	Bell's Wynd
Baillie,	Mrs		Dallas's	Blackfriar's Wynd
Baillie,	Robert	Merchant	Baillie's	Milne Square
Baillie,	Thomas	Wright	Baillie's	Cant's Close Foot
Baillie,	Thomas	W.S. *of Polkemmet*		James Court
Baillie,	William	Wright	Riddel's	Paterson's Court
Baillie,	William	Hosier	Wardrop's	Libberton's Wynd
Baillie,	William	Merchant	Seton's	Luckenbooths
Bain,	John			
Bain,	Mrs	Washer	Nisbet's	Bell's Wynd
Bain,	Mrs		Humbie's	Dickson's Close
Baird,	David	Merchant/Agent Sun Fire Insurance	Baird's	Currie's Land
Baird,	David	Doctor	Innes's	Cowgate South
Baird,	James	Ale Seller	Gibson's	Custom House Stairs Parliament Close
Baird,	John	Ale Seller	Nisbet's	Niddry's Wynd
Baird,	Lady		Adams's	Cowgate South
Baird,	John	Stationer	Allan's	High Street North at Baillie Fyfe's
Baird,	John	Bookseller		Old Post Office Close
Baird,	Miss		Scott's	Brown's Land opposite Tolbooth
Baird,	Mrs	Shopkeeper/Ale Seller	Peter's	Horse Wynd
Baird,	William	Smith	Reid's	Cant's Close Foot
Baird,	William *of Brankston*		Baird's	Castlehill South
Bairnsfather,	George	Plumber	Oliphant's	Niddry's Wynd
Bake,	Mrs	Ale Seller	Bell's	West Bow Middle
Balcarres,	Lady		Her Own	Dickson's Close
Balderstone,	Misses	Milliners	MacPherson's	Horse Wynd West
Balderstone,	Mrs		Williamson's	Fleshmarket Close
Balderstone,	Thomas	Wheelwright	Mason's	Kinloch's/Cant's Cowgate North
Balfour,	Helen	Merchant	Finlayson's	High Street North at Kinloch's Close
Balfour,	James	Coffee House	Hogg's	Mary King's Close
Balfour,	James	Merchant	Custom House Stairs	Parliament Close

NAME		OCCUPATION	ADDRESS	
Balgowan,	Lady		Her Own	Blackfriar's Wynd
Ballantyne,	James	Wheelwright	Baillie's	Cant's Close Foot
Ballantyne,	William	Printer	Barclay's	Lyon's Close
Balmerino,	Lady			Milne Square
Bank, Royal			Hamilton's	New Bank Close
Bank of Scotland			Bank's	Bank Close
Banks,	Charles	Stabler		Hammermen's Close
Bannatyne,	Maitland	Linen Merchant	Rae's	Bull's Close & Dickson's Close
Barclay,	Adam			Mary King's Close
Barclay,	John	Skinner	Stevenson's	Upper Baxter's Close
Barclay,	Miss	Merchant	Shearer's	Luckenbooths
Barclay,	Mrs		Bruce's	Forrester's Wynd Head
Barclay,	Robert	Taylor	Scougall's	Advocate's Close
Barclay,	William	Optician	Tailfair's	Baillie Fyfe's Close
Barclay,	William	Wright	Mitchell's	Fishmarket Close
Barclay,	Mr			Blackfriar's Wynd
Barclay,	Mrs		Crockett's	West Bow Foot
Barr,	Robert	Stabler/Ale Seller	Cochrane's	Grassmarket Mid
Barr,	William		Sinclair's	Blackfriar's Wynd
Barrowman,	Peter	Stabler	Gray's	Grassmarket East
Barrowman,	William		Galloway's	Castlehill South
Bartram & Williamson		Linen Merchants	Speir's	Lawnmarket North
Bartram,	Mr	Teacher	Riddel's	Cap & Feather Close
Bartram,	William	*of Nisbet*	Innes's	Halkerston Wynd
Batchelor,	Jenet		Batchelor's	High Street North at Baillie Fyfe's
Bavelaw,	Lady		Stewart's	Milne Square
Baveridge,	Alex.		Gavinlock's	Forrester's Wynd
Baveridge,	James	Merchant	Lauder's	Gosford's Close & Argylle Square
Baverly,	Elspit	Grocer	Carmichael's	World's End Close
Baxter,	James	Meal Seller	Cleghorn's	Society
Baxter,	Mrs		Cumming's	Peebles Wynd East
Beasey,	George	Buckle-maker	Finlayson's	High Street North at Kinloch's Close
Beat,	David	Writing Master	Sibbald's	Carruber's Close
Beatt,	Mr jr.			Skinner's Close
Beech,	Mrs		Her Own	Libberton's Wynd
Begbie,	Charles	Stabler	Mitchell's	Baillie's Land Cowgate North
Begbie,	George	Locksmith	Mylne's	West Bow Foot
Begbie,	George	Baxter	Lamb's	Lawnmarket North at Galloway's
Begbie,	Walter		Scott's	Cowgate North
Begg,	Allan	Merchant	Munro's	Lawnmarket North at Wardrope's
Begg,	William	Gauger (Excise)	Herriot's	Cowgate Head South
Belches,	John *of Innermay*	Clerk to Trustees	Sheriff Clerk's Office	Edinburgh Turnpike Roads Niddry's Wynd
Belches,	Miss		Dewar's	Forrester's Wynd Head
Belches,	Thomas	Depute Sheriff Clerk	Anderson's	Fishmarket Close West
Belhaven,	Lord		Lindsay's	Libberton's Wynd
Bell,	Alexander	Wigmaker	Cunningham's	Lawnmarket North at Galloway's
Bell,	Andrew	Engraver	Bell's	Mary King's Close
Bell,	Bartholomew	Brewer	Cleghorn's	Grassmarket South
Bell,	Edward	Smith	Mitchell's	Fishmarket Close
Bell,	John	Baxter	Hay's	Trunk Close
Bell,	John	Stabler	Braidwood's	President's Close
Bell,	John	Stabler	Jollie's	Cowgate Head North
Bell,	Mrs	Tobacconist	Hewit's	Fleshmarket Close Head
Bell,	Mrs		Cleghorn's	Horse Wynd
Bell,	Mrs		Mitchell's	Fishmarket Close

NAME		OCCUPATION	ADDRESS	
Bell,	Widow		Robertson's	Skinner's Close
Bell,	Widow		Mitchell's	Kennedy's Close
Bells,	Messrs	Brewers	Cleghorn's	Grassmarket South West
Benazeck,	Mdme.	French Teacher	at Mdme. Le Blanc's	Cant's Close
Bennet,	Mrs		Halyburton's	Trunk Close
Bennet,	Widow		Her Own	Grassmarket/Cowgate
Berrey,	David	Cobbler	Davie's	Blackfriar's Wynd
Bertram,	Mr of Nisbet		Skinner's	Castlehill North
Betts,	Mrs Thomas			Fleshmarket Close
Biggar,	John	Merchant	Chalmer's	Candlemaker Row
Binnie,	John	Distiller	Robertson's	Pearson's Close
Binnie,	Mr	Cobbler	Mouat's	Meal Market
Binning,	Charles	Advocate		Cullen's/Fisher's
Binning,	Mrs		Somervail's	High Street North at Carruber's Close
Birnie,	Widow		Ferguson's	Con's Close
Black,	John	Merchant	Robb's	Byre's Close
Black,	John	Ale Seller	Livingston's	Craig's Close
Black,	John	Poultryman	Stenhouse's	Marlin's Wynd
Black,	William	Wright	Gordon's	Chamber's Close
Black,	William	Stabler/Ale Seller	Bruce's	Grassmarket South West
Blackadder,	Mrs		Schaw's	Castlehill South
Blackie,	Mrs		Telfer's	West Bow Head
Blackwood,	Mistress		Crichton's	Luckenbooths
Blackwood,	Mrs		Mylne's	Castlehill South East
Blackwood,	Mrs	Merchant	Brand's	Castlehill South
Blackwood,	Mrs			Marlin's Wynd East
Blackwood,	Robert	Merchant		James Court
Blair,	Archibald	Writer	Blair's	Castlehill South
Blair,	Charles	Goldsmith	Mylne's	Castlehill South East
Blair,	Mr	Exciseman	Syme's	Blackfriar's Wynd
Blair,	Mrs			Dickson's Close
Blair,	Patrick	Vintner	see (John's Coffee House)	Parliament Close
Blair Drummond,	Lady		Farquhar's	Cantore's/Advocate's High Street North
Bland,	Mrs		Seton's	Libberton's Wynd
Bland,	General	Soldier		Milne's Court
Bland,	Miss		Sideserf's	West Bow Foot
Blantyre,	Lady		Watson's	Niddry's Wynd
Blyth,	Robert	Trunk Maker	Blyth's	Chamber's Close
Boggie,	Widow		Her Own	Halkerston's Wynd
Boggie,	James	Stabler/Ale Seller	Carfrae's	Candlemaker Row
Boghall,	Lady		Maul's	West Bow Middle
Bogle,	Mrs		Lithgow's	Paterson's Court
Bogle,	Mrs		Her Own	Halkerston's Wynd
Boid,	George	Merchant	Robertson's	James Court
Boid,	Miss		Messenger's	Horse Wynd
Bomana,	Lady		Murray's	Niddry's Wynd
Bonnar,	Andrew	Merchant	Schaw's	Castlehill South
Bonnar,	David		Fulton's	Blackfriar's Wynd
Bonnar,	John	Painter	Blair's	Castlehill South
Bonsie,	James	Manservant	Norie's	Kinloch's Close
Borthwick,	Mrs		Gedd's	Byre's Close
Boswall,	Alexander	Painter	mason's	Plainstone Close
Boswall,	Alexander	Advocate	Custom House Stairs	Parliament Close
Boswall,	David	Glazier	Deuchar's	Lawnmarket South
Boswall,	David	Merchant		Forrester's Wynd East
Boswall,	George	Saddler	Hamilton's	High Street North at Halkerston's Wynd
Boswall,	George	Writer	Boswall's	High Street North at Baillie Fyfe's

NAME		OCCUPATION	ADDRESS	
Boswell,	John	Doctor	Brand's	Castlehill South
Boswell,	Mrs		Boswall's	Lawnmarket North
Boswell,	Thomas	Writer		Parliament Close
Boswell,		*of Balminto*		Lady Stair's Close
Bower,	Alexander	Weaver	Clerk's	Castlehill South
Bowie,	Archibald	Merchant	Hepburn's	Don's Close
Bowie,	Archibald	Shipping Agent		Libberton's Wynd
Bowie,	David	Mason		Colledge Wynd
Bowie,	John	Clerk	Webster's	West Bow
Bowie,	John	Stabler	Marshal's	Grassmarket South West
Bowie,	Patrick	Merchant	Penman's	Advocate's Close
Bowie,	Patrick	Haberdasher	"Eagle & Globe"	Luckenbooths
Bowie,	Robert	Distiller	Bowie's	Cowgate South
Bowman,	William	Taylor	Stewart's	Con's Close
Boyd,	Miss		Messenger's	Horse Wynd
Boyd,	Robert	Merchant	Currie's	Lawnmarket North
Boyes,	Thomas	Writer	Monro's	Milne's Court
Braehead,	Lady		Johnstone's	Cowgate North
Braid,	John	Glover	Brown's	Mary King's Close
Braidfoot,	Mrs		Hendry's	Milne's Court
Braidwood,	John	Stabler	Donaldson's	Grassmarket North West
Braidwood,	Mrs	Candlemaker	Somervail's	Society
Braidwood,	William	Candlemaker		Castlehill
Brand,	John	Merchant	Bowie's	James Court
Brand,	John		Brand's	Society
Brand,	Mrs		MacVey's	Libberton's Wynd
Brandon,	Charles	Bonnetmaker		
Bremner,	Robert	Musical Instruments	"Golden Harp"	High Street opposite Blackfriar's Wynd
Briggs,	Alexander	Merchant	Cleghorn's	Horse Wynd
Brodie,	Francis	Wright	Little's	Cullen's Close
Brodie,	James	Surgeon	Walker's	Galloway's Close
Brodie,	Thomas	W.S.	Montgomery's	Niddry's Wynd
Brown & Hepburn		Merchants	Inglis's	Luckenbooths
Brown,	Alexander		His Own	Craig's Close
Brown,	Charles	Stabler	Cleghorn's	Grassmarket South West
Brown,	David	Ale Seller	Young's	Blackfriar's Wynd
Brown,	David		Syme's	Kennedy's Close
Brown,	George	*of Colston*		Byre's Close
Brown,	James	Bookseller		Parliament Close
Brown,	James	Weaver	Chalmer's	Castlehill South
Brown,	James	Wright	Brown's	Brown's Land Opposite Tolbooth
Brown,	James	Glover	His Own	Brown's Land Opposite Tolbooth
Brown,	James & Co.	Merchants	Blair's	Writer's Court
Brown,	John	Ironmonger	"Iron Monkey"	High Street opposite Cross
Brown,	John			Galloway's Close
Brown,	John	Cork Cutter	Wilson's	Borthwick's Close
Brown,	Lawrence	Wigmaker	Norie's	Kinloch's Close
Brown,	Malcolm	Saddler	Barber's	Fleshmarket Close
Brown,	Mathew	Merchant	Chine's	Cowgate at Scott's/Baillie's
Brown,	Thomas	*of Blackford*	Stewart's	Lawnmarket North at Upper Baxter's Close
Brown,	Mr		Knox's	Lady Stair's Close
Brown,	Mr	Gauger	Bull's	Cowgate South
Brown,	Mr		Riddel's	Cowgate South
Brown,	Mr	Writer	Hay's	Anderson's Land West Bow
Brown,	Mrs	Merchant		Wardrope's Court
Brown,	Mrs		Penman's	Warriston's Court
Brown,	Mrs	Bookseller	Brown's	Byre's Close
Brown,	Mrs	Watchmaker	Wright's	High Street at North Foulis
Brown,	Mrs & Son	Merchants	Brown's	Halkerston's Wynd
Brown,	Mrs	*of Carseleath*	Bull's	Cowgate South

NAME		OCCUPATION	ADDRESS	
Brown,	Mrs			Her Own	Forrester's Wynd Foot
Brown,	Miss	Merchant	Corsbie's	Gladston'e Land
Brown,	Nicol	Flesher	Williamson's	Fleshmarket Close
Brown,	Patrick	Ale Seller	Annandale's	Bull's Close
Brown,	Robert	Taylor		Under Baxter's Close
Brown,	Robert	Furrier	Paton's	Writer's Court
Brown,	Robert	Taylor	Fisher's	Mary King Close
Brown,	Robert	Furrier	Dick's	Kinloch's Close
Brown,	Samuel	Watchmaker		North Foulis Close
Brown,	Widow	Ale Seller	Wardrop's	Foulis's Close
Brown,	Widow		Divistob's	Plainstone Close
Brown,	William	Manservant	Newlands	Milne Square
Brown,	William	Merchant		Bess Wynd, Middle
Brownlie,	John		Nisbet's	Bell's Wynd
Bruce,	Alexander	Upholsterer	Panmure's	Netherbow North
Bruce,	Alexander	Merchant	Fairholm's	West Bow Middle
Bruce,	Alexander	Writer	McKinlay's	West Bow Foot
Bruce,	Alexander	Surgeon		West Bow at Grassmarket
Bruce,	Alexander	Surgeon	Tod's	Kennedy's Close
Bruce,	Betty		Bruce's	Grassmarket South
Bruce,	Charles,	Glazier	His Own	Lawnmarket North
Bruce,	David	Writer	Scale Stairs	Old Assembly Close West
Bruce,	John	Printer	Hutton's	Gosford's Close
Bruce,	Mr	Printer	Edmonston's	Lawnmarket South
Bruce,	Mrs	*of Kinnaird*	Campbell's	Parliament Close
Bruce,	Mrs		Baird's	Upper Baxter's Close
Bruce,	Mrs		Bruce's	Forrester's Wynd West
Bruce,	Mrs		Her Own	Grassmarket West
Bruce,	T.	Merchant	McKinlay's	West Bow Foot
Bruce,	Thomas	Writer		James Court
Bruce,	William	Merchant	McKinlay's	West Bow Foot
Bruce,	William jr.	Merchant	Hallyburton's	Grassmarket North
Bruntone,	Robert	Merchant	Finlayson's	Grassmarket South West
Brymer,	George	Staymaker	Gibson's	Lady Stairs Close
Brymer,	James	Mealmaker/Ale Seller	Cleghorn's	Meal Market
Brymer,	Mr	Merchant	Paton's	Writer's Court
Brymer,	William		Spence's	Mary King's Close
Bryson,	John	Merchant	Burn's	Mary King's Close
Buchan,	Andrew	Merchant	Naismith's	Cant's Close
Buchan,	Duncan	Manservant/Ale Seller	Erskine's	Niddry's Wynd
Buchan,	Duncan		Wight's	New Stairs Parliament Close
Buchan,	George	Writer	His Own	Dickson's Close
Buchan,	Mrs		Edmonstone's	Lawnmarket South
Buchan,	Thomas			Lawnmarket North
Buchan,	William	Ale Seller	Brown's	Wardrope's Close
Buchanan,	Andrew			Todrick's Wynd
Buchanan,	John	Printer	Fleming's	Pearson's Close
Buchanan,	Mrs		Buchan's	Murdoch's Close
Bunckle,	Henry		Ogilvie's	Cowgate South
Budge,	William	W.S.		Anchor Close
Buller,	Jerome	Druggist	Lithgow's	Candlemaker Row
Burd,	Edward	Merchant	Wight's	Forrester's Wynd
Burn,	James		Burn's	Forrester's Wynd
Burnet,	Andrew	W.S.		Miln's Court
Burnet,	James	(*Lord Monboddo*) W.S. *of Barns*		Writer's Court
Burnet,	Mr		Hay's	Anderson's Land
Burnet,	William	Merchant	Little's	High Street at Bell's/Covenant
Burnett,	Mrs		Callander's	Lawnmarket North
Burns & Finlayson		Merchants	Mansfield's	Byre's Close
Burns,	James	Wright	Burn's	Forrester's Wynd Head
Burns,	James		Burn's	Mary King's Close
Burns,	Mrs		Burn's	Forrester's Wynd Head

NAME		OCCUPATION	ADDRESS	
Burns,	Patrick	Sheriff's Officer	Black's	Fleshmarket Close
Burton,	Alexander	Glazier	Chalmer's	High Street at New Assembly Close
Burton,	Mrs		Mitchell's	Fishmarket Close
Butter,	Charles	Wright	Lithgow's	Advocate's Close
Butter,	Charles	Wright	Butter's	Carruber's Close
Butter,	James		Cleghorn's	Horse Wynd
Butter,	Jerome	Druggist		Cowgate Head at Candlemaker Row
Caddel,	James	Upholstery/Ale Seller	Colvill's	Trunk Close
Cairns,	Mr	Flesher	Millar's	Grassmarket South West
Cairns,	Mrs		Thomson's	Dickson's Close
Cairns,	Mrs	Merchant	Brown's	World's End Close
Cairns,	Mrs			Stonelow's Close
Caithness,	Edward	Merchant	Arthur's	Advocate's Close
Caithness,	David	Cook	Murray's	Halkerston's Wynd
Caithness,	Lady		Buchan's	Murdoch's Close
Calder,	Thomas	Merchant	Robertson's	Grassmarket East
Calder,	Thomas		Colvill's	Trunk Close
Callander & Hamilton		Merchants	Veitch's	Warriston Close
Callander,	Andrew	Cordiner		
Callander,	Jenet		Her Own	Carruber's Close
Callander,	John	Glover	Cant's	High Street at Carruber's Close
Callander,	John	Merchant		Lawnmarket South between Cullen's & Fishers
Callander,	William	Ale Seller	Wight's	Society
Cameron,	James		Ainslie's	Baillie Fyfe's Close
Cameron,	Mrs		Baillie's	Cant's Close Foot
Cameron,	Ronald		Purdie's	Sandilands Close
Campbell,	Alexander	Manservant	Davidson's	High Street at Carruber's Close
Campbell,	Alexander	Brewer	His Own	Argylle Square
Campbell,	Archibald	W.S.		James Court
Campbell,	Archibald	Merchant	Dean's	Don's Close
Campbell,	Archibald	Ale Seller	Mein's	Fleshmarket Close
Campbell,	Archibald	Brewer	Bruce's	Grassmarket South West
Campbell,	Captain	*of Finnab*	Barclay's	Craig's Close
Campbell,	Charles	Gauger (Excise)	Good's	Colledge Wynd
Campbell,	Charles	Horse Hirer	Noble's	Candlemaker Row
Campbell,	Colin	Merchant	Robertson's	Lyon's Close
Campbell,	Colin	Bookbinder	Gilchrist's	President's Close
Campbell,	David	Ale Seller	Wilson's	Borthwick's Close
Campbell,	Duncan	Dye Merchant/Ale Seller	Downie's	Grassmarket Mid
Campbell,	Duncan	Painter	Good's	Colledge Wynd
Campbell,	George	Wright/Factor	Campbell's	Argylle Square
Campbell,	Henrietta	Lady	Greenhill's	Libberton's Wynd
Campbell,	Hugh	Grocer/Ale Seller		Craig's Close
Campbell,	John	Taylor	Campbell's	Bell's Wynd
Campbell,	John	Ale Seller	Bairfoot's	Peebles Wynd
Campbell,	John		Young's	Covenant Close
Campbell,	John	Manservant	Peter's	Horse Wynd
Campbell,	John		Gairn's	Grassmarket East
Campbell,	John	Writing Master		Niddry's Wynd West
Campbell,	*of Monse*			Bull's Close
Campbell,	Mrs		Wardrop's	Wardrope's Court
Campbell,	Mrs		Brown's	Fleshmarket Close
Campbell,	Mrs		Main Building	Infirmary
Campbell,	Mrs	*of Arbuckle*		Marlin's Wynd
Campbell,	Misses		Murray's	Upper Baxter's Close
Campbell,	Misses		Peter's	Horse Wynd
Campbell,	Robert			Paterson's Court
Canning,	Mrs		Scott's	

NAME		OCCUPATION	ADDRESS	
Carfrae,	Martin	Wright	Carmichael's	Bell's Wynd
Cargill,	James	Merchant	Mein's	Old Post Office Close
Cargill,	John			Old Post Office Close
Carlowrie,	Lady		Wight's	James Court
Carmichael	David		Hamilton's	Grassmarket West
Carmichael,	James	Ale Seller	Watson's	Custom House Stairs Parliament Close
Carmichael,	James	Ale Seller	Riddock's	Covenant Close
Carmichael,	John			Writer's Close
Carmichael,	John	Merchant		Royston's Close
Carmichael,	Mrs		Gairn's	Grassmarket
Carmichael,	Robert		Stevenson's	Erskine's Land
Carmichael,	William	(ex) Porter	Hamilton's	Grassmarket West
Carnegie,	John	Merchant	Halyburton's	Trunk Close
Carnegie,	John	Merchant	Somervail's	Society
Cavers Kerr	Lady		Gillon's	President's Close
Chaipland,	Mrs			Sandiland's Close
Chalmers,	Alexander	Writer	MacLenan's	West Bow
Chalmers,	Andrew	Writer	His Own	Jackson's Close
Chalmers,	George	W.S.	Divistob's	Plainstone Close
Chalmers,	George	Merchant		Lawnmarket at Bank/Cullen's
Chalmers,	Mrs		Chalmer's	Allan's Close
Chalmers,	Mrs		Melvil's	Foulis Close
Chalmers,	William	Taylor	Keltie's	Forrester Wynd West
Chalmers,	William	Merchant	Chalmer's	Society Gate Candlemaker Row
Chalmers,	William	Surgeon	Chalmer's	Society Gate Candlemaker Row
Chapman,	Andrew	Meal Seller	Ewing's	New Stairs, Meal Market
Charles,	John		Peter's	Horse Wynd
Chartries,	Francis	Gentleman	Chartries'	Post Office Stairs Parliament Close
Chartries,	Lady		Bruce's	Libberton's Wynd
Chatto,	Mrs		Chatto's	Dickson's Close
Chatto,	Miss		Kennedy's	Cant's Close Foot
Cheap,	William	Linen Merchant	Magdalen's	High Street above Tron
Cheeslie,	Mrs		Laboratory	Cowgate South
Cheeslie,	Mrs	Mantua maker	Selkirk	Royston's Close Foot
Cheyne,	Charles	Merchant	Cheyne's	James Court
Cheyne,	William	Printer	Millar's	Craig's Close
Chisholm,	John	Merchant		Lawnmarket South
Christie,	John	Merchant	Stewart's	Trunk Close
Christie,	George	Baxter	Lawrie's	Blackfriar's Wynd
Christie,	Mr	Cordiner	Grant's	Trunk Close
Christie,	Mrs		Biggar's	Miln's Square
Christie,	Mrs		Ramsay's	Forrester's Wynd Foot
Christie,	Mrs		Sinclair's	Blackfriar's Wynd
Christie,	Patrick	Wright	Hamilton's	High Street at Halkerston's Wynd
Christie,	Patrick	Printer	Christie's	Borthwick's Close
Christopher's (St.) Sugar House			Armour's	High Street at North Foulis Close
Clapperton,	Alex.	Writer's Clerk	at Wm. Wilson's	Niddry's Wynd
Clapperton,	William	Merchant	Blair's	Byre's Close
Clark,	Alexander	Ale Seller/Glover	Biggar's	Miln Square
Clark,	Alexander	Stabler/Ale Seller	Clerk's	Skinner's Close
Clark,	Baron			Blackfriar's Wynd
Clark,	David	Wigmaker/Ale Seller		High Street at Baillie Fyfe's Close
Clark,	Doctor		Galloway's	Horse Wynd
Clark,	George	Merchant	Crockate's	Bull's Close
Clark,	George	Merchant		Wardrope's Court
Clark,	Hugh	Captain/Merchant		Milne Square

NAME		OCCUPATION	ADDRESS	
CLARK,	James	Grocer	Clerk's	Fountain Close
CLARK,	James	Weaver	Lithgow's	Grassmarket West
CLARK,	John	Glazier	Pearson's	Pearson's Close
CLARK,	John	Jeweler	Blair's	Luckenbooths
CLARK,	Mr	Mason	Nairn's	Trunk Close
CLARK,	Mrs			Gray's Close
CLARK,	Robert	Vintner	Loch's	Writer's Court
CLARK,		Commissary	Smith's	Niddry's Wynd
CLARKSON,	John	Baxter	Schiell's	Swan's Close
CLARKSON,	John	Merchant	Smith's	Monteith's Close
CLARKSON,	Thomas	Baxter	Clarkson's	Fleshmarket Close
CLARKSON,	Thomas	Baxter		Cant's Close
CLEGHORN & LIVINGSTONE		Merchants	Hathorn's	Luckenbooths
CLEGHORN,	Adam	Merchant	Cleghorn's	Grassmarket West
CLEGHORN,	James	Baxter	Schiell's	Covenant Close
CLEGHORN,	Jean			Society
CLEGHORN,	John	Brewer	Hunter's	Flint's Land Cowgate South
CLEGHORN,	Mrs	Cooper	Lithgow's	Grassmarket West
CLEGHORN,	Mrs	Brewer/Ale Seller	Cleghorn's	Candlemaker Row
CLELLAND,	John	Merchant	Todd's	Castlehill North
CLELLAND,	Margaret			Burnet's Close Foot
CLELLAND,	Mrs		Gray's	Chambers Close
CLELLAND,	Mrs		Clelland's	Stonelaw's Close
CLELLAND,	Mrs	Widow	Aikman's	Marlin's Wynd
CLELLAND,	Peter	Vintner		Byre's Close
CLELLAND,	Rachel		Todd's	Horse Wynd
CLELLAND,	Thomas	Saddler	His Own	Milne Square
CLEMENT,	Thomas	Cordiner	Arthur's	Libberton's Wynd
CLERK, STEVENSON & CO.		Merchants	Stewart's	President's Stairs Parliament Close
CLERK,	Hugh	Wright	His Own	
CLERK,	Mrs	Widow	Black's	Fleshmarket Close
CLEUGH,	Alexander	Skinner		
CLEUGH,	Robert	Merchant	Sinclair's	Anderson's Land, West Bow
COBZIER,	Peter	Exciseman	Heriott's	Cowgate Head South
COCHRANE & HAMILTON		Merchants	Crawford's	Advocate's Close
COCHRANE,	Betty			Colledge Wynd South
COCHRANE,	Christian		Scott's	Murdoch's Close
COCHRANE,	James & Co.	Printers (Scots Mag.)	Millar's	Craig's Close
COCHRANE,	John	of Ravelridge	His Own	Foulis Close
COCHRANE,	Mrs		Clerk's	West Bow Middle
COCHRANE,	Mrs		Young's	Dickson's Close
COCHRANE,	Mrs			Lawnmarket at Libberton's Wynd
COCHRANE,	Mrs		Her Own	Meal Market
COCHRANE,	Mrs		Gillon's	President's Close
COCHRANE,	Mrs		Watson's	Cowgate North
COCK,	William	Cordiner	Schaw's	President's Close
COCKBURN,	Andrew	Hammerman	Johnstone's	Royston's Close
COCKBURN,	Ann			Mary King's Close
COCKBURN,	Sir James			Skinner's Close
COCKBURN,	Isobel			Mary King's Close
COCKBURN,	Mrs		Handyside's	Trunk Close
COCKBURN,	Mrs		Learmonth's	Skinner's Close
COCKBURN,	Mrs		Knox's	Blackfriar's Wynd
COCKBURN,	Thomas	of Rowchester W.S.	Smith's	Monteith's Close
COCKBURN,	Thomas		Montgomery's	Niddry's Wynd
COCKPEN,	Lady		Brownhills	Cowgate North
COLLIE,	John	Teacher	Stirling's	Bell's Wynd
COLQHOUN,	Patrick's Children		Rankin's	Milne Square
COLQHOUN,	Allan			Milne Square
COLVILLE,	Walter	Baxter	Reoch's	Plainstone Close
COLVIN,	Elizabeth		Naismith's	Bell's Wynd

NAME		OCCUPATION	ADDRESS	
Combs,	William		Thomson's	New Stairs, Parliament Close
Comiston,	Laird of		Dewar's	West Bow Foot
Congleton,	Charles	Surgeon	His Own	Foulis Close
Congleton,	Mrs			Old Post House Stairs
Copeland,	Charles	Writer (*Home*) (*Office*)	Somervail's	Grassmarket Mid Parliament Close
Corbet,	Mistress		Ancrum's	Grassmarket East
Corse,	James	Stabler	Galloway's	Horse Wynd West
Cossenot,	Mrs		Grant's	Trunk Close
Cossor,	Walter	Dep. Controller, Excise & Writing Master	Granger's	High Street below Tron
Couden,	Robert	Wright	Shearer's	Chamber's Close
Coulter,	Mrs	Pewterer	Stewart's	Candlemaker Row
Coulteraws, (see Menzies, Robert)	Lady		Cooper's	High Street at Borthwick's/Fishmarket
Couper,	Mr	Weaver	Cairn's	Mary King's Close
Couper,	Mrs	Upholsterer	Elliot's	Upper Baxter's Close
Couper,	Mrs		Hutton's	Gosford's Close
Coutts & Trotter Co.		Merchants	Charteris'	Post Office Stairs Parliament Close
Coutts,	James	Merchant	President's Stairs	Paliament Close
Coutts,	John	Merchant	President's Stairs	Parliament Close
Cowan,	Barbara			Anchor Close
Cowan,	George	Wright	Somervail's	Society
Cowan,	Janet	Room Setter	Innes's	Bull's Close
Cowan,	Helen			High Street at Clamshell Turnpike
Cowan,	James	Watchmaker		Parliament Close
Cowan,	William		Inglis's	Bell's Wynd
Cowie,	Mr	Chairmaster	Campbell's	Bell's Wynd
Cowie,	Patrick	Ale Seller	Wardrope's	Milne Square
Coventry,	Cath.		Moffat's	Peebles Wynd East
Craich,	Mrs		Bruce's	Forrester's Wynd West
Craig,	Charles	Tobacconist	Craig's	Fleshmarket Close
Craig,	Charles	Merchant		Upper Baxter's Close
Craig,	James	Baxter	Stark's	Cowgate North
Craig,	John	Clerk *to Presbytery of Edinburgh*	Brymer's	Lawnmarket at Bank/Cullen's
Craig,	John	Cordiner	Johnstone's	Royston's Close
Craigentinny,	Lady		Foulis's	Kinloch's Close
Craigie,	Charles	Merchant	Willson's	Baillie Fyfe's Close
Craigie,	Kilgriston		Fisher's	Lawnmarket South
Craigie,	Lawrence	W.S.	Fisher's	Lawnmarket South
Craigie,	Robert	Advocate	Fisher's	Lawnmarket South
Cranstone,	James	Shopkeeper/Ale Seller	Scheil's	Blackfriar's Wynd
Cranstone,	George	of Dewar	Anderson's	Grassmarket Mid
Crass,	James			Horse Wynd
Craw,	James	Brewer		Marlin's Wynd
Craw,	Mrs		Craw's	High Street at Baillie Fyfe's Close
Craw,	Mrs	Room Setter	McKenzie's	Blackfriar's Wynd
Crawford,	Alexander	Baxter	Alexander's	President's Stairs, Parliament Close
Crawford,	John	Fruiterer	"Orange Wench"	High Street opposite Niddry's Wynd
Crawford,	Gideon	Bookseller	Alexander's	President's Stairs, Parliament Close
Crawford,	Hugh		McGowan's	Lawnmarket South
Crawford,	Jenet		Good's	Colledge Wynd
Crawford,	John	Ale Seller	Gavinlock's	Forrester's Wynd
Crawford,	Mrs		Colt's	Cant's Close Foot
Crawford,	Mrs		Wight's	Cowgate Head
Crawford,	Peter	Merchant	McGhie's	West Bow Mid
Crawford,	Ronald	*of Restalrig* W.S.		Cant's Close Foot

NAME		OCCUPATION	ADDRESS	
CRAWFORD,	Ronald	*of Jordanhill* W.S.	McGowan's	Bess Wynd
CRAWFORD,	William	Manservant	Brownhills	Cowgate North
CRICHTON,	Patrick & Co.	Merchants	Wright's	North Foulis Close
CRICHTON,	Patrick	Merchant	Peacock's	High Street opposite Cross
CRICHTON,	Penelope	Lady	Rutherford's	Lawnmarket at Forrester's Wynd
CRICHTON,	Mrs		Little's	Cullen's Close
CRICHTON,	Mary	Lady	Pencaitland's	Niddry's Wynd
CRINZIN,	Alexander		Dallas's	Blackfriar's Wynd
CROCKATE,	Mrs	Minister's Widow	Hedderwick's	High Street at Baillie Fyfe's Close
CROCKETT,	Mr			Colledge Wynd
CROCKETT,	Thomas	Merchant	Crockett's	West Bow Foot
CROOKS,	William	Baxter	Allan's	Castlehill
CROSS,	John			Chamber's Close
CROSS,	John			Horse Wynd
CRUTHERS,	Christopher		Lindsay's	West Bow Head
CUDDIE,	Robert	Ale Seller	Fullerton's	Lawnmarket North
CUMMING,	Alex.	Cook	Paterson's	Lawnmarket North
CUMMING,	James	Weaver		Milne Square
CUMMING,	Jenet		Aitken's	Cowgate South
CUMMING,	Mrs	Room Setter	Peacock's	Lyon's Close
CUMMING,	Mrs		Scott's	Cowgate at Forrester's Wynd
CUMMING,	Mrs	Boarding School		Cap and Feather Close
CUMMING,	Patrick	Minister	Old Kirk	Milne's Court
CUMMING,	Thomas	Bonnetmaker	Gray's	Grassmarket East
CUMMING,	William	Merchant	Borthwick's	Luckenbooths
CUMMING,	William	Cordiner	President's Stairs	Parliament Close
CUNNINGHAM,	Alex.	*of Lathrisk* W.S.		Writer's Court
CUNNINGHAM,	Ann		Crockett's	West Bow Foot
CUNNINGHAM,	Charles	Baxter	Hutton's	Blackfriar's Wynd
CUNNINGHAM,	David	Baxter	Crawford's	West Bow South
CUNNINGHAM,	Sir David		His Own	Niddry's Wynd
CUNNINGHAM,	George			Wardrope's Close
CUNNINGHAM,	George	(ex) Porter	Foulis's	Lawnmarket
CUNNINGHAM,	George	Surgeon		James Court
CUNNINGHAM,	Lady		Dick's	Cullen's Close
CUNNINGHAM,	Mrs	Teacher	Cunningham's	Stonelaw's Close
CUNNINGHAM,	Mrs		Good's	Colledge Wynd
CURRIE,	Margaret		Clerk's	Upper Baxter's Close
CUSTOM HOUSE			Dewar's	Custom House Stairs
CUTHBERTSON,	Mrs		Bull's	Cowgate South
CUTHBERTSON,	Peter		Seton's	Libberton's Wynd
DALE,	John	Wigmaker	Kinneir's	Candlemaker Row
DALGLEISH,	James	Merchant	Murray's	Gosford's Close
DALGLEISH,	John	Watchmaker (*home*) (*shop*)	Paterson's Post Office Stairs	Paterson's Court Parliament Close
DALGLEISH,	John	Skinner	Forrest's	West Bow South
DALGLEISH,	Mrs		Spalding's	Candlemaker Row
DALKEITH,	Earl of		Kennedy's	Castlehill South
DALL,	Andrew		Bell's	Brownhills Land
DALLAS,	Alexander	Silk Dyer	Dallas's	Blackfriar's Wynd
DALLAS,	Hugh	Merchant	Colvill's	Trunk Close
DALLAS,	Mrs			Fountain Close
DALLAS,	Mrs		Garbiston's	High Street at Clamshell Turnpike
DALLAS,	Thomas	Surgeon	Lithgow's	Grassmarket West
DALLAS,	William	Wright	Hunter's	Anchor Close
DALRYMPLE,	Hugh		Miln's	Mealmarket
DALRYMPLE,	John	Merchant	Sym's	High Street at Kennedy Close
DALRYMPLE,	Lady		Dalrymple's	Lady Stairs Close

NAME		OCCUPATION		ADDRESS
Dalziel,	Lady		Hope's	Barringer's Close
Danwick,	Lady		Eccles'	Chamber's Close
David,	Mr	Wright	Blair's	Castlehill South
Davidson,	Alex.	Cordiner	Bavelaw's	Cowgate Southat President's/Scott's
Davidson,	Elizabeth	Merchant	Inglis's	High Street opposite Cross
Davidson,	James	Printer	Scott's	Cowgate South
Davidson,	John	W.S.		Advocate's Close
Davidson,	John	Merchant	Smith's	Blackfriar's Wynd
Davidson,	John	Factor	Fisher's	Lawnmarket
Davidson,	William	Manservant	Cant's	High Street at Carruber's Close
Davie,	Angus	Merchant	Angus's	Luckenbooths
Davie,	William	Goldsmith	Stonehouse's	Fishmarket Close
Dawson,	John	Cordiner	Foulis's	Castlehill South
Dawson,	Mr	Prof. of Hebrew		Colledge Wynd South
Dawson,	Mrs		Armour's	Jackson's Close
Dean,	Lady		Gordon's	Gosford's Close
D'Effrene,	Mlle.	Dancing Mistress		Carruber's Close
Dempster,	William	Goldsmith (*home*)	Smith's	Jackson's Close
		(*shop*)	Exchange Stairs	Parliament Close
Deuchar,	Andrew	Writer	His Own	Bull's Close
Dewar,	James	*of Vogrie*		Cowgate Head North
Dewar,	Robert	Writing Master	Galloway's	Lawnmarket North High Street at Clamshell Turnpike
Dewar,	Robert	Glazier	Taylor's	President's Close
Dewar,	Robert	Glazier	McLenan's	West Bow Middle
Dewar,	William	Merchant	Hunter's	West Bow Foot
Dick,	Alexander	Vintner	Armour's	High Street at North Foulis Close
Dick,	James	Mason	Dick's	Jackson's Close
Dick,	James	Brewer	Burnett's	Borthwick's Close
Dick,	John sr.	Mason		Kennedy's Close
Dick,	Mr	Hair Merchant	Jollie's	Cowgate North
Dick,	Mrs		Stewart's	Candlemaker Row
Dick,	Robert	Writer	New Stairs	Parliament Close
Dick,	Mrs Thomas	Cordiner		Fleshmarket Close
Dickie,	Andrew	Watchmaker	His Own	Lawnmarket at Forrester's/Libberton's
Dickie,	John sr.	W.S.	His Own	Kennedy's Close
Dickie,	John jr.		Hellistob's	Cowgate South
Dickson,	Alex.	Glazier	His Own	Bull's Close
Dickson,	Charles	Goldsmith	Robertson's	
Dickson,	Mrs		Marshall's	Pearson's Close
Dickson,	Robert	Webster		
Dickson,	William	Dyer/Bonnetmaker	Selkirk's	Grassmarket South East opposite Cowgate
Dingwall,	John			Marlin's Wynd
Dinning,	Alex.	Stationer	Sinclair's	Milne's Court
Dirleton,	Lady		Schaw's	Castlehill South
Doig,	David	Linen Merchant	Eglinton's	High Street at North Foulis Close
Donald,	Thomas	Smith	Davidson's	Carruber's Close
Donaldson,	Alex.	Stationer	Crichton's	Luckenbooths
Donaldson,	Alex.			Gosford's Close
Donaldson,	John	Gilder	Moffat's	Trunk Close
Donaldson,	Mrs			Kennedy's Close
Donaldson,	Mrs		Stewart's	Forrester's Wynd Foot
Donaldson,	Robert	Glover	Robertson's	James Court
Dougall,	Mrs		McCulloch's	Mary King's Close
Douglas,	Alex.	Wright	Petrie's	Burnett's Close
Douglas,	Andrew	Provision Merchant	"Crown & Limon Tree"	High Street at Marlin's Wynd

NAME		OCCUPATION	ADDRESS	
Douglas,	Andrew		Veitch's	Forrester's Wynd West
Douglas,	Archibald	Merchant	Brown's	Lawnmarket North
Douglas,	Belle	Lady	Smith's Land	High Street North
Douglas,	George	Farmer	Friershaw's	Grassmarket South
Douglas,	John	Armourer (*home*)	Garbiston's	Kinloch's Close South
		(*shop*)		Above Niddry's Wynd
Douglas,	John	Architect	Hyndwood's	Todrick's Wynd
Douglas,	John	Surgeon	His Own	Custom House Stairs Parliament Close
Douglas,	Mary	Lady	Smith's Land	High Street North
Douglas,	Mrs		Learmonth's	Skinner's Close
Douglas,	Mrs		Smetholm's	Fountain Close
Douglas,	Mrs			Gosford's Close
Douglas,	Mr			Dickson's Close
Douglas,	Robert	Writer	Wordie's	Niddry's Wynd
Douglas,	Robert	Ale Seller	Aitken's	West Bow South
Douglas,	William		Foulis's	Castlehill South
Douglas,	William	Merchant	Seton's	Luckenbooths
Dow,	James	Merchant	Hunter's	President's Close
Dow,	John	Writer	Legat's	Fishmarket Close
Dow,		Lady		
Dow,	Mis		McConachie's	Halkerston's Wynd
Dow,	William	Merchant	His Own	Niddry's Wynd
Dowie,	David	Merchant	Crockett's	West Bow Foot
Dowie,	David	Mason	Good's	Colledge Wynd
Dowie,	William		Speir's	Lawnmarket North
Down,	Mrs		Middleton's	Trunk Close
Downie,	John	Dancing Master (*home*)		Carruber's Close
		(*school*)	Crawford's	Niddry's Wynd below Mary's Chapel
Downie,	Mrs		MacLelland's	Society
Drummond & Austain,		Surgeons	Cockburn's	Lawnmarket at Bank/Cullen's
Drummond,	Adam	Surgeon	Fisher's	Lawnmarket South
Drummond,	Andrew	Seedsman		Carruber's Close Head
Drummond,	George	Comm. of Excise		Dickson's Close Head
Drummond,	George	Hammerman	Denholm's	Lawnmarket at Wardrope's Court
Drummond,	James	Merchant	Scirving's	Good Town's Land
Drummond,	John	Chair Master	Paterson's	Milne Square
Drummond,	John	Lord	President's Stairs	Parliament Close
Drummond,	John		McIlwraith's	Blackfriar's Wynd
Drummond,	Mr	*of Excise*	Muschet's	Grassmarket East
Drummond,	Mr	*of Hawthorndean*	Drummond's	Blackfriar's Wynd
Drummond,	Mrs	Ale Seller	Hamilton's	Old Post Office Close
Drummond,	Mrs		Ancrum's	Monteith's Close
Drummond,	Mrs			Tweedales Court
Drummond,	Miss		Blair's	Castlehill South
Drummond,	Patrick	Seed Merchant	Galloway's	Lawnmarket North
Drummond,		Professor	Hanty's	Monteith's Close
Drummond,	Robert	Printer		Swan's Close
Drummond, & Co.		Printers	Schiell's	Swan's Close
Drummore,	Hew	Lord of Session		Geddes' Close
Drysdale,	Joseph	Cordiner	Weaver's	New Assembly Close
Drysdale,	Mr	Cordiner	Bryden's	West Bow Mid.
Drysdale,	Mr	Exciseman	Simpson's	Libberton's Wynd
Drysdale,	Mrs		Pollock's	Foulis Close
Drysdale,	Thomas	Stabler	Duncan's	Argylle Square
Duff,	John	Hair Merchant	Hepburn's	James Court
Duff,	John		Wilkie's	High Street at New Assembly Close
Duff,	Miss	Merchant	Penman's	Parliament Close
Duguid,	George		Schaw's	Kennedy's Close
Dumfries,		Earl of	Dumfries'	Kennedy's Land Castlehill South

NAME		OCCUPATION	ADDRESS	
Dun,	Lord			Milne Square
Dun,	William	Merchant	Foulis's	Lawnmarket South
Dunbar & McGhie			Inglis's	Writer's Court
Dunbar,	George	Merchant	Dunbar's	James Court
Dunbar,	James	Stabler	Thomson's	Grassmarket East
Dunbar,	John	Skinner	Lithgow's	Grassmarket West
Dunbar,	Lady			
Dunbar,	Ronald	W.S.		Gosford's Close
Dunbar,	William	Barber	Dunbar's	Lawnmarket at Milne's Court
Dunbar,	William		Chatto's	Dickson's Close
Duncan,	Alexander	Druggist	Seton's	Lawnmarket at Royston's
Duncan,	Elizabeth		Fairholm's	Allan's Close
Duncan,	Helen		Chalmer's	Bell's Wynd East
Duncan,	Jean		Kinneir's	Royston's Close
Duncan,	Ludovic		Hepburn's	Don's Close
Duncan,	Robert	Trunkmaker	Houston's	Mealmarket
Duncanson,	Thomas	Stabler	Hamilton's	Grassmarket West
Dundas,	Betty		Scott's/Wilson's	Plainstone Close
Dundas,	James	*of Castlecarry*	Anderson's	West Bow Middle
Dundas,	John			Milne's Court
Dundas,		Doctor	His Own	Fountain Close
Dundas,	Ralph	Merchant	Marjoribanks	Warriston's Close
Dundas,	Robert	Merchant	His Own	New Stairs Parliament Close
Dundas,	Robert	*of Arniston*	Bishop's	Carruber's Close
Dundas,	Thomas & Co.	Merchants	Dundas's	Luckenbooths
Dundas,	Thomas			Hyndford's Close
Dundas,	Thomas	Merchant	Dundass's	President's Stairs Parliament Close
Dundas,	William		Johnstone's	Upper Baxter's Close
Dundonald,	Lady		Her Own	Carruber's Close
Dunlop,	Lady		Sinclair's	Skinner's Close
Dunlop,	Thomas	Wright	Schaw's	President's Close
Dunlop,	Lady		Nevey's	Fountain Close
Dunsmuir,	George	Merchant	Lindsay's	West Bow Head
Dunsmuir,	John	Merchant		Lawnmarket opposite Forrester's Wynd
Dunsmuir,	Mrs	Merchant	Brown's	Lawnmarket North
Dunstaffnage,	Lady		Kilkerran's	Lawnmarket at Forrester's/Libberton
Durham,	Miss		Spence's	Murdoch's Close
Eagle,	Archibald	Seed Merchant	McKay's	High Street at Smith's Land
Eason,	James	Gauger (Excise)	Johnstone's	West Bow South
Easton,	Mrs		Easton's	
Eccles,	Martin	Surgeon	Campbell's	Foulis's Close
Edgar,	Mr	Cordiner	Lindsay's	Cant's Close
Edgar,	Mrs		Her Own	Lyon's Close
Edgar,	Mrs		Henderson's	Forrester's Wynd Foot
Edman,	John		Penman's	Advocate's Close
Edmonstone,	Alex.	Merchant (*Shop*)	Barclay's	Luckenbooths
		(*Home*)	Johnstone's	Royston's Close
Ednum,	Lady		Hay's	Smith's Land
Elchies,	Lord		Surgeon's Hall	High School Yards
Elder,	Betty	Ale Seller	Glover's	Niddry's Wynd
Elder,	John	Shoemaker	Stenhouse's	Marlin's Wynd
Elliot,		Doctor	Hope's	Trunk Close
Elliot,	Alexander	Baxter	Hendry's	Cowgate North
Elliot,	Gilbert	(see Lord Minto)		
Elliot,	Mr		Inglis's	Bell's Wynd
Elliot,	Mrs		Turnbull's	Brown's Land opposite Tolbooth
Elliot,	Widow	Stabler	Tod's	Horse Wynd West

NAME		OCCUPATION	ADDRESS	
Elliot,	William	Writer		Kennedy's Close
Ellis,	Mrs		Innes's	Cowgate South
Elphingstone,	Anne		Her own	Carruber's Close
Elphingstone,		Master of	Kinloch's	Kinloch's Close
Elphingstone,	Mr		Douglas's	Skinner's Close
Elphingstone,	Mrs		Anderson's	West Bow Middle
Elphingstone,	Thomas		Duncan's	Argylle Square
Erskine,	Alexander	Smith	Halyburton's	Grassmarket West
Erskine,	Charles	*of Tinwald;* *Lord Justice Clerk*		Bull's Stairs/Milne Square
Erskine,	James	Advocate	Campbell's Buildings	Argylle Square
Erskine,	Mr	*of Carnock*		Marlin's Wynd East
Erskine,	Mrs	*of Carnock*		Byre's Close
Erskine,	Mrs	Widow		Milne's Court
Erskine,	Mrs		Anderson's	West Bow Middle
Espline,	Charles	Merchant	Burns'	Swan's Close
Espline,	Mary	Widowed — now Mrs Laurence	at "Hand and Pen"	
Ewart,	James	Accomptant	Cleghorn's	Grassmarket West
Ewing,	Mrs	Room Setter	Brown's	Galloway's Close
Excise Office		Merchant's/Wight's	Cowgate South	
Ezat,	Neil	Ale Seller	Munro's	Lawnmarket at Wardrope's Court
Fairfoull,	Mrs		Wilkie's	Robertson's Close
Fairholm, Adam & Co.		Merchants	Fairholm's	Craig's Close
Fairholm,	Adam	Merchant	Fairholm's	Craig's Close
Fairholm,	John	Furrier		
Fairholm,	Mr & Mrs	*of Pilton*	Fairholm's	West Bow Middle
Fairholm, Thomas	Mr, Mrs	Merchants	Smith's	Niddry's Wynd
Fairlie,	Patrick	Webster		
Fairlie,	Patrick jr.	Webster		
Falconer,	George	Ale Seller	Clerk's	West Bow Head
Falconer,	Lady	*of Mountaine*	Her Own	Bull's Close
Falconer,	Mr			Cullen's Close
Falconer,	Mr			World's End Close
Falconer,	Peter		McRabbie's	Warriston Close
Farquhar,	Alexander	Skinner		Lawnmarket
Farquhar,	James	Merchant	Farquhar's	Lawnmarket at Roxburgh's Close
Farquharson,	Francis	Accomptant	His Own	Craig's Close
Farquharson,	Mrs		Marshal's	Cowgate South
Farquharson,	Miss		Foggo's	Horse Wynd West
Farquharson,	Walter	Doctor		Borthwick's Close
Farras,	David		Anderson's	Grassmarket Mid
Fenwick,	John	Chairman	Wright's	High Street at North Foulis Close
Fergus,	Mrs		Wardrop's	Libberton's Wynd
Ferguson,	Miss B.			Carruber's Close
Ferguson,		Doctor	Sharp's	Kinloch's Close
Ferguson,	James	Coppersmith	Lauder's	West Bow
Ferguson,	James			Lawnmarket at Roxburgh's Close
Ferguson,	John		Reid's	Cant's Close Foot
Ferguson,	John	Merchant	Wright's	Con's Close
Ferguson,	Mrs		Hay's	West Bow Middle
Ferguson,	Mrs	Widow	Bavelaw's	Cowgate South at President's/Scott's
Ferguson,	Walter	Writer	Laigh Coffee House	
Ferguson,	William		Wright's	Con's Close
Ferrier,	David	Stabler	Crighton's	Grassmarket West
Fettes,	James	Porter	Clerk's	Fountain Close
Fettes,	John	Merchant	Hutton's	Lawnmarket North
Fiddes,	Robert		Moncour's	Horse Wynd

NAME		OCCUPATION	ADDRESS	
FIFE,	James	Linen Merchant	2nd Laigh Shop	above Bank Close
FIFE,	John	Merchant	Geddes'	Bell's Wynd
FINLAY,	Daniel	Wright	Hope's	Monteith's Close
FINLAY,	David	Wright	Hope's	Monteith's Close
FINLAY,	Francis	Goldsmith	Dallas's	Todrick's Wynd
FINLAY,	James	*of Walliford*	Christie's	Borthwick's Close
FINLAY,	John	Merchant	Hunter's	West Bow Foot
FINLAY,	Misses		Duncan's	Libberton's Wynd
FINLAY,	Miss		Burn's	Libberton's Wynd
FINLAY,	Robert	Brewer	Messenger's	Horse Wynd
FINLAY,	William	Glassgrinder	Jolley's	Burnet's Close
FINLAYSON,	Alex	Underclerk of Session		Lawnmarket at Bank/Cullen's
FINLAYSON,	Duncan	Merchant	Thomson's	Cullen's Close
FINLAYSON,	James	Manservant	at Mr Belches, John	Niddry's Wynd
FINLAYSON,	John	Instrument Maker	Dowie's	Cowgate South
FINLAYSON,	Mrs		Scirving's	Good Town's Land
FINLAYSON,	Mrs			Paterson's Court
FISH,	John	Linen Merchant	Mein's	Lawnmarket North
FISHER,	Charles	Merchant	Thomson's	Grassmarket West
FISHER,	Isobel	Ale Seller	Bruce's	Under Baxter's Close
FISHER,	Mr	Servant	Robertson's	Lawnmarket at Gladstone's Land
FISHER,	Mrs		Aikman's	Lady Stair's Close
FLEMING,	Agnes			Under Baxter's Close
FLEMING,	George	Printer	Fleming's	Pearson's Close
FLEMING,	Miss		Forbes	Murdoch's Close
FLEMING,	Robert	Printer/Bookseller	Edinburgh Evening Courant	Pearson's Close
FLETCHER,	Mrs		Baillie's	Cant's Close
FLINT,	James	Merchant	Hunter's	Flint's Land Grassmarket South
FOGGO,	Mrs		Foggo's	Horse Wynd
FOGGO,	Walter	Wigmaker	His Own	Halkerston's Wynd
FORBES,	Hugh	Advocate		Lady Stairs Close
FORBES,	James	Merchant	Johnstone's	Castlehill South
FORBES,	James	Merchant	Mitchell's	Fishmarket Close
FORBES,	John	Clerk	Kennedy's	Castlehill South
FORBES,	John	Ale Seller	Cleghorn's	Horse Wynd
FORBES,	Mr	Teacher	Dalrymple's	Bull's Close
FORBES,	Mrs	Widow	Grant's	Trunk Close
FORBES,	Mrs		Forbes's	Milne's Court
FORBES,	Mrs	*of Knapernie*	Hogg's	High Street at Carruber's Close
FORBES,	Mrs		Mason's	Blackfriar's Wynd
FORBES,	William			Jackson's Close
FORBES,	William	Room Setter	Baillie's	Bull's Close
FORBES,	William	W.S.		Custom House Stairs
FORDICE,	Thomas	Writer	His Own	Dickson's Close
FORDICE	Thomas			President's Stairs Parliament Close
FORDYCE,	John	Merchant		
FORREST,	Andrew	Waulker	Veitch's	Forrester's Wynd West
FORREST,	James	*of Comiston*	Dewar's	West Bow
FORREST,	Elizabeth			Old Assembly Close
FORREST,	John	Merchant	Dalrymple's	Castlehill North
FORREST,	Mrs		Her Own	Lawnmarket North
FORRESTER,	Barbara	Room Setter	Spence's	Bull's Close
FORRESTER,	James	Writer	Sideserf's	West Bow Foot
FORRESTER,	John		Newland	Lawnmarket
FORRESTER,	Robert	Merchant	Foster's	Grassmarket East
FORTUNE,	Thomas	Tanner	Veitch's	Forrester's Wynd West
FOTHERINGHAME	Isobel	Merchant/Ale Seller	Norrie's	High Street at Kinloch's Close

NAME		OCCUPATION	ADDRESS	
Fowler,	James	Ale Seller	Robertson's	James Court
Fowles,		Doctor	Riddle's	Royston's Close
Fowles,	George		Foulis's	Castlehill South
Fowles,	Grizell		McRabbie's	Stonelaw's Close
Fowles,	John			Milne's Square
Fowles,	William	Ale Seller	Biggar's	Swan's Close
Foy,	Dennis	Silk Dyer	Oliphant's	Niddry's Wynd
Francis,	Hugh		Campbell's	Grassmarket West
Fraser,	Daniel	Footman	Wardrop's	Cant's Close
Fraser,	Hugh		Chatto's	Dickson's Close
Fraser,	Hugh	Ale Seller	Nisbet's	Niddry's Wynd
Fraser,	John			Milne's Court
Fraser,	John	Ale Seller	Kerr's	Carruber's Close
Fraser,	Robert	Room Setter	Clerk's	Lyon's Close
Fraser,	Thomas		Aikman's	Candlemaker Row
Fraser,	William	Manservant	Hunter's	Kinloch's Close
Fraser,	William	W.S.	President's Stairs	Parliament Close
Frazer,	William			Old Post House Stairs
Freebairn,	Mrs		Murray's	High Street at Fleshmarket Close
Frogg,	Robert	Merchant	Jameson's	Lawnmarket
Fyfe,	Alexander	Ale Seller	Hutton's	Gosford's Close
Fyfe,	James	Merchant	Grahame's	Lawnmarket at Bank Close
Fyfe,	John	Merchant		Bell's Wynd
Fyfe,	John	Writer	Mylne's	Mary King's Close
Fyfe,	Patrick	Stabler	Burd's	Grassmarket East
Gachan,	Mrs			Lawnmarket at Bank Close
Gachan,	Mrs			Lyon's Close
Gair,	James	Cordiner	Dalie's	Blackfriar's Wynd
Gairdner,	A.		Lindsay's	Castlehill South
Gairns,	Mrs		Somervail's	Grassmarket Mid
Gairns,	Robert	Waiter	McRabbie's	Stonelaw's Close
Gall,	Alexander		Hewit's	Fleshmarket Close Head
Gallatly,	William	Merchant	Tytler's	Wardrope's Court
Gallatrie,	Mrs		Petrie's	Burnet's Close
Galloway,	Alex.	Stabler	Allan's	Grassmarket West
Galloway,	Earl of		Galloway's	Horse Wynd West
Galloway,	James	Furrier		
Galloway,	Mrs	Corkcutter	Jameson's	Kennedy's Close
Galston,	Lady		Whiteburgh's	Fleshmarket Close
Garden,	James	Wright	Scheil's	Sandiland's Close
Garden,	William			Goudilock's Land
Gardiner,	Fanny	Vintner/Ale Seller	Don's	Don's Close
Gardiner,	James	Hammerman	Gray's	Grassmarket East
Gardiner,	Mrs	Merchant	More's	Lawnmarket
Gardiner,	Mrs		Craig's	Grassmarket East
Gardiner,	William	Candlemaker	Syme's	Barringer's Close
Gardiner,	William	Bonnetmaker	Bavelaw's	President's Close
Garroch,	John	Ale Seller	MacLeish's	Covenant Close
Garroch,	Mrs		Her Own	Dickson's Close
Gedd,	Dougal	Goldsmith	Gedd's	Byre's Close
Gedd,	Mrs		Bruce's	Libberton's Wynd
Gedd,	Robert	Dyer	Weaver's	New Assembly Close
Gedd,	Robert	Dyer	Christie's	Borthwick's Close
Geddes,	James	Watchmaker	Geddes's	Bell's Wynd
Geddes,	Miss	Milliner	Ferguson's	Kennedy's Close
Geddes,	Miss			Cant's Close Foot
Geddes,	Mrs		Geddes's	West Bow/Lawnmarket
Geddes,	William	Poulterer	Monro's	Geddes' Close
G.P. Office			Campbell's	President's Stairs Parliament Close
Gibb,	Andrew	Ale Seller	Jackson's	Luckenbooths

NAME		OCCUPATION	ADDRESS	
Gibb,	Elizabeth		Bannatyne's	Trunk Close
Gibb,	Mrs		Gibb's	Lady Stairs Close
Gibb,	Robert	Vintner	Alison's	New Stairs Parliament Close
Gibson,	Archibald	Cordiner	Tod's	Grassmarket East
Gibson,	Archibald	*of Cliftonhall*		Bull's Close
Gibson,	Hendry	Flesher	Pollock's	Foulis Close
Gibson,	James	Sclater	Thomson's	Grassmarket West
Gibson,	John	Auctioneer	His Own	High Street opposite Cross-Well
Gibson,	Mr	Slater	Young's	Society
Gibson,	Mrs		Her Own	Fleshmarket Close
Gibson,	Mrs		Bruce's	Grassmarket West
Gibson,	Mrs			High Street at Todrick's Wynd
Gibson,	Margaret		Veitch's	West Bow Foot
Gibson,	Thomas	W.S.	Fisher's	Lawnmarket South
Gibson,	Thomas	*of Cliftonhall*	Bull's Stairs	Milne Square
Gibson,	William	Cordiner		
Gifford,	Thomas	Hammerman	His Own	Candlemaker Row
Gilbert,	James	Ale Seller	McClelland's	Society
Gilchrist,	David	Flesher	Greig's	Fleshmarket Close
Gilchrist,	Robert	Cooper	Kelie's	West Bow Middle
Gilchrist,	William	Goldsmith	His Own	Anchor Close
Gill,	Baillie	Glazier	His Own	Lawnmarket North
Gillane,	Mrs		Clerk's	Castlehill South
Gilles,	Mrs		Hedderwick's	Lawnmarket North
Gilles,	Margaret		Bannatyne's	Trunk Close
Gillespie,	Alex.	Ale Seller	Baillie's	Meal Market
Gillespie,	James	Merchant	Armour's	High Street at North Foulis Close
Gilliland,	James	Jeweler	Blair's	Luckenbooths
Gilmore,	Mrs Ann		Little's	Cullen's Close
Gilmore,	James		Legat's	Fishmarket Close
Givan,	Alexander	Glover	Stonehouse's	Fishmarket Close
Glasgow,	Lady			Paterson's Court
Glass,	Mr	Writer	Fraser's	Milne's Back Court
Glass,	Mrs			High Street at North Foulis
Glass,	Mrs Helen	Mantua Maker	Finlayson's	Kinloch's Close
Glassie,	Lady		Bain's	Niddry's Wynd
Glen,	John	Minister	Haddo's Hole	Milne's Court
Glendinning,	Mr			Cant's Close
Glendinning,	William			Grassmarket East
Godsman,	John	Fishmonger		Old Fishmarket Close
Goldie,	Alex.	*of Ryes* W.S.		James Court
Goldie,		Professor		Colledge Wynd
Goldie,	Thomas	Carrier	Flint's	Grassmarket Mid.
Goldman,	John	Turner	Legat's	Fishmarket Close
Golston,	Lady		Whiteburgh's	Fleshmarket Close E.
Good,	Andrew	Wright	Good's	Colledge Wynd
Good,	William	Wright	Good's	Colledge Wynd
Goodale,	Walter		New Stairs	Parliament Close
Gordon's		Barley Office	Wardrop's	Cowgate at Cant's/Dickson's Close
Gordon,	Ann		Callander's	Foulis Close
Gordon,	James	Saddler	Scheil's	Chamber's Close
Gordon,	James	Merchant	Ferguson's	Cowgate Head South
Gordon,	James	Dyer	Aitken's	West Bow South
Gordon,	John		Weemy's	Niddry's Wynd
Gordon,	John	Stabler	Innes's	Horse Wynd West
Gordon,	John		Gavinlock's	Forrester's Wynd
Gordon,	John		Bruce's	Libberton's Wynd
Gordon,	John	Merchant	Riddle's	Royston's Close
Gordon,	Kenneth		Nairn's	Castlehill North

NAME		OCCUPATION		ADDRESS
Gordon & Irvine				Libberton's Wynd
Gordon,	Mrs		Stewart's	West Bow Head
Gordon,	Mrs		Anderson's	Foulis Close
Gordon,	Mrs			Fountain Close
Gordon,	Mrs		Watson's	Forrester's Wynd W.
Gordon,	Patrick	Watchmaker		Skinner's Close
Gordon,	Robert	Goldsmith		Parliament Close
Gordon,	William	Bookseller	Robertson's	James Court
Gordon,	William	Litster	Peter's	Horse Wynd
Gordon,	William	Bookseller	Jameson's	Parliament Close
Gordon,	William	Ale Seller		Cullen's Close
Gourlie,	Thomas	Weaver	McArthur's	Kennedy's Close
Govan,	Archibald			Trunk Close
Govan,	Stephen	Merchant	Govan's	James Court
Govan,	William	Glazier	Govan's	James Court
Gow,	Gilbert	Vintner	Arbuthnot's	Writer's Court
Gow,	Mrs	Tavern Keeper		Anchor Close
Gowan,	James	Wig-maker	Blair's	Swan Close
Grahame,	David	Merchant	Allan's	Grassmarket West
Grahame,	David	Merchant	Post Office Stairs	Parliament Close
Grahame,	David	Barber	Laing's	Gladstone's Land
Grahame,	Hugh	Writer	Barber's	New Stairs Parliament Close
Grahame,	James	Confectioner	Dickson's	Cowgate Head
Grahame,	James	W.S.	Bishop's	Carruber's Close
Grahame,	James			Milne Square
Grahame,	John	Printer	Muschet's	Grassmarket East
Grahame,	Mrs		Fyfe's	Marlin's Wynd
Grahame,	Mrs		Gavinlock's	Forrester's Wynd
Grahame,	Mrs	Wig-maker	Young's	Society
Grahame,	Miss		Cochrane's	
Grahame,	Samuel	Bookbinder	Young's	Society
Grahame,	Samuel & John	Bookbinders	Young's	Society
Grahame,	Thomas	Brewer	Ogilvie's	Cowgate
Grahame,	William	Saddler	Veitch's	Cowgate Head North
Granier,	Mr & Mrs	Dancers		Marlin's Wynd Head
Grant,	Alexander	Merchant		
Grant,	Donald		Cleghorn's	Horse Wynd
Grant,	Mrs Frances			James Court
Grant,	James	Merchant	Sinclair's	West Bow Foot
Grant,	John		Gavinlock's	Forrester's Wynd
Grant,	Ludovic	Writer (Office) (Home)	MacKenzie's Thom's	Parliament Close Monteith's Close
Grant,	Mr			Libberton's Wynd
Grant,	Reverend	Teacher		Halkerston's Wynd
Grant,	Misses		Cullen's	Upper Baxter's Close
Grant,	Mrs		Gray's	Grassmarket East
Grant,	Mrs		Gavinlock's	Forrester's Wynd
Grant,	Robert	*of Ruthrie* W.S.		Halkerston's Wynd
Grant,	Thomas	Brewer	Mitchell's	Erskine's Land
Grant,	Lord William	*of Prestongrange* Lord Advocate		Advocate's Close
Grant,	William		Nisbet's	Bell's Wynd
Gray,	Alexander			James Court
Gray,	George	Merchant		
Gray,	Mrs Henry	Ale Seller	Hammermen's	Cowgate Head South
Gray,	John	Cordiner	Whitehead's	Mary King's Close
Gray,	Mrs	Merchant	Hamilton's	High Street at Halkerston's Wynd
Gray,	Mrs	Vintner	Mercer's	High Street at Borthwick's Close
Gray,	Mrs		Keltie's	Forrester's Wynd W.
Gray,	Robert			Wardrope's Court
Gray,	Robert	Writer	Simpson's	Cowgate South

NAME		OCCUPATION		ADDRESS
GRAY,	William	Sootie-man	Thomson's	Lawnmarket at Fisher's Land
GRAY,	William	Printer	Wight's	Cowgate Head South
GREAT,	David	Mends China	Nisbet's	Niddry's Wynd
GREENLEES,	Mrs	Room Setter	Hutton's	Lawnmarket 1st entry below James Court
GREENLEES,	Robert	Merchant	Montgomerie's	Lawnmarket at Wardrope's Court
GREIG,	Andrew	Flesher		Fleshmarket Close
GREIG,	David	Vintner	Armour's	Jackson's Close
GREIG,	John	Flesher		
GREIG,	Robert	Writer	Forrest's	Castlehill North
GREIG,	Mrs	Widow	Cleghorn's	Horse Wynd
GREIG,	Robert	Merchant	Mylne's	Milne Square
GREIG,	William	Manservant	Riddle's	Niddry's Wynd
GRIERSON,	David		Hamilton's	High Street at Halkerston's Wynd
GRIERSON,	James	Merchant	Robertson's	Lawnmarket at Gladstone's Land
GRIEVE,	John	Merchant	Livingstone's	Under Baxter's Close
GRIEVE,	John	Merchant		Byre's Close
GRIEVE,	John	Manservant	Lauder's	Niddry's Wynd
GUILD,	Mr	Writer	Swinton's	Dickson's Close
GULLANE,	Mrs		Innes's	High Street at Carruber's Close
GUSTARD,	William Rev.	Minister	Fairholm's	West Bow Middle
GUTHRIE,	Alex.	Limner	Bell's	Castlehill
GUTHRIE,	Charles	Writer	Bruce's	Libberton's Wynd
GUTHRIE,	Mrs	Room Setter	Blair's	Warriston Close
HACKET,	Sir Peter		Surgeon's Hall	High School Yards
HACKNEY,	David	Ale Seller	Clerk's	Castlehill South
HADDINGTON,	Lady		Infirmary	Robertson's Close
HADDINGTON	Lord		Blair's	Castlehill South
HAIGGS,	Colin	Lint Dresser	Haiggs'	Baillie Fyfe's Close
HAIGGS,	William	Baxter	Willson's	Plainstone Close
HAINING,	Lord			West Bow Head
HALDEN,	Jean		Hunter's	Kinloch's Close
HALDEN,	Patrick	H.M. Solicitor		James Court
HALKERSTONE,	Lady		Halkerstone's	Lawnmarket at Bank Close
HALL,	Amelia			Under Baxter's Close
HALL,	Lady			Gosford's Close
HALLEY,	John		Hamilton's	High Street at Halkerstone's Wynd
HALLYBURTON,	Henrietta		Magdalen's	High Street above Tron
HALLYBURTON,	James	W.S.	Thom's	Libberton's Wynd
HALLYBURTON,	John	Merchant	Grant's	Lawnmarket at Forrester's Wynd
HALLYBURTON,	John			Milne's Court
HALLYBURTON,	Mr			Gray's Close
HALLYBURTON,	Mrs		Easton's	High Street
HALLYBURTON,	Misses		Cummings	Fishmarket Close E.
HALYDAY,	Mistress		Ewart's	Murdoch's Close
HALYDAY,	Mistress		Wilkie's	High Street at New Assembly Close
HAMILTON & BALFOUR		Booksellers	Hay's	High Street at Old Post Office Close
HAMILTON & BRUCE		Merchants	Foster's	Grassmarket East
HAMILTON,	Andrew	Merchant	Ranie's	West Bow South
HAMILTON,	Archibald	*of Dalserf*		Milne's Court
HAMILTON,	Archibald	*of Dalserf*	Lindsay's	West Bow Head
HAMILTON,	Charles	Stabler	Alexander's	Candlemaker Row
HAMILTON,		Doctor		Borthwick's Close E.
HAMILTON,	Gavin & Co.	Merchants	Infirmary	Robertson's Close

NAME		OCCUPATION	ADDRESS	
Hamilton,	Gavin	Merchant	Cleghorn's	Society
Hamilton,	George	Taylor	Mylne's	Bull's Close
Hamilton,	Gordon Charles		Foulis's	Castlehill South
Hamilton,	Hugh	Merchant	Hepburn's	Blackfriar's Wynd
Hamilton,	Hugh	Sir	Hog's	Castlehill South
Hamilton,	James	Surgeon	Hellistob's	Cowgate South
Hamilton,	John	Cordiner	Gray's	Grassmarket East
Hamilton,	John			New Stairs Parliament Close
Hamilton,	John	Cordiner		Milne's Court
Hamilton,	Mary	Lady, *of Pencaitland*	Brownhills	Cowgate North
Hamilton,	Mr	Merchant	Crawford's	West Bow South
Hamilton,	Mr	*of Gilderscleugh*	Kennedy's	Cant's Close
Hamilton,	Mrs	Seedmerchant	"Gardiner's"	Veitch's Land
Hamilton,	Mrs		Dallas's	Todrick's Wynd
Hamilton,	Mrs		Baird's	Hyndfoord's Close
Hamilton,	Mrs	Teacher	McRabbie's	Stonelaw's Close
Hamilton,	Mrs		Capell's	Colledge Wynd
Hamilton,	Mrs		Somervail's	Society
Hamilton,	Misses		Millar's	Grassmarket West
Hamilton,	Robert	Merchant	Stewart's	Anchor Close
Hamilton,	Robert Rev.	Minister		Halkerston's Wynd
Hamilton,	Robert	*of Monkland* W.S.	Crawford's	Colledge Wynd
Hamilton,	William	Bookseller	His Own (shop)	James Court High Street opposite Cross
Hamilton,	William	Brewer	Hamilton's	Grassmarket Mid.
Hardy,	Andrew	Baxter	His Own	Peebles Wynd
Hardy,	Hendry	Baxter	Brown's	Wardrope's Court
Hardy,	James	Wright	Murray's	Bull's Close
Hardy,	John	Baxter	Barridge's	Gosford's Close
Hardy,	Mrs	Ale Seller	Gray's	Grassmarket East
Harley,	Alexander	Merchant	Hamilton's	Cowgate North
Harley,	Mr	Taylor		Pearson's Close
Harper,	William			Foulis Close
Harries,	Betty			Covenant Close
Harrison & Davison,	Misses		Reid's	Stonelaw's Close
Hart,	Archibald	Merchant	Dewar's	Milne Square
Hart,	Archibald			Baillie Fyfe's Close
Harvey,	Mrs		Syme's	Cant's Close Foot
Harvey,	Florence	Merchant (home) (shop)	Lundie's	High Street opposite Cross High Street at Fishmarket/Borthwick's
Harwood,	Lady		Wight's	Cowgate Head South
Hastie,	George	Ale Seller	Hamilton's	Grassmarket
Hathorn,	Hugh	Merchant	Forbes's	High Street at Forrester's/Libberton's
Hathorn,	Mrs		Duncan's	Argyll Square
Hay,	Adolphus		His Own	Cant's Close
Hay,	Alexander	Wright	Hay's	Geddes Close
Hay,	Alexander	Lady	Hay's	Hyndfoord's Close
Hay,	Andrew		Ancrum's	Cowgate Head North
Hay,	Andrew		McLenan's	West Bow Mid.
Hay,		Doctor	Blair's	Warriston's Close
Hay,	George	Printer	Campbell's	New Stairs Parliament Close
Hay,	James	W.S.	Scale Stairs	Old Assembly Close W.
Hay,	James			Paterson's Court
Hay,	John	Wigmaker	Chalmer's	Bell's Wynd East
Hay,	John	Writer	Wordie's	Niddry's Wynd
Hay,	John	Baxter	Laboratory	Cowgate South
Hay,	William	Merchant		Tweeddale Court
Hay,	Mrs		Blyth's	Castlehill North
Hay,	Mrs	Room Setter	McKenzie's	Milne Square
Hay,	Mrs		Scheil's	Sandiland's Close

NAME		OCCUPATION		ADDRESS
Hay,	Mrs		Hunter's	Todrick's Wynd
Hay,	Mrs		Lothian's	Blackfriar's Wynd
Hay,	Mrs Alexander			Foulis's Close
Hay,	Mrs		Nairn's	Stonelaw's Close
Hay,	Mistress		Hamilton's	Cowgate North
Hay,	Thomas	Baxter	Hay's	Dickson's Close
Hay,	Thomas		Craigleith's	Peebles Wynd East
Hay,	William	*of Charterfield*	Syme's	Kennedy's Close
Hay,	William		Miln's	Meal Market
Hay,	William	Lady	Dundas's	Paterson's Court
Hedderwick,	Thomas	Baxter	His Own	Lawnmarket
Hempseed,	John	Merchant	Hempseed's	West Bow Foot
Henderson,	Alex.	Vintner	His Own	High Street North at Brown's Close
Henderson,	Alexander	Cordiner	Myln's	Mary King's Close
Henderson,	Andrew	Merchant	Wallace's	West Bow Mid.
Henderson,	John	*of Liston*	His Own	Wardrope's Court
Henderson,	Lady		Riddle's	Royston's Close
Henderson,	Lady		Surgeon's Hall	High School Yards
Henderson,	Mr		Kennedy's	Cant's Close Foot
Henderson,	Miss	Ale Seller	Corsbie's	Gladstone's Land
Henderson,	Mrs	Merchant	Clerk's	Fountain Close
Henderson,	Mrs			Kinloch's Close
Henderson,	Mrs		Henderson's	Niddry's Wynd
Henderson,	Patrick	Tea Merchant	Garbiston's	High Street 1st Stair below Tron
Henderson,	Thomas	Cutlery and Sporting Goods	Scheil's	High Street opposite Cross
Hendry,	William			Anchor Close
Hepburn,	Alex.	Merchant	Hepburn's	Don's Close
Hepburn,	John		Campbell's Bldgs.	Argylle Square
Hepburn,	Mrs		Innes's	Castlehill West
Hepburn,	Mrs		Crockett's	West Bow Foot
Hepburn,	Mrs		Johnstone's & Keltie's	Royston's Close Forrester's Wynd
Hepburn,	William	Surgeon	Knoye's	Lady Stair's Close
Herriot,	James	Wright	Heriot's	Craig's Close
Herriot,	John	Candlemaker	Boswall's	Carruber's Close
Herriot,	John	Cordiner	Schiel's	Con's Close
Herriot,	Mrs		Norrie's	High Street at Kinloch's Close
Herriot,	Mrs (Widow)	Ale Seller	Cumming's	Peebles Wynd
Herriot,	Thomas	Ale Seller	Craig's	Grassmarket East
Herriot,	William	Gunsmith	Fisher's	Hyndfoord's Close
Herron,	Alexander	Cordiner	Fairlie's	Forrester's Wynd
Heslop,	John		Campbell's	Castlehill North
Highyards,	Lady		Infirmary	High School Yards
Hill,	David	Wright	Stewart's	Trunk Close
Hill,	John	Skinner	Syme's	High Street at Baillie Fyfe's Close
Hill,	Mrs	Merchant	Dunbar's	Writer's Court
Hill,	Mrs		Peter's	Horse Wynd
Hill,	Mrs		Hutton's	Gosford's Close
Hill,	Thomas	Tanner	Paterson's	Under Baxter's Close
Hill,	William	Letter Carrier	Fairholm's	Allan's Close
Hill,	William	Clerk	Howie's	Milne Square
Hill,	William	Merchant		Stonelaw's Close
Hodge,	William	Baxter	Wauch's	Murdoch's Close
Hogg,	Alexander	Merchant	Main's	Byre's Close Head opposite Back of T'booth
Hogg,	George	Brewer	Colt's	Cant's Close Foot
Hogg,	James	Merchant	Myln's	Mary King's Close
Hogg,	James	Merchant	Stewart's	High Street at Fishmarket Close

NAME		OCCUPATION	ADDRESS	
Hogg,	John	Corkcutter	Bell's	President's Close
Hogg,	Thomas	Schoolmaster	Chatto's	Dickson's Close
Hogg,	Walter	Merchant	Hay's	Gosford's Close
Hogg,	Walter & Co.	Merchants	Hogg's	Paterson's Court
Hogg,	William	Merchant	Currie's	Castlehill South
Hogg,	William & Son		Hogg's	Castlehill South
Hollands,	Archibald		Peter's	Horse Wynd
Home,	Andrew	Accomptant	Montgomerie's	Lady Stair's Close
Home,		Captain	Brown's	World's End Close
Home,	David	Merchant	Thomson's	Roxburgh's Close
Home,	George	Baxter	Craigleith Ct.	Peebles Wynd East
Home,	George	Baxter	Home's	Lawnmarket at Bank/Cullen's
Home,	John	Teacher	Wilkison's	Lawnmarket at Forrester's Wynd
Home,	Mr		Home's	Covenant Close
Home,	Mrs		Andrew's	Tweeddale Court
Home,	Robert	Wright	Wright's	Con's Close
Hope,	Archibald	Accomptant	Royal Bank	New Bank Close
Hope,	John	Merchant	"The Globe"	President's Stairs Parliament Close
Hope,	Mrs		Carnegie's	Trunk Close
Hope,	Thomas	Brewer		Campbell's Brewery
Horne,	Mrs		Inglis's	Kennedy's Close
Horner,	Mrs	Pastry Cook	Rae's	Peebles Wynd
Horseburgh,	Wm.	Doctor	Cummings	Back of Infirmary
Houston,	John	Manservant	Kerr's	Blackfriar's Wynd
Houston,	John	Writer		Paterson's Court
Houston,	Lady		Her Own	Carruber's Close
Houston,	Mrs		Good's	Colledge Wynd
Houston,	Misses		Houston's	Gray's Close
Howboise,	Mr	Vintner	Don's	Don's Close
Howison,	Charles	Wright	Howison's	Lawnmarket at Cullen's Close
Hue,	Michael,	Gilder	Brown's	President's Stiars
Hugh,	Michael			Fleshmarket Close
Humbie,	Lady		Her Own	Gray's Close
Hume,	Alexander	His Majesty's Advocate Depute		Marlin's Wynd
Hunter,	Alexander	Merchant	Hunter's	Stonelaw's Close
Hunter,	Andrew			Paterson's Court
Hunter,	Archibald	Vintner	Inglis's	Allan's Close
Hunter,	Betty		Penman's	Warriston Close
Hunter,	James	Wright	Hunter's	Kinloch's Close
Hunter,	John	Apothecary	Hunter's	West Bow Mid
Hunter,	Lauchlan	Bookseller	Lumsden's	Post Office Stairs Parliament Close
Hunter & Lauder			Hutton's	Gosford's Close
Hunter,	Mr		Colledge	Cowgate South
Hunter,	Mr	Pewterer	Craig's	Grassmarket East
Hunter,	Mrs		Forrest's	Lady Stair's Close
Hunter,	Miss		Chalmer's	Lawnmarket at Forrester's/Libberton's
Hunter,	Robert	Ale Seller	Lithgow's	Grassmarket West
Husband & Bogg,	Miss		Lothian's	Warriston Close
Husband,	Paul	Merchant	His Own	Bull's Close
Hutchison,	James		Colvill's	Trunk Close
Hutchison,	James	Merchant (*home*)	Livingston's	Craig's Close
Hutchison,	James	Fishing & Fowling Nets (*shop*)	"Peacock & Crown"	Luckenbooths
Hutton,	Alexander	Ale Seller	Shiell's	Covenant Close
Hutton,	Andrew	Brewer	Kinneir's	Candlemaker Row
Hutton,	James	Merchant	Spence's	Mary King's Close
Hutton,	James	Brushmaker	Gilles's	Old Post Office Close

NAME		OCCUPATION	ADDRESS	
Hutton,	John	Brushmaker	Gilles's	Old Post Office Close
Hutton,	Mary	Ale Seller	Hutton's	Cowgate South (Gosford's Close)
Hutton,	Mrs		Cumming's	Fishmarket Close East
Hutton,	William			Barringer's Close
Hutton,	William	Merchant	Ramsay's	Luckenbooths
Hutton,	William	Merchant		High Street South at Cross
Imrie,	Alexander		Grant's	Trunk Close
Ingles,	Archibald	*of Auchendinny*		Craig's Close
Ingles,	John	Merchant		Pearson's Close
Inglis,	Archibald	Pewterer	Inglis's	Kennedy's Close
Inglis,	Charles			Custom House Stairs
Inglis,	Claud	Linen Merchant	Barclay's	Luckenbooths
Inglis,	David	Linen Merchant	Davidson's McLenan's	at Craig's Close West Bow
Inglis,	Edward	Druggist	Inglis's	Lawnmarket at Wardrope's Court
Inglis,	George		Smith's	Niddry's Wynd
Inglis,	Hugh	Wright	Wardrope's	Wardrope's Court
Inglis,	James	Merchant	Bodie's	Murdoch's Close
Inglis,	Sir John		Cave's	Cowgate at Robertson's Close
Inglis,	Mr William	Surgeon	Kinloch's	Kinloch's Close
Inglis,	Mrs			Bess Wynd, Middle
Inglis,	Thomas	Wright	Dick's	Burnet's Close
Inglis,	William		Hogg's	Gray's Close
Inglish,	Miss	Merchant	Corsbie's	Gladstone's Land
Innes,	Alexander	Writer	Watson's	Covenant Close
Innes,	Alexander		Innes's	New Stairs Meal Market
Innes,	Andrew	Wright	Good's	Colledge Wynd
Innes,	George		Pencaitland's	Niddry's Wynd
Innes,	Jean		Robertson's	Blackfriar's Wynd
Insurance Office			New Stairs	Parliament Close
Inverary,	Lady			Blackfriar's Wynd
Ireland,	James	Ale Seller	Schaw's	Bess Wynd
Ireland,	Mrs	Merchant	Callander's	Skinner's Close
Irvine,	John	*of Burleigh*	Blythe's	Castlehill North
Irvine,	Mrs		Crinzen's	Blackfriar's Wynd
Irvine,	Thomas	Stabler	Muschet's	Grassmarket East
Jack,	George	Merchant	Lithgow's	Grassmarket West
Jackson,	Andrew	Merchant	Innes's	New Stairs Meal Market
Jackson,	Gideon	W.S.		Dickson's Close
Jackson,	John		Rules'	Grassmarket Mid
Jackson,	Mrs		Willson's	Lawnmarket at Cullen's Close
Jaffrey,	Francis	Wigmaker	Galloway's	Lawnmarket
Jameson,	Andrew	Merchant	Jameson's	Warriston's Close
Jameson,	Andrew	Mason	Jameson's	Borthwick's Close
Jameson,	James	Ale Seller	Crawford's	Colledge Wynd
Jameson,	John	Merchant	Finlayson's	Allan's Close
Jameson,	Mr & Mrs, John		Sinclair's	Skinner's Close
Jameson,	John	Lodging House		Halkerston's Wynd
Jameson,	Patrick	Ironmonger	"Scots Arms"	High Street opposite Cross
Jameson,	Robert	Ale Seller	Fyfe's	James Court
Jameson,	Robert	Mason	Mitchell's	Borthwick's Close
Jameson,	Thomas	Glover	Halyburton's	Trunk Close
Jardin,	Lady		Burn's	Forrester's Wynd
Jardine,	Mrs	Merchant	McKinlay's	Grassmarket East
Jarvie,	Mathew	Printer	New Stairs	Meal Market

NAME		OCCUPATION	ADDRESS	
Jarvie,	Thomas	Merchant	Anthonius'	Erskine's Land
John's Coffee House		Tavern		Parliament Close
Johns,	John	Manservant	Campbell's	Bell's Wynd
Johnston,	Charles	Druggist	Foulis's	Forrester's Wynd
Johnston,	Mrs			World's End Close
Johnstone,	Andrew	Stabler	Somervail's	Grassmarket Mid
Johnstone,		Captain	Messenger's	Horse Wynd
Johnstone,	James		Sinclair's	Blackfriar's Wynd
Johnstone,	Jean	Merchant	Paton's	Byre's Close
Johnstone,	John	Schoolmaster		Fountain Close
Johnstone,	Mr		Marshall's	Pearson's Close
Johnstone,	Mr	Surgeon	Weir's	Chamber's Close
Johnstone,	Mrs		Brown's	West Bow Middle
Johnstone,	Mrs	Milliner	McDuff's	High Street at North Foulis Close
Johnstone,	Mrs			Baillie Fyfe's Close
Johnstone,	Mrs		Carnegie's	Trunk Close
Johnstone,	Mrs			High Street at Foulis' Close
Johnstone,	Mrs		Sinclair's	World's End Close
Johnstone,	Mrs	Poultrywoman	Dean's	Marlin's Wynd
Johnstone,	Mrs		Peter's	Horse Wynd
Johnstone,	Mrs		Henderson's	High Street 1st below Blackfriar's
Johnstone,	Miss		Burnet's	Borthwick's Close
Johnstone,	Richard	Vintner	Woodhouselee's	Anchor Close
Johnstone,	Robert	Merchant	Wilson's	Galloway's Close
Johnstone,	Thos.	Linen Merchant	Johnstone's	Luckenbooths at Byre's Close Head
Johnstone,	William	Sheriff's Officer	Gray's	Grassmarket East
Johnstone,	Walter		Clerk's	Blackfriar's Wynd
Johnstone,	William	Wigmaker	Hogg's	Mary King's Close and 1st stair above New Bank Close
Jolly,	Patrick		Jolly's	Castlehill North
Jones,	Jonathan	Ale Seller	Stewart's	Trunk Close
Kaimes,	Lord		New Land	Lawnmarket at Advocate's/Cantore's
Kay,	James		Post Office Stairs	Parliament Close
Kay,	James	Wright	Millar's	Stonelaw's Close
Kay,	Mrs	Merchant	Lithgow's	Advocate's Close
Keir,	Adam	Baxter	His Own	Horse Wynd
Keir,	Magdalen		Surgeon's Hall W.	High School Yards
Keir,	William	Baxter	His Own	Fishmarket Close
Keith,	Alexander		Custom House Stairs	Parliament Close
Kellie,	Mrs		Veitch's	Forrester's Wynd
Kello,	Earl of		Pitcairn's	Kinloch's Close
Kello,	Lady			Kinloch's Close
Kelso,	Mrs	Milliner	Chalmer's	High Street behind Guard
Keltie,	Alexander		Keltie's	Forrester's Wynd W.
Keltie,	Robert	Merchant	Cleghorn's	Grassmarket West
Keltie,	William	Merchant	Sheill's	Stonelaw's Close
Kemptie,	Francis	Merchant	Malloch's	Dickson's Close
Kendall,	Mr	Slater	McPherson's	Horse Wynd W.
Kennedy,	Alex.	Linen Manufacturer		West Bow Foot
Kennedy,	Betty		Brand's	Castlehill South
Kennedy,	David	Advocate		Barringer's Close
Kennedy,	James	Horse Hirer	Brown's	Brownhill's Land
Kennedy,	John	Surgeon	His Own	Milne's Square
Kennedy,	John	Surgeon		Cant's Close Foot
Kennedy,	Marion		Kennedy's	Castlehill South
Kennedy,	Mrs	*of Kilkingie*	Munro's	Baillie Fyfe's Close
Kennedy,	Robert	Cooper	Anderson's	Fishmarket Close
Kenny,	John			Roxburgh's Close

NAME		OCCUPATION	ADDRESS	
Kerr & Dempster		Jewelers	Kerr's	Luckenbooths
Kerr, Cavers-	Lady		Kerr's	President's Close
Kerr,	James	Goldsmith		Allan's Close
Kerr,	Mr	Writer	Taylor's	President's Close
Kerr,	Mrs		Paterson's	Grassmarket West
Kerr,	Mrs		Bell's	Todrick's Wynd
Kerr,	Mrs		Surgeon's Hall	High School Yards
Kerr,	Mrs William		Douglas Lane	Forrester's Wynd
Kerr,	Patrick		Good's	Colledge Wynd
Kidd,	James	Merchant	Stewart's	Galloway's Close
Kidd,	John	Merchant	Thomson's	Cowgate Head North
Kidd,	Mrs		Jollie's	Bain & Jollie's Land
Kidd,	Mrs		McLenan's	West Bow Mid.
Kidd,	Mrs		Inglis's	Cowgate Head North
Kilkerran,	Lord		His Own	Forrester's Wynd Head
Killicranky,	Lady		Crawford's	West Bow South
Kincaid,	Alex.	Bookseller		President's Close
Kincaid & Donaldson		Booksellers		
Kincardine,	Lady		Baillie's	Chamber's Close
King,	Charles	Ale Seller		Brown's Land opposite Tolbooth
Kinloch,	Robert	Glover	Brownhills	Cowgate North
Kinloch,	Robert		Mein's	Fleshmarket Close
Kinnaird,	David		Hendry's	Sandilands Close
Kinnaldie,	Lady		Denholm's	Wardrope's Court
Kinneir,	Andrew	Pewterer	Naismith's	Lady Stair's Close
Kinneir,		Doctor		Skinner's Close
Kinneir,	Robert	Merchant	Dundas's	Don's Close
Kinneir,	Thomas	Merchant	Dick's	New Stairs Parliament Close
Kinneir,	Thomas	Shipping Agent	"Picardy Lawn & Caroline Warehouse" (home)	Opp. Luckenbooths Roxburgh's Close
Kintore,	Lady		Hellistob's	Cowgate South
Kirkcudbright,	Lord		Nairn's	Trunk Close
Kirkland,	James	Merchant	His Own	Grassmarket West
Kirkland,	Mrs	Merchant	Goudlilocks	Lawnmarket North
Kirkwood,	Alex.	Merchant		Gray's Close
Knox,	Miss		Knox's	Allan's Close
Knox,	Isobel			Lady Stair's Close
Knox,	Misses		Fyfe's	Lady Stair's Close
Laigh Coffee House		Tavern		Head of Pearson's Close
Laing,	Mrs	Merchant	Mein's	Fleshmarket Close
Laing,	William	Factor	Peter's	Horse Wynd
Lake,	Richard	Merchant		Sandilands Close
Lamb,	George	Wright	Grant's	Trunk Close
Lamb,	John	Wright	Pencaitland's	Niddry's Wynd
Lamb,	Thomas	Gardiner	Inglis's	Fleshmarket Close
Lammond,	Charles		Colvill's	Trunk Close
De Lamotte,	Pierre	Dancing Master	Baxter's	Baxter's Close
Lancashire,	Mr	Coachmaker	Ferguson's	Kennedy's Close
Lauder,	Ann			Bess Wynd Head
Lauder, †.8:5:52	George	Surgeon	Dalrymple's	World's End Close
Lauder,	Mrs		Cleghorn's	Horse Wynd
Lauder,	Mrs	Merchant	Lauder's	Gosford's Close
Lauder,	William	Staymaker		
Law,	David	Ale Seller	Dewar's	Milne's Square
Law,	Jean		Brown's	World's End Close
Law,	Mrs		Carbiston's	Kinloch's Close South
Law,	Mrs		Johnstone's	Cowgate Head North
Lawrence,	Charles		Lithgow's	Candlemaker Row
Lawrence,	James		Colt's	Cant's Close Foot
Lawrence,	Simon	Ale Seller	Wilson's	Borthwick's Close

NAME		OCCUPATION	ADDRESS	
Lawrence,	Simon	Merchant	Lowrie's	Robertson's Close
Lawrence,	Simon		Nairn's	Castlehill North
Lawrie,	John	Flesher	Anderson's	Grassmarket Mid
Lawrie,	Gilbert	Druggist		Niddry's Wynd Head
Lawrie,	Gilbert			Kinloch's Close South
Lawrie,	Mrs	Minister's Widow	Fairholm's	West Bow Middle
Lawrie,	Mrs		Bairfoot's	Peebles Wynd
Lawrie,	Thomas	Manservant	Syme's	High Street at Niddry's Wynd
Lawson,	Charles		Riddoch's	Cowgate South
Lawson,	George	Upholsterer	Handyside's	Trunk Close
Lawson,	Margaret		Hewit's	Fleshmarket Close Head
Lawson,	Mrs	Widow	Miller's	Fleshmarket Close Head
Lawson,	Mrs		Schaw's	President's Close
Lawson,	Mrs			Carruber's Close
Lawson,	Patrick	Weaver	Good Town's	Candlemaker Row
Lawson,	Thomas		Hawthornden's	Cowgate North
Lawson,	William	Teacher	His Own	Carruber's Close
Learmonth,	Alex.	Merchant		St Mary's Wynd
Learmonth,	John	Merchant	Millar's	Craig's Close
Learmonth,	Miss		Innes's	Halkerston Wynd
Le Blanc,	Mme	Boarding School		Cant's Close Middle
Lees,	John	Teacher	Surgeon's Hall	High School Yards
Lees,	Robert	Ale Seller	Ogilvie's	Horse Wynd
Leishman,	Alex.	Lint Dresser	Scirving's	Good Town's Land
Leishman,	Thomas		Keltie's	Forrester's Wynd West
Leget,	John		Kirktonholm's	Kennedy's Close
Leitch,	Isobell	Ale Seller	Ramsay's	Trunk Close
Leith,	Alexander		Brown's Land	Opposite Tolbooth
Lesslie,	Alexander	Vintner	Montgomerie's	Writer's Court
Lesslie,	Charles	Merchant	Reid's	Lawnmarket North
Lesslie,	David	Meal Seller	Hammermen's	Cowgate Head South
Lesslie,	James jr.	Writer		Mary King's Close
Lesslie,	James		Adam's	Kinloch's Close Foot
Lesslie,	Mrs		Forrest's	Gray's Close
Lethem,	Mrs	Baxter	Cleghorn's	Grassmarket West
Lethem,	Thomas	Smith	Selkirk's	Grassmarket East
Libberton,	Lady		Little's	Cullen's Close
Liddell,	Agnes		Craigleith's	Peebles Wynd East
Lind,	George	Merchant		
Lind,	James	Doctor	Lind's	Paterson's Court
Lind,	Miss		Taylor's	President's Close
Lindsay,	Alex.	Merchant	Clerk's	West Bow Middle
Lindsay,	David	Writer		1st turnpike above Weigh-house Castlehill South
Lindsay,	David		Jolley's	Burnet's Close
Lindsay,	James	Tobacconist	Laing's	West Bow Middle
Lindsay,	John	Skinner		Burnet's Close Foot
Lindsay,	Katharine	Lady		World's End Close
Lindsay,	Mrs		Skinner's	Castlehill North
Lindsay,	Mrs		Lindsay's	West Bow Head
Lindsay,	Martin		Bruce's	Libberton's Wynd
Lindsay,	Patrick	Merchant		Milne's Court
Lindsay,	Robert	Merchant	McRabbie's	Stonelaw's Close
Linton,	John	Cowfeeder	Douglas's	Grassmarket West
Lithgow,	Agnes	Grass Seller	Lithgow's	Candlemaker Row
Lithgow,	James	Merchant	Lithgow's	West Bow Foot
Lithgow,	Robert	Merchant	Lithgow's	Paterson's Court
Little,	Charles	Tavern Keeper	L'mkt. Coffee Hse.	Lawnmarket North
Littlejohn,	Mrs (heirs)		Watson's	New Stairs Foot Parliament Close
Livingstone,	George	Vintner	Bain's	Advocate's Close
Livingstone,	George		Tait's	Lawnmarket
Livingstone,	Jean			Craig's Close

NAME		OCCUPATION	ADDRESS	
Loch,	John	Tavern Keeper	Laigh Coffee Hse.	Pearson's Close
Loch,	Mr		Aitken's	
Loch,	Mrs		Callander's	Skinner's Close
Loch,	Robert		Weaver's	New Assembly Close
Loch,	William	Writer		Paterson's Court
Lochere,	Margaret		Dickson's	Candlemaker Row
Lockhart,	Alex.	of Craighouse	New Stairs Foot	Parliament Close
Lockhart,	George	of Carnwath	Carnwarth's Ct.	Niddry's Wynd
Lockhart,	Mary		Kerr's	President's Close
Logan,	Rev. George	Minister	(College Kirk)	Milne's Court
Lord Justice Clerk	Charles Erskine of Tinwald			Bull's Stairs
				Milne Square
Lorimer,	James	Merchant	Halkerston's	Lawnmarket at Bank/Cullen's
Lothian,	Edward	Goldsmith	Goudilocks	opp. Forrester's Wynd
Lothian,	George	Merchant	Brown's	Gladstone's Land
Lothian,	James	Skinner	Watson's	Upper Baxter's Close
Lothian,	John	Merchant		
Lothian,	Miss		Reoch's	President's Close
Lothian,	Richard		Lothian's	Bain & Jolley's Land
Louden,	John		Scott's	Cowgate South
Lovatt,	Lady		Learmonth's	Blackfriar's Wynd
Love,	James	Stabler	Millar's	Grassmarket West
Lovebone,	Mr			Lawnmarket at Forrester's/Libberton's
Low,	David		Watson's	Forrester's Wynd W.
Low,	Robert	Goldsmith	Goldsmith's	Luckenbooths
Lowrie,	Andrew	Precentor, New Kirk:	Forrest's	President's Close
Lowrie,	Jenet		Armour's	High Street at North Foulis Close
Lowrie,	Mr	Schoolmaster	Tod's	Geddes' Close
Lowrie,	Mrs	Minister's Widow	Crockett's	West Bow Foot
Lowrie,	William	Cutler	Dalgleish's	Society
Lumsden & Robertson			Anderson's	Fishmarket Close West
Lumsden,	Andrew		Post Office Stairs	Parliament Close
Lumsden,	Mrs		Orphan's	Kennedy's Close
Lyle,	Alexander	Chairmaster	Crawford's	Cowgate South
Lyle,	Mrs	Widow	Bell's	
Lyle,	Mrs		McLelland's	Society
Lyon,	David	Vintner	Allan's	Milne Square
Lyon,	James	Merchant	Hastie's	Borthwick's Close
Lyon,	Mrs		Taylor's	President's Close

All Mc and Mac Surnames are given as Mc.

McAlister,	Mathew	Merchant	Stewart's	Luckenbooths
McArra	Andrew		Aitken's	Robertson's Close
McArthur,	John	Writer	at McKenzie's	Parliament Close
McAulay,	Archibald	Merchant		World's End Close
McAulay,	Patrick		Anderson's	Milne's Court
McCalla,	Mrs			Cap & Feather Close
McCarter,	Mrs	Gauger	Thomson's	Grassmarket Mid
McCarter,	William		Tod's	Horse Wynd W.
McClachlane,	Duncan	Cordiner	Reid's	Cant's Close Foot
McConachie,	Alex.	Writer	Hallyburton's	Cowgate Head South
McConachie,	William	Linen Merchant	Dewar's	West Bow Foot
McCormack,	Samuel	Excise	Henderson's	Forrester's Wynd Foot
McCormack,	Samuel	Tavern Keeper	New Inn	Paterson's Grassmarket West
McCoull & Watson Co.		Merchants	Heriot's	Luckenbooths
McCoull,	Archibald	Merchant	Stewart's	Advocate's Close
McCoull,	John	Cordiner	Norrie's	High Street at Kinloch's Close
McCulloch & Tod		Merchants and at	Butter's Gullane's	Carruber's Close Lawnmarket at Forrester's/Libberton's

NAME		OCCUPATION	ADDRESS	
M<small>C</small>C<small>ULLOCH</small>,	Archibald			Milne's Court
M<small>C</small>C<small>ULLOCH</small>,	Archibald			Milne's Square
M<small>C</small>C<small>ULLOCH</small>,	Daniel		Ancrum's	Monteith's Close
M<small>C</small>C<small>ULLOCH</small>,	Jeremiah	Coachman	Cant's	High Street at Carruber's Close
M<small>C</small>C<small>ULLOCH</small>,	Mr		Boswall's	Todrick's Wynd
M<small>C</small>C<small>ULLOCH</small>,	Thomas		Murray's	Halkerston's Wynd
M<small>C</small>C<small>ULLOCH</small>,	William	Merchant	Brown's	Lawnmarket at Wardrope's Court
M<small>C</small>C<small>ULLOCH</small>,	William		Drummond's	Blackfriar's Wynd
M<small>C</small>D<small>ERMOTT</small>,	William	Ale Seller	Chalmer's	High Street at New Assembly Close
M<small>C</small>D<small>ONALD</small>,	Donald	Merchant	Crinzen's	Blackfriar's Wynd
M<small>C</small>D<small>ONALD</small>,	Donald		McCruther's	Stonelaw's Close
M<small>C</small>D<small>ONALD</small>,	Duncan	Druggist	Gibson's	Lady Stair's Close
M<small>C</small>D<small>ONALD</small>,	John		Peter's	Horse Wynd
M<small>C</small>D<small>ONALD</small>,	Mrs		Scott's	Cowgate North at Cant's/Dickson's
M<small>C</small>D<small>OUGALL</small>,	Andrew			James Court
M<small>C</small>D<small>OUGALL</small>,	Betty		Kinloch's	Kinloch's Close
M<small>C</small>D<small>OUGALL</small>,	Christian		Orphans'	Milne's Court
M<small>C</small>D<small>OUGALL</small>,	Isobell	Ale Seller	Oliphant's	Niddry's Wynd
M<small>C</small>D<small>OUGALL</small>,	James	Merchant	McFarlane's	High Street at Fishmarket Close
M<small>C</small>D<small>OUGALL</small>,	Margaret			Roxburgh's Close
M<small>C</small>D<small>OUGALL</small>,	Mrs			Colledge Wynd Foot
M<small>C</small>D<small>OUGALL</small>,	Mr			World's End Close
M<small>C</small>D<small>OUGALL</small>,	Miss		McDougall's	Lawnmarket North
M<small>C</small>D<small>OWALL</small>,	James of Canonmills	Waulker		High Street at Back of Cross
M<small>C</small>D<small>OWALL</small>,	William	Merchant	Surgeon's Hall	High School Yards
M<small>C</small>D<small>UFF</small>,	Robert	Goldsmith	McRabbie's	Stonelaw's Close
M<small>C</small>E<small>WAN</small>,	Mrs	Ale Seller		Gray's Close
M<small>C</small>F<small>AIT</small>,	Dr	Prof. of Mathematics		University
M<small>C</small>F<small>ARLANE</small>,	Andrew	Stabler/Ale Seller	Baillie's	Grassmarket East
M<small>C</small>F<small>ARLANE</small>,		Doctor	His Own	New Assembly Close
M<small>C</small>F<small>ARLANE</small>,	James	Wigmaker	Baillie's	Bull's Close
M<small>C</small>F<small>ARLANE</small>,	John		Jamieson's	Cowgate North
M<small>C</small>F<small>ARLANE</small>,	John	Writer		Anchor Close
M<small>C</small>F<small>ARLANE</small>,	Mr	Schoolmaster	Divistob's	Plainstone Close
M<small>C</small>F<small>ARLANE</small>,	Robert	Insurance Agent	Anderson's 2nd Land at Fountainwell	West Bow Mid.
M<small>C</small>F<small>ARQUHAR</small>,	Mr	Wigmaker		High Street
M<small>C</small>G<small>HIE</small>,	William	Writer		James Court Lawnmarket at Kinloch's Close
M<small>C</small>G<small>HIE</small>,	William	Merchant	Innes's	James Court
M<small>C</small>G<small>IBBON</small>,	James	Merchant	Mein's	Fleshmarket Close
M<small>C</small>G<small>IBBON</small>,	James		Todd's	New Assembly Close
M<small>C</small>G<small>ILL</small>,	Mrs		Her Own	Marlin's Wynd East
M<small>C</small>G<small>ILL</small>,	Mrs of Rankeillor		Buchan's	Lawnmarket at Bowhead
M<small>C</small>G<small>IVAN</small>,	John		Robertson's	Grassmarket East
M<small>C</small>G<small>LASHAN</small>,	James	Ale Seller	Spence's	Burnet's Close
M<small>C</small>G<small>LASHAN</small>,	John	Merchant	Norrie's	Kinloch's Close
M<small>C</small>G<small>LASHAN</small>,	Miss	Merchant	Finlayson's	Kinloch's Close
M<small>C</small>G<small>OWAN</small>,	John	W.S.	McGowan's	Bess Wynd
M<small>C</small>G<small>REGOR</small>,	Mrs	Vintner	Frogg's	James Court
M<small>C</small>G<small>RIGOR</small>,	Alex.		Tod's	Candlemaker Row
M<small>C</small>G<small>RIGOR</small>,	Hugh	Ale Seller	Weigh House	Lawnmarket at Milne's Court
M<small>C</small>G<small>RIGOR</small>,	John	Billiard Tables	Turpie's	Jackson's Close
M<small>C</small>G<small>ROGAN</small>,	Thomas	Merchant	Temple's	Lawnmarket at Wardrope's/Paterson's
M<small>C</small>G<small>UFFOCK</small>,	Mrs		Moffat's	Trunk Close
M<small>C</small>H<small>ARDIE</small>,	John	Merchant	Peacock's	High Street opposite Cross

NAME		OCCUPATION		ADDRESS
McHardie,	John	Grocer		High Street at back of Fountainwell
McIlwreath,	John		Hamilton's	High Street at Halkerston's Wynd
McIntosh,	Alex.	Writer	Mylne's	Halkerston's Wynd
McIntosh,	John	Staymaker/Ale Seller	Pringle's	James Court
McIntosh,	John	Ale Seller/Grocer	His Own (W'house) (Shop)	Baillie Fyfe's Close Cant's Close
McIntosh,	Mr	Writer	Hope's	Monteith's Close
McIntosh,	Mrs	Merchant	Gray's	Bull's Close
McIntosh,	Robert	Writer	Spence's	Warriston Close
McIntosh,	William	Ale Seller	Armour's	High Street at North Foulis Close
McIntyre,	Nicol		Livingstone's	Craig's Close
McKain,	James	Merchant	Inglis's	Lawnmarket at Wardrope's Court
McKain,	James		Sommervail's	Society
McKain,	John	Merchant	Livingstone's	Byre's Close
McKay,	Charles	Professor of History		New Stairs
McKay,	Hugh			Chamber's Close
McKay,	James	Coppersmith	Moffat's	West Bow Middle
McKay,	Mr	Ale Seller	Howison's	Lawnmarket at Cullen's
McKay,	Miss		Garbiston's	Clamshell Turnpike
McKay,	Miss		Campbell's	Castlehill North
McKechnie,	James	Shopkeeper	Old Stage Coach Office:	High Street at Back of Guard
McKechnie,	William	Merchant	Dallas's	Bell's Wynd
McKellar,	Patrick	Writing Master	Swinton's	Old Post Office Close
McKellar,	Peter		Smith's	High Street at Baillie Fyfe's Close
McKeltope,	James	Merchant	Herriot's	Kennedy's Close
McKenzie,	Alex.	Vintner	Petrie's	Custom House Stairs
McKenzie,		Doctor	Duncan's	Forrester's Wynd
McKenzie,	Francis	Ale Seller	Seton's	Libberton's Wynd
McKenzie,	Harry		Braidwood's	President's Close
McKenzie,	James	Goldsmith	McKenzie's	Luckenbooths
McKenzie,	John	Corkcutter	Bruce's	Kennedy's Close
McKenzie,	John		Peter's	Horse Wynd
McKenzie,	Kenneth	Law Professor		University
McKenzie,	Mr		McCulloch's	Forrester's Wynd
McKenzie,	John	Writer	McKenzie's	Parliament Close
McKenzie,	Mr			Tweedale's Court
McKenzie,	Mr		Brownhills	Cowgate North
McKenzie,	Mrs		Scheil's	Sandilands Close
McKenzie,	Mrs	Vintner	Cairn's	President's Stairs Parliament Close
McKenzie,	Mrs		Gavinlock's	Forrester's Wynd
McKenzie,		Doctor	Burn's	Libberton's Wynd
McKenzie,		Doctor		Bank Close
McKenzie,	Miss		Clelland's	Covenant Close
McKenzie,	Richard	Vintner	Schiell's	Covenant Close
McKinlay,	Janet		Cochrane's	Grassmarket East
McClachlane,	Ann	Widow	Her Own	Writer's Court
McClachlane,	D.	Cordiner	Reid's	Cant's Close Foot
McClagan,	Mrs		Grant's	Trunk Close
McLaren,	Andrew		McRabbie's	Stonelaw's Close
McLean,	Allan	Flesher	Black's	Fleshmarket Close
McLean,	Duncan	Ale Seller	Inglis's	High Street opposite Cross
McLean,	George		Lerson's	Cowgate Head North
McLean,	Malcolm		Allan's	Grassmarket West
McLean,	William	Ale Seller	Dick's	Burnet's Close
McClellan,	Robert	Clerk		Edinburgh Shipping Co.
McLeod,	Roderick	*of Sunbank* W.S.		Craig's Close
McLure,	John	Writing Master	Temple's	Lawnmarket at Wardrope's/Paterson's

NAME		OCCUPATION	ADDRESS	
McMichan,	John	Grocer	Moffat's	West Bow Middle
McMichan & Stewart		French Masters		Wardrope's Court
McMillan,	Alex.	W.S.		James Court
McMurray,	Robert		Clerk's	West Bow Middle
McNab,	John	Merchant	Henderson's	High Street 1st below Blackfriar's
McNat,	Mrs		Bull's	Cowgate South
McNaughtone,	Peter		McCulloch's	Mary King's Close
McNeill,	Andrew		Bairfoot's	Peebles Wynd
McNeill,	James	Distiller	Selkirk's	Grassmarket East
McNeill,	Miss		Chapman's	New Stairs Foot Parliament Close
McNeill,	John			
McNiven,	Donald		Bairfoot's	Peebles Wynd
McNiven,	John	Merchant	Selkirk's	Grassmarket East
McPhail,	Hector	Vintner	Watson's	High Street at Fishmarket/Borthwick's
McPhail,	Mrs			Warriston's Close
McPherson,	Angus	Taylor	Cockburn's	Luckenbooths
McPherson,	Duncan			Writer's Court
McPherson,		Doctor	Cockburn's	Bess Wynd
McPherson,	Duncan	Room Setter	Clerkson's	Anchor Close
McPherson,	Mr		Hay's	Grassmarket Middle
McPherson,	Mrs		Elphinstone's	Blackfriar's Wynd
McPherson,	Mrs		Riddoch's	Cowgate South
McPherson,	Mr	Musician	Bain & Jolley's	Blackfriar's Wynd
McQueen,	Andrew	Schoolmaster	Little's	Cullen's Close
McQueen,	Robert	*Lord Braxfield*		Covenant Close
McRabbie,	Miss	Milliner	Nairn's	Stonelaw's Close
McVey,	William	Wright	Learmonth's	Skinner's Close
McVey,	Mrs	Printer's Widow	Fairholm's	Craig's Close
Maben,	John		McCulloch's	Mary King's Close
Mack,	Charles	Mason	Hunter's	Cant's Close Foot
Mack,	Daniel	Ale Seller	Napier's	Carruber's Close
Mack,	John	Mason	Adamson's	Horse Wynd
Mackie,	George	Merchant	Bavelaw's	President's Close
Main,	Mrs		Neil's	Fleshmarket Close
Mair,	Thomas	Merchant	Halyburton's	Grassmarket East
Maitland,	Mrs	Room Setter	Marjoribanks and at Bishop's	Bull's Close Carruber's Close
Maitland,	Mistress		Cramond's	West Bow Middle
Maitland,	Obrian	Shoemaker	Forglen's	Anchor Close
Maitland,	William	Historian	c/o Stewart's Bookseller	West Bow
Malcolm,	Charles		Ewing's	Lady Stair's Close
Malcolm,	Mrs		Grant's	Lawnmarket North
Malice,	George	Flesher		Fleshmarket Close
Malice,	John	Ale Seller		Allan's Close
Manderson,	Patrick	Merchant	Oliphant's	Milne's Square
Manners,	Alexander	Merchant	Auchinleck's	Peebles Wynd East
Manners,	John	Dyster	Dallas's	Blackfriar's Wynd
Mansfield,	James & Co.	Merchants	Mansfield's	Byre's Close
Mansfield,	Mrs			Cantore Close
Manuel,	Hugh	Writer	Clerk's	Castlehill South
Manuel,	John	Merchant	Dickson's 2nd Land	Libberton's Wynd
March,	Lady of		Gordon's	High Street at Baillie Fyfe's Close
Marjoribanks,	Andrew	Merchant	His Own	Foulis Close
Marjoribanks,	James		His Own	Blackfriar's Wynd
Marjoribanks,	Mrs		Ancrum's	Sandiland's Close
Marjoribanks,	Mrs		Wright's	Meal Market
Marjoribanks,	Mrs		Infirmary	High School Yards
Marjoribanks,	Robert		Hogg's	High Street at Carruber's Close

NAME		OCCUPATION	ADDRESS	
Marishall,	Mr		Anderson's 2nd Land	West Bow Middle
Marshall,	David	Porter	Bell's	Geddes Close
Marshall,	Francis	Merchant	Robb's	Byre's Close
Marshall,	Mr	Ale Seller	Dick's	Blackfriar's Wynd
Marshall,	Mrs	Widow	Straton's	Milne Square
Marshall,	William	Writer	Lindsay's	West Bow Head
Martin,	Alexander	Herald	His Own	James Court
Martin,	Alexander		McClelland's	Society
Martin,		Doctor	Law's	Cant's Close
Martin,	George	Ale Seller	Wilson's	Borthwick's Close
Martin,	James' Children		Simpson's	Candlemaker Row
Martin,	John	Merchant	Bavridge's	Campbell's Brewery
Masson,	James	Merchant		Todrick's Wynd Head
Mason,	Miss	Ale Seller	Gibson's	Lady Stair's Close
Mathew,	Thomas			Fleshmarket Close
Mathie,	John	Weaver	Smith's	Baillie Fyfe's Close
Mathie,	Mrs		Jolly's	Bain & Jolly's Land
Mathie,	Thomas	Manservant	Smith's	Baillie Fyfe's Close
Mathison,	Patrick	Ale Seller	Lumsden's	Burnet's Close
Maule,		Baron of Exchequer		Trunk Close (Panmure)
Maunderson,	Miss			Kennedy's Close
Maxwell,	John		Young's	Lawnmarket at Libberton's Wynd
Maxwell,	Lady		Burnet's	Gray's Close
Maxwell,	Mr			Lawnmarket at Royston's/Anderson's
Maxwell,	Mrs		Knox's	Lady Stair's Close
Mayelstone,	Charles	Grocer	Hunter's	Niddry's Wynd Foot
Meals,	Alexander		Good's	Colledge Wynd
Medina,	John	Limner	Grant's	Trunk Close
Meggat,	James	Bookbinder	Young's	Society
Mein,	John	Slater	Mein's	Under Baxter's Close
Mein,	William	Merchant	His Own	Lawnmarket at Royston's
Melli(e)s,	George	Flesher	Black's	Fleshmarket Close
Melli(e)s,	John	Flesher/Ale Seller	Blair's	Allan's Close
Menzies,	Alexander	Wigmaker	His Own	Brown's Land opposite Tolbooth
Menzies,	James	Merchant	Menzies'	Castlehill North
Menzies,	Mrs	Merchant	Crockate's	Lawnmarket
Menzies,	Robert	W.S. *of Culteraws*		High Street at Roxburgh's Close
Mercer,	Mrs		Mercer's	Borthwick's Close
Mercer,	William	Apothecary		High Street opposite Tron
Michie,	Thomas	Ale Seller	Gedd's	Byre's Close
Michie,	William	Merchant	Hastie's	Hyndford's Close
Michison,	Isobell		Cumming's	Fishmarket Close
Michon & Stewart		French Masters	Brown's	Paterson's Court
Middlemist,	John	Baxter	Baxter's	Lady Stair's Close
Middleton,	Alex.		Wight's	Cowgate at Cant's/Dickson's
Miles,	James		Ramsay's	Trunk Close
Mill,	John		Schiel's	West Bow South
Mill(s),	Mrs	Midwife	Myll's	Kinloch's Close
Millar,	Alexander	Painter	His Own	Marlin's Wynd
Millar,	Andrew	Wheelwright	Mitchell's	Fishmarket Close
Millar,	Benjamin	Merchant	Colvill's	Trunk Close
Millar,	Catharine	Merchant	Armour's	High Street at North Foulis Close
Millar,	David		Mein's	Trunk Close
Millar,	David	Printer	New Stairs	Meal Market
Millar,	David	Ale Seller	Brown's	Forrester's Wynd Foot
Millar,	George	Merchant	Campbell's	Argylle Square
Millar,	James	Painter	Baird's	Hyndford's Close
Millar,	James	Tailor		Pipe Close Castlehill North

NAME		OCCUPATION	ADDRESS	
MILLAR,	John	Caddie	Hogg's	Mary King's Close
MILLAR,	Mrs		Jolly's	Castlehill North
MILLAR,	Thomas	Merchant	Armour's	High Street at North Foulis Close
MILLAR,	William	Ale Seller	McGowan's	Bess Wynd
MILLAR,	William	Bookseller		Marlin's Wynd
MILLER,	David		Hamilton's	Grassmarket West
MILLER,	James	Auctioneer		Lawnmarket at Bank Close
MILLER,	Mr		Schaw's	Castlehill South
MILLER,	Thomas			Paterson's Court
MILLER,	William	Bookseller		High Street
MILLIGAN,	John	Merchant	Marshal's	Cowgate South
MILNE,	John	Hammerman (Founder) and at "Golden Church Branch"	Dick's	Chamber's Close
			Bishop's	Carruber's Close
MILROY,	James	Merchant		
MILTON, (Andrew Fletcher)	Lord	Lord Justice Clerk		Bull's Close & Hyndford's Close
MINTO, (Gilbert Elliot)	Lord	Lord of Session	Paton's	West Bow Head & Horse Wynd
MINTO,	Lady		Wordie's	Halkerston's Wynd
MIRTLE, see Myrtle				
MIRRIE,	Mr	Manservant	Clerk's	Fountain Close
MIRRIE,	Mrs		Handyside's	Trunk Close
MITCHELL,	Anna	Merchant	Muschet's	Luckenbooths
MITCHELL,		Doctor	Foulis's	Castlehill South
MITCHELL,	James	Goldsmith	His Own	Anchor Close
MITCHELL,	James	Saddler		Marlin's Wynd
MITCHELL,	John		Brown's	World's End Close
MITCHELL,	John	Wright	Clerk's	Warriston's Close
MITCHELL,	Mr	Cordiner	Veitch's	Cowgate Head North
MITCHELL,	Mrs		Hay's	Trunk Close
MITCHELL,	Mrs		Nielsen's	Forrester's Wynd Foot
MITCHELL,	Mrs		Weir's	Gosford's Close
MITCHELL,	Robert		Gairn's	Grassmarket South
MITCHELL,	Thomas	Jeweller	Laing's	Gladstone's Land
MITCHELL,	Thomas		Peter's	Horse Wynd
MITCHELL,	William	Fur Merchant	Robertson's	James Court
MITCHELL,	William	Ale Seller	Lawrie's	Cowgate at Forrester's Wynd
MITCHELLHILL,	Robert	Merchant	Weir's	Forrester's Wynd
MITCHELSON,	James	Goldsmith	His Own	Milne's Court
MITCHELSON,	Samuel	Writer		Carruber's Close
MOFFAT,	William	Glass Grinder	Moffat's	Trunk Close
MOFFAT,	William	Room Setter	Jolly's	Bain & Jolly's Land
MOIR,	John	Merchant	Forbes's	Anchor Close
MOIR,	John	Merchant	Somervail's	Society
MOLLISON,	John	Writer	Commissary Office:	Parliament Close
MOLLISON,	Mrs		Watson's	Cowgate North
MONCRIEF,	David	Writer: Secretary to Exchequer Chamber:	West Scale Stair	Parliament Close Old Assembly Close
MONCRIEF,	Mrs		Alves's	Murdoch's Close
MONRO,	Alexander	Surgeon	His Own	Gosford's Close
MONRO,	George		Geddes'	Lawnmarket at West Bow Head
MONRO,	John	Ale Seller	Lumsden's	Burnet's Close
MONRO,	Mr	Cordiner	Keltie's	Forrester's Wynd W.
MONRO,	Mrs		Anderson's 2nd Land	West Bow
MONTEITH,	Betty		Dunbar's	Carruber's Close
MONTGOMERY,	Mr	*of Langshaw*		James Court
MONTGOMERY,	David	Manservant	Riddock's	Covenant Close
MONTGOMERY,	Helen		Clerk's	West Bow Middle
MONTGOMERY,	Mrs James	Milliner	Bruce's	Kinloch's Close

NAME		OCCUPATION	ADDRESS	
Montgomery,	John	Wright	Dallas's	Blackfriar's Wynd
Montgomery,	Lady		Scott's	Plainstone Close
Montgomery,	Margaret			Foulis's Close
Montgomery,	Miss		Burn's	Lawnmarket at Forrester's Wynd
Montgomery,	Robert	Brewer	Hay's	Grassmarket Middle
Montgomery,	Mrs			High Street at North Foulis Close
Montgomery,	Walter	Manservant	McKay's	Cap & Feather Close
Montgomery,	Sir Walter		Montgomerie's	Blackfriar's Wynd
Moodie,	Alexander	Wright	Marshal's	Pearson's Close
Moodie,	Alexander	Vintner	Stevenson's	Custom House Stairs Parliament Close
Moodie,	James	Taylor	Riccarton's	Fleshmarket Close
Moodie,	Thomas		Foulis's	Castlehill South
Moodie,	William		Ivie's	
More,	George	Merchant	Grahame's	Lawnmarket at Bank/Cullen's
More,	John & Co.	Merchants	More's	Lawnmarket North
More,	John	Bookbinder	Brown's	Byre's Close
More,	John			Cullen's Close
More,	John			Stonelaw's Close
More,	Thomas	Vintner	Barclay's	Old Post Office Close
Morgan,	John	Manservant	Riddock's	Covenant Close
Morrison,	James	Agent for Edinburgh Whale Fishing Co.		
Morrison,	James	Glover	Weaver's	New Assembly Close
Morrison,	John	Wigmaker/Ale Seller	Auchinleck's	Peebles Wynd East
Morrison,	Mrs	Ale Seller	Watson's	Bull's Close
Morrison,	Robert	Wigmaker	Schiel's	Sandiland's Close
Morrison,	William	Hatter	Robertson's	Lyon's Close
Mortimore,	Robert	Glover	Hunter's	West Bow Middle
Morton,	Sir Robert		Morton's	Foulis Close South
Mosman,	Hugh	Writer	His Own	Forrester's Wynd Foot
Mosman,	John	Linen Merchant		Lawnmarket Middle
Mosman,	William	Merchant		Craig's Close
Mouatt,	Andrew	Merchant	Hellistob's	Cowgate South
Mouatt,	Archibald		Kinneir's	Don's Close
Mouatt,	John	Cowfeeder/Ale Seller	Mouatt's	Meal Market
Moubray,	Alex.	Wigmaker	Lindsay's	Blackfriar's Wynd
Moubray,	John	Hair Merchant	Dunbar's	Carruber's Close
Moubray,	John	Mason	His Own	Todrick's Wynd
Moubray,	Mrs		Hawthornden's	Cowgate North
Mucklewraith,	Janet		Quaker's	Peebles Wynd East
Muir,	Andrew		Murray's	Bain & Jolly's Land
Muir,	John	Ale Seller	Finlayson's	Allan's Close
Muir,	William	Stabler/Ale Seller	Douglas's	Grassmarket West
Muirhead,	Mr		Kinloch's	Kinloch's Close
Muirhead,	Mrs		Gray's	Grassmarket Middle
Mundell,	James	Teacher	Aitken's	West Bow
Munro,	Albert	Treasurer Heriot's Hospital Trust	Munro's	Lawnmarket at Wardrope's Court
Munro,	Alexander	Surgeon	see Monro	
Murdoch,	John	Teacher	Jack's	Halkerston's Wynd
Murdoch,	Thomas		Penston Letter's	Lawnmarket North
Murray,	Adam	Baxter	Laing's	Upper Baxter's Close
Murray,	Alexander	Printer (Scots Mag.)	Fairholm's	Craig's Close
Murray,	Andrew	Wigmaker	Gibson's	Lady Stair's Close
Murray,	Archibald			James Court
Murray,	Daniel	Merchant	McConachie's	Cowgate Head South
Murray,	David	Stabler	Veitch's	Cowgate Head North
Murray,		Skinner	Clerk's	West Bow Head
Murray,		Doctor	Herriot's	Cowgate Head North
Murray,	George	Cordiner	Skinner's	West Bow Middle
Murray,	James	Spirit Merchant	Robertson's	Todrick's Wynd

NAME		OCCUPATION	ADDRESS	
Murray,	James	Candlemaker	Moffat's	Peebles Wynd East
Murray,	James	Ale Seller	Candlemaker's	Candlemaker's Row
Murray,	James	Dyster		High Street opposite Cross
Murray,	Janet		Hellistob's	Cowgate South
Murray,	John	Glass Grinder	Chalmer's	Chamber's Close
Murray,	John	Druggist	(*Home*) Baillie's (*Shop*) "The Mermaid"	Cant's Close Foot High Street at Dickson's Close
Murray,	Lady		Smith's	Niddry's Wynd
Murray,	Lady	*of Broughton*	Mitchell's	Baillie's Land
Murray,	Margaret		Morison's	West Bow Middle
Murray,	Mr	Manservant	McRabbie's	Stonelaw's Close
Murray,	Mrs		Blair's	Milne's Court
Murray,	Mrs		Hepburn's	Don's Close
Murray,	Mrs		Jameson's	Warriston Close
Murray,	Mrs	Room Setter	Marjoribanks	Bull's Close
Murray,	Mrs		Smith's	Monteith's Close
Murray,	Mrs		Anderson's	Foulis Close South
Murray,	Mrs		Colt's	Cant's Close Foot
Murray,	Mrs		Divistob's	
Murray,	Mrs		Nisbet's	Niddry's Wynd
Murray,	Mrs		Bruce's	Forrester's Wynd
Murray,	Mrs		Rigg's	Gosford's Close
Murray,	Mrs		Crawford's	West Bow South
Murray,	Mrs		Candlemaker's	Candlemaker's Row
Murray,	Miss & Kidd	Merchants	Kidd's	Warriston's Close
Murray,	Patrick	Linen Merchant	Bryden's	Mary King's Close
Murray,	Robert	Skinner	Cramond's	West Bow Middle
Murray,	Robert	Manservant	Haig's	Baillie Fyfe's Close
Murray,	Thomas	Baxter	His Own	Forrester's Wynd East
Murray,	Thomas	Skinner	Sommervail's	Society
Murray,	Thomas	Baxter	Turnbull's	Cowgate Head North
Murray,	Walter	*of Halmyre*	Thomson's	Grassmarket West
Murray,	William	Haberdasher	"Royal Tent"	High Street at Cantore's Close
Murray,	William	Colonel	Smith's	High Street at Baillie Fyfe's Close
Muschet,	Miss & Co.		Spence's	Luckenbooths
Mutter,	Elionora	Ale Seller	Wilkie's	High Street at New Assembly Close
Mutter,	Miss	Milliner	Nairn's	Stonelaw's Close
Mutter,	Thomas	Merchant	Todd's	New Assembly Close
Myles,	Alexander	Brewer	Capell's	Colledge Wynd
Mylne,	Patrick	Ale Seller	Whitehead's	Mary King's Close
Mylne,	William	Mason	Halyburton's	Trunk Close
Mylestone,	Charles:	see Mayelstone		
Myrtle,	Thomas	Brewer	His Own	Mirtle's Land
Myrtle,	William	Baxter	His Own	Kennedy's Close
Nairn,	Alexander	Advocate		Bull's Close
Nairn,	George		Sandilands	Warriston Close
Nairn,	Mrs		Aitken's	West Bow
Naismith,	James	Writer		Gray's Close
Naismith,	John	Chairmaster	Wilkie's	High Street at New Assembly Close
Naismith,	Mrs	Merchant	Chalmer's	Lawnmarket at Milne's Court
Naismith,	Mrs		Naismith's	Bell's Wynd
Napier,	Gabriel	Writer	His Own	Writer's Court
Napier,	Jean	Lady	Willson's	Lawnmarket at Cullen's Close
Napier,	Mrs		Crockett's	West Bow Foot
Napier,	Robert	Ale Seller	Clerk's	West Bow Head
Naughtone,	Alex.		Robertson's	Lady Stair's Close

NAME		OCCUPATION	ADDRESS	
Neilsen,	James	Ale Seller	Brown's	Galloway's Close
Neilsen,	Jean		Muschet's	Grassmarket East
Neilsen,	John	Glass Grinder	Simpson's	Trunk Close
Neilsen,	John	Ale Seller	Montgomerie's	Lawnmarket at Royston's
Neilsen,	William	Merchant	Scott's	Cowgate North
Nevay,	David	Merchant	His Own	Craig's Close
Nevay,	David	Merchant	Cumming's	Fishmarket Close
Newton,	Hugh	Webster		
Newton,	Richard		Guthrie's	Libberton's Wynd
Nicoll,	George	Merchant	Nicoll's	Brown's Land opposite Tolbooth
Nicoll,	George	Cordiner	Weaver's	New Assembly Close
Nicoll,	James	Trunk maker	Winter's	Chamber's Close
Nicoll,	James	Trunk maker	Callander's	Skinner's Close
Nicoll,	John	Wright	Clerk's	Warriston Close
Nicoll,	John	Baxter	Gavinlock's	Forrester's Wynd
Nicoll,	Margaret	Ale Seller	Dickson's	Candlemaker Row
Nicoll,	Mr & Mrs		Clerk's	Castlehill South
Nicoll,	William	Watchmaker	Henderson's	High Street at Clamshell Turnpike
Nicolson,	Alex.	Mason	Jolly's	Castlehill North
Nicolson,	John	Manservant	Ferguson's	Con's Close
Nicolson,	Thomas	Stabler	Johnstone's	West Bow Foot
Nimmo,	Elizabeth		Kirkton's	Milne's Court
Nimmo,	James	Ale Seller	Grange's	Peebles Wynd
Nimmo,	Mr	Lint Dresser	Simpson's	Candlemaker Row
Nimmo,	Richard	Stationer	Moubray's	Castlehill South
Nimmo,	Thomas			Peebles Wynd
Nisbet,	Alex.	Weaver	Crawford's	Colledge Wynd
Nisbet,	Alex.	Surgeon	Nisbet's	Peebles Wynd
Nisbet,	James	Wheelwright	McMillan's	Stonelaw's Close
Nisbet,	James		Smith's	High Street at Baillie Fyfe's Close
Nisbet,	John	Merchant		Libberton's Wynd
Nisbet,	John		Scott's	West Bow Foot
Nisbet,	John		Gairn's	Grassmarket East
Nisbet,	Mr	Manufacturer	Forrest's	President's Close
Nisbet,	Lady			High Street at Gosford's/Bank
Noble,	Alexander	Candlemaker	Munro's	Lawnmarket at Wardrope's Court
Noble,	Alexander	Hair Merchant	Stonehouse's	Fishmarket Close
Noble,	Robert	Merchant	Brown's	Wardrope's Court
Noble,	Robert	Cordiner	Dalgleish's	Society
Norrie,	James	Painter	Norrie's	Kinloch's Close N.
Norrie,	Mrs	Paints & Dyes Mcht.	Norrie's	Kinloch's Close N.
Norrie,	Mrs		Dunbar's	Carruber's Close
Norrie,	Richard			Upper Baxter's Close
Norrie,	Robert	Painter	Norrie's	Chamber's Close
Northesk,	Lady		Guild's	Covenant Close
Ogilvie,	Alex.	Glover		
Ogilvie,	Captain			Foulis Close South
Ogilvie,	David	Ale Seller	Benzie's	Lawnmarket at West Bow Head
Ogilvie,	James		Cumming's	Forrester's Wynd
Ogilvie,	Malcolm	Merchant	Kirkton's	Milne's Court
Ogilvie,	Malcolm	Skinner	Weigh House	West Bow Head
Ogilvie,	Mr	*of Coul*	Lock's	World's End Close
Ogilvie,	Mrs		Moriston's	Foulis Close South
Ogilvie,	Mrs	Midwife	Adams's	Kinloch's Close South
Ogle,	Mary	Vintner	Exchange Coffee House	Craig's Close
Ogston,	Mrs	Room Setter		Goudilock's Land

NAME		OCCUPATION	ADDRESS	
OLD,	John			Horse Wynd
OLD,	Mrs	Stabler	Galloway's	Horse Wynd
OLIPHANT,	Ebenezer	Goldsmith	Gavinlock's	Forrester's Wynd
			(shop) Forbes's	Parliament Close
OLIPHANT,	Langton Oliphant's	Children	Oliphant's	Niddry's Wynd
OLIPHANT,	Lawrence	Goldsmith		Brown's Land opposite Tolbooth
OLIPHANT,	Mr	Weaver	Chalmer's	Castlehill South
OLIPHANT,	Mrs		Callander's	Skinner's Close
OLIPHANT,	Mrs			Borthwick's Close
ORAM,	Alexander	Writer	Marjoribank's	High Street at Bull's Close
ORAM,	David	Writer	Taylor's	President's Close
ORBISTON,	Lady		McGill's	Foulis Close South
ORMISTON,	William	Manservant	Norrie's	Kinloch's Close North
ORMISTON,	William	Coppersmith	Duncan's	Cowgate South
ORR,	Alexander	Writer	Milne's	Meal Market
ORR,	John	Stabler	Douglas's	Grassmarket West
ORR,	John	Wigmaker	Fisher's	Mary King's Close
ORR,	Mr	Baxter/Room Setter		Warriston's Close
ORROCK,	John		Cumming's	Fishmarket Close
ORROCK,	Robert	*of that ilk*	Dalrymple's	Castlehill North
OSBURN,	John	Merchant	His Own	Covenant Close
OSBURN,	Margaret		Hammermen's	Cowgate Head South
OSWALD,	John	Tavern Keeper	Moncrief's	Mary King's Close
OSWALD,	Mrs		Kennedy's	Cant's Close Foot
PALE,	Mr	Cobbler	Callander's	Foulis Close South
PARK,	John	Shoemaker	Wardrop's	Cant's Close
PATERSON,	David	Merchant	Wight's	Allan's Close
PATERSON,	George	Merchant	Dunbar's	James Court
PATERSON,	George	Teacher	1st Tunrpike in	Horse Wynd Foot
PATERSON,	Hugh	Taylor	Schaw's	Brown's Land opposite Tolbooth
PATERSON,	James	Taylor	Paterson's	Galloway's Close
PATERSON,	James	Advocate	Paterson's	Blackfriar's Wynd
PATERSON,	Robert	Brewer	Paterson's	Grassmarket West
PATON,	John	Bookseller	(*home*) Paton's	Castlehill South
			(*shop*)	Parliament Close
PATON,	Miss		Smellie's	West Bow in Anderson's Land
PATON,	Thomas	Merchant	Livingston's	Byre's Close
PATON,	Thomas	Bookbinder	Sandiland's	Forrester's Wynd East
PATRICK,	Gordon			Skinner's Close
PATULLO,	John	Merchant	Foulis'	Foulis Close South
PATULLO,	John	Bookseller		Kinloch's Close North
PAUL,	Alexander	Stabler/Ale Seller	Watson's	Grassmarket West
PAXTON,	John	Coachman	White Lion Tavern	West Bow Head
PEACOCK,	John	Glazier	Adams'	Kinloch's Close
PEAT,	Mrs		Stenhouse's	Marlin's Wynd
PEDDIE,	Thomas	Ale Seller	Veitch's	West Bow Foot
PENMAN,	George	Cordiner	His Own	Cap & Feather Close
PENMAN,	Hugh	Goldsmith		Fleshmarket Close
PENMAN,	Hugh	Goldsmith	Penman's	Cap & Feather Close
PENMAN,	Miss		Moffat's	West Bow Middle
PENMAN,	Mistress		Penman's	Cap & Feather Close
PENNEY,	James		Taylor's	President's Close
PERRIE,	John		Kersie's	Lawnmarket at Forrester's Wynd
PERRIE,	Mrs		Bull's	Cowgate South
PETERS,	Alexander	Wright	His Own	Horse Wynd
PETERS,	Mr	Printer	Blair's	Castlehill South
PETRIES,	Andrew	Wright	Finlayson's	High Street at Allan's Close

NAME		OCCUPATION	ADDRESS	
Petries,	Jean		Custom House Stairs	Parliament Close
Petries,	William & Jean		Petrie's	Cowgate at Fishmarket/Borthwick's
Philip,	John	Manservant	Lawrie's	Blackfriar's Wynd
Philip,	Robert		Clerk's	Trunk Close
Philipshaugh,	Lady			Royston's Close
Philp,	John	Auditor in Exchequer		Wardrop's Court
Picard,	Msr.	Fencing Master		Don's Close
Picque,	Msr.	Dancing Master	Learmonth's	Skinner's Close
Pillans,	Hector	Baxter	Taylor's	President's Close
Pillans,	Miss	Merchant		Lawnmarket North at Gladstone's Land
Piper,	Mrs	Milliner	Piper's	Kinloch's Close North
Piper,	Mrs		Millar's	Grassmarket West
Pitcairn,	Andrew			Milne Square
Pitcairn,	George	Merchant	Hepburn's	James Court
Pitcairn,	George	Merchant	Thom's	Libberton's Wynd
Pitcairn,	Mrs		Pitcairn's	Kinloch's Close South
Pitcairn,	Mr		Aitken's	Cowgate South
Pitcairn,	Lady		Pitcairn's	Kinloch's Close South
Pitcarty,	Lady		Ancrum's	Monteith's Close
Pitfour Hay,	Lady		Craigie's	Libberton's Wynd
Plenderlieth,	Mrs			Tweeddale's Court
Plummer,		Doctor	Colt's	Cant's Close Foot
Police Office				Lawnmarket at Bank/Cullen's
Polkemmet,	Lady		Aitken's	Cowgate South
Pollock,	Richard		Reid's	President's Close
Polson,	John	Ale Seller	Bell's	Kennedy's Close
Porteous,	Mrs	Mantua Maker	Hay's	Grassmarket Mid
Porteous,	Nathan	Glover	Dunbar's	Carruber's Close
Porterfield,		Doctor	Farquhar's	High Street at Advocate's/Cantore's
Porterfield,		Doctor		Kinloch's Close North
Porterfield,	William	Doctor		Covenant Close
Post Office			Campbell's	Post Office Stairs Parliament Close
Powfowlis,	Lady		Monro's	Geddes Close
Preston,	Lady			Writer's Court
Preston,	Misses		Preston's	Milne's Court
Pringle,	Alexander	Wright	Mitchell's	Kennedy's Close
Pringle,	Andrew	H.M. Solicitor	Scale Stairs	Old Assembly Close W.
Pringle,		Captain	Naismith's	Brownhill's Land
Pringle,	George	Furrier		Borthwick's Close
Pringle,	James	*of Bowland* W.S.	Scale Stairs	Old Assembly Close W.
Pringle,	John	Skinner	Bell's	West Bow Middle
Pringle,	John	Captain	Manson's	Fleshmarket Close
Pringle,	John	W.S.	Dickson's 2nd Land	Libberton's Wynd
Pringle,	Mr	*of Crighton*	Syme's	Kennedy's Close
Pringle,	Mr	Manservant	Stewart's	Covenant Close
Pringle,	Mrs		Schaw's	President's Close
Pringle,	Misses		Burn's	Lawnmarket at Forrester's Wynd
Pringle,	Robert	Merchant	Pringle's	Old Post Office Close
Pringle,	Robert	Merchant	Lundie's	High Street at Borthwick's/Fishmarket
Pringle,	Robert		Smith's	Niddry's Wynd
Pringle,	Robert			Monteith's Close
Pumpherston,	Lady		Somervail's	High Street at Kinloch's Close
Punton,	Archibald		His Own	Borthwick's Close
Punton,	Archibald	Baxter	Anderson's	Cowgate South
Purdie,	George	Druggist	Holburn's	High Street at Baillie Fyfe's Close

NAME		OCCUPATION	ADDRESS	
Purdie,	Mr	Merchant	Young's	Society
Purdie,	Thomas	Merchant	Blair's	Craig's Close
Purvis,	Alexander	Merchant	Stewart's	Luckenbooths
Purvis,	James	W.S.		Under Baxter's Close
Purvis,	Lady		Carmichael's	Under Baxter's Close
Purvis,	William	Ale Seller	His Own	
Quesnot,	John	French Teacher		Stonelaw's Close Head
Rae,	James	Surgeon	Rae's	High Street at Fleshmarket Close
Rae,	John	Teacher	Good's	Colledge Wynd
Raeburn,	Andrew	Wright	Hastie's	Hyndford's Close
Ramage,	James	Meal Seller	Mouat's	Meal Market
Ramage,	John	Port Waiter	Paterson's	Grassmarket West
Ramage,	John	Merchant	Scriving's	Candlemaker Row at Good Town's Land
Ramsay,	Allan	Bookseller	Ramsay's	Castlehill Head
Ramsay,	James	Merchant	Callander's	Foulis Close South
Ramsay,	Katharine	Milliner		Jackson's Close
Ramsay,	Mrs	Room Setter	Elliot's	Upper Baxter's Close
Ramsay,	Mrs		Brown's	Byre's Close
Ramsay,	Mrs		Ramsay's	Todrick's Wynd
Ramsay,	Mrs		Hay's	West Bow in Anderson's Land
Ramsay,	Misses	Milliner's	Armour's	North Foulis Close
Ramsay,	Peter	Tavern Keeper	Red Lion Inn	West Bow Foot
Ramsay,	Robert	Taylor	Mylne's	Skinner's Close
Ramsay,	Samuel	Stabler	Dickson's	Candlemaker Row
Ramsay,	William	Banker		High Street at Kinloch's Close North
Rankine,	Andrew	Coppersmith	Veitch's	West Bow Foot
Rankine,	James	Wright		Cullen's Close
Rankine,	Mrs		Dickson's	Candlemaker Row
Rankine,	Mrs		Todd's	Horse Wynd East
Rankine,	Miss		Todd's	Horse Wynd West
Rannie,	Andrew	Merchant	Crawford's	West Bow South
Rannie,	David	Wigmaker	Jack's	Covenant Close
Rannie,	Mrs	Room Setter	Turnbull's	Custom House Stairs Parliament Close
Rannie,	Miss & Wood	Merchants	Lothian's	Warriston Close
Rannie,	Thomas	Merchant	Crichton's	Luckenbooths
Rannie,	William	Stabler	Hamilton's	Grassmarket Mid
Rattray,	John	Surgeon	Rattray's	Foulis Close South
Rattray,	John			Kinloch's Close North
Rattray,	John		Dickson's	Candlemaker Row
Rattray,	Mr		Campbell's	New Stairs Parliament Close
Ravenscroft,	Mrs		Shearer's	Chamber's Close
Reid & Chalmers		Merchants	Alison's	Luckenbooths
Reid,	George	Ale Seller	Brown's	Paterson's Court
Reid,	John	Manservant	Legat's	Fishmarket Close
Reid,	John		Stevenson's	
Reid,	John	Printer	Chalmer's	Candlemaker Row
Reid,	Margaret	Merchant	Gladstone's	Lawnmarket North
Reid,	Mr	Schoolmaster	Penicuik's	Kinloch's Close South
Reid,	Mr	Merchant	Young's	Society
Reid,	Mrs	Merchant	Morrison's	West Bow Middle
Reid,	Mrs	Widow	Blair's	Castlehill South
Reid,	Mrs	Merchant	Forrest's	Lady Stair's Close
Reid,	Mrs		McRabbie's	Warriston Close
Reid,	Mrs		Marshall's	Murdoch's Close
Reid,	Mrs		Reid's	President's Close
Reid,	Robert	W.S.		Geddes Close

NAME		OCCUPATION	ADDRESS	
REID,	Thomas	Chairman	Jolly's	Burnet's Close
REID,	William	Chairman	Bryden's	Mary King's Close
REID,	William	Taylor	McClellan's	Society
RENTON,	Mrs	Merchant	Mein's	Pearson's Close
REOCH,	James	Procurator	His Own	Blackfriar's Wynd
REOCH,	James	Ale Seller	Borthwick's	High Street at Borthwick's/Fishmarket
REOCH,	John	Musician	Hart's	Carruber's Close
REOCH,	Mrs		Reoch's	President's Close
REOCH,	William	Wright	Dick's	Carruber's Close
RICCARTON,	Lady		Menzie's	Lawnmarket at Roxburgh's Close
RICHARDSON,	Archibald	Bookbinder	Turpie's	Jackson's Close
RICHARDSON,	George	Writer	Paton's	Byre's Close
RICHARDSON,	John	Merchant	Downie's	Grassmarket East
RICHARDSON,	William	Smith	Wedderburn's	Gray's Close
RICHARDSON,	William	Farrier		Warriston's Close
RICHIE,	Thomas	Glazier	Legat's	Fishmarket Close
RICHMONT,	John	Teacher	Peter's	Horse Wynd
RIDDLE,	George	Wright	Royston's	Royston's Close
RIDDLE,	Mrs		Riddle's	Craig's Close
RIDDOCH,	David		Crinzen's	Blackfriar's Wynd
RIDDOCH,	Jean		Riddoch's	Covenant Close
RIGG,	George	Grocer	McCulloch's	Lawnmarket at Gosford's Close
RIPPATH,	John		Knox's	Lady Stair's Close
RITCHIE,	Alex.	Merchant	Brown's	Lawnmarket at Wardrope's Court
RITCHIE,	George	Fishmonger	New Stage Coach Office	
ROBB,	James		Henderson's	Wardrope's Court
ROBERT,	Anna	Merchant	Dallas's	Bell's Wynd
ROBERTSON & McFARQUHAR		Painters	"Queen's Head"	Libberton's Wynd
ROBERTSON,	Alex.	Merchant	Boswall's	High Street at Carruber's Close
ROBERTSON,	Alexander	Spirit Merchant	"Golden Dog"	High Street opposite Guard
ROBERTSON,	Alexander	W.S. *of Parson's Green*		Carruber's Close
ROBERTSON,	Andrew	Ale Seller	Tod's	Niddry's Wynd
ROBERTSON,	Charles	Flesher	Inglis's	Fleshmarket Close
ROBERTSON,	Charles	Professor	New Stairs	Parliament Close
ROBERTSON,	Colin	Wigmaker	His Own	Old Post Office Close
ROBERTSON,	David	Smith	Adams'	Foot of Kinloch's Close South
ROBERTSON,	Duncan	Manservant	Fouler's	Cant's Close Foot
ROBERTSON,	Gilbert	Merchant	Halyburton's	Foulis Close South
ROBERTSON,	Hugh	Indweller	Sandiland's	Forrester's Wynd East
ROBERTSON,	James	Merchant	McCulloch's	Mary King's Close
ROBERTSON,	James	Poulterer	Mylne's	Milne Square
ROBERTSON,	James	Waiter	Hammerman's	Cowgate Head South
ROBERTSON,	James	Professor of Hebrew		University
ROBERTSON,	Mrs Jean		Gladstone's	Lawnmarket North
ROBERTSON,	John		Foster's	Peebles Wynd
ROBERTSON,	John	Chairman	Bairfoot's	Peebles Wynd
ROBERTSON,	John	Vintner	McRabbie's	Stonelaw's Close
ROBERTSON,	John		Hammerman's	Cowgate Head South
ROBERTSON,	John	Writer		Todrick's Wynd
ROBERTSON,	John			Pearson's Close
ROBERTSON,	Mary		Candlemaker's	Candlemaker Row
ROBERTSON,	Mr	Gauger	Hamilton's	Grassmarket West
ROBERTSON,	Mr	Gentleman	Bell's	Mary King's Close
ROBERTSON,	Mr	Smith	Adams'	Foot of Kinloch's Close South
ROBERTSON,	Mr			Colledge Wynd
ROBERTSON,	Mrs		Robertson's	Lady Stair's Close
ROBERTSON,	Mrs		Winter's	Chamber's Close
ROBERTSON,	Mrs	Room Setter	Jolly's	Bain & Jolly's Land

NAME		OCCUPATION	ADDRESS	
Robertson,	Mrs		Lauder's	Niddry's Wynd
Robertson,	Mrs		Wallace's	Forrester's Wynd Foot
Robertson,	Mrs	Widow	Scirving's	Good Town's Land
Robertson,	Mrs			Upper Baxter's Close
Robertson,	Miss	Merchant	Chalmer's	Lawnmarket at Milne's Court
Robertson,	Miss	Milliner	Langland's	Gladstone's Land
Robertson,	Miss	Milliner	Carmichael's	World's End Close Foot
Robertson,	Patrick	Ale Seller	Livingstone's	Byre's Close
Robertson,	Patrick	Jeweller	McKay's	Luckenbooths
Robertson,	Thomas	Flesher	Williamson's	Fleshmarket Close
Robertson,	Thomas	Writer	Hogg's	High Street at Carruber's Close
Robertson,	Thomas	Taylor	Legat's	Fishmarket Close
Robertson,	William	Manservant	Hunter's	Cant's Close Foot
Robertson,	William	Writer	Scale Stairs	Old Assembly Close West
Robson,	William	Teacher	1st Stair above Guard:	High Street
Rochead,	Betty		Her Own	Craig's Close
Rochead,	James	Merchant		Craig's Close
Rochead,	James	Distiller	Allan's	Milne's Square
Rochead,			Robertson's	Cowgate South
Rollo,	Mrs		Finlayson's	Kinloch's Close South
Ronalds,	Mrs		Cathcart's	Foulis's Close
Ronalds,	William	Ale Seller	Straton's	High Street at Niddry's Wynd
Ronaldson,	Anna	Ale Seller	Ure's	Libberton's Wynd
Ronaldson,	James	Glazier	Ferguson's	Kennedy's Close
Ronaldson,	James	Baxter	McCulloch's	Lawnmarket at Forrester's Wynd
Ronaldson,	James	Baxter	Hogg's	High Street at Carruber's Close
Ronaldson,	John	Merchant	Robertson's	Skinner's Close
Ronaldson,	Mrs		Bruce's	Cowgate at Cant's/Dickson's
Ronaldson,	Stephen	Cordiner	Winter's	Chamber's Close
Rose,	Mr	Painter	Gray's	Dickson's Close
Ross,	Alexander	Ale Seller	Baillie's	Bull's Close
Ross,	Alexander	Writer		
Ross,	Alexander	Ale Seller	Shiel's	Stonelaw's Close
Ross,	Charles	Merchant	Kinloch's	Kinloch's Close South
Ross,	Daniel	Merchant	McKinlay's	Grassmarket East
Ross,	Daniel	Upholsterer	Ainslie's	Baillie Fyfe's Close
Ross,	Isobel	Ale Seller	Shiel's	High Street at Lyon's Close
Ross,	John	Stationer	Cumming's	President's Stairs Parliament Close
Ross,	John		Scale Stairs	Old Assembly Close
Ross,	Mr	Flesher	Simpson's	Cowgate South
Ross,	Mr		Pencaitland's	Niddry's Wynd
Ross,	Mrs	Ale Seller	Baird's	Hyndford's Close
Ross,	Mrs		Ramsay's	Meal Market
Ross,	Mrs	Widow	Hammerman's	Cowgate Head South
Ross,	Miss & Paton	Merchants	Stonehouse's	Con's Close
Ross,	Patrick	Merchant		High Street at Fleshmarket Close
Ross,	William	Writer: Secretary to SPCK	(home)	Warriston Close Milne's Court
Rothiemay,	Lady		Her Own	Lawnmarket at Forrester's/Libberton's
Royal Bank; see **Bank, Royal.**				
Ruddiman Brothers		Publishers: Caledonian Mercury		New Stairs Parliament Close
Ruddiman,	Thomas	Publisher	Warrender's	Parliament Close
Ruddiman,	Walter	Printer	Ruddiman's (home)	Meal Market Under Baxter's Close

NAME		OCCUPATION	ADDRESS	
Russell,	Francis	Surgeon		Dickson's Close Head
Russell,	James		Dean's	Libberton's Wynd
Russell,	James	Merchant	McGowan's	Grassmarket East
Russell,	James	Surgeon	Surgeon's Hall	High School Yards
Russell,	James		Russell's	High Street at Cantore's Close
Russell,	James	Doctor	Herring's	Grassmarket Middle
Russell,	John	*of Roseburne* W.S.	Swinton's	Forrester's Wynd East
Russell,	John jr.		Campbell's Bldgs.	Argylle Square
Russell,	Mary			Bess Wynd Middle
Russell,	Mrs	Shipping Agent	Weigh House	Lawnmarket at West Bow Head
Russell,	Robert	Merchant		Advocate's Close
Russell,	Robert	Merchant	Home's	Byre's Close
Russell,	William	Clerk	Stewart's	Trunk Close
Rutherford,	John	Milliner	"Cap & Lappets"	Forrester's Wynd East
Rutherford,	John	Doctor	His Own	Custom House Stairs Parliament Close
Rutherford,	Edward	Writer	Morrison's	West Bow Middle
Rutherford,	Mrs		Wardrope's	Wardrope's Court
Rutherford,	Mrs	Ale Seller	Millar's	Craig's Close
Rutherford,	William	Hair Merchant	Legat's	Fishmarket Close
Ruthven,	Lady		Gray's	Chamber's Close
Samson,	Mr		Hunter's	West Bow Middle
Samuel,	David		Hamilton's	Grassmarket West
Samuels,	Robert	Merchant	Samuel's	Horse Wynd East
Sanders,	Mr	Printer	Pearson's	Pearson's Close
Sanders,	Mrs	Vintner	Armour's	North Foulis Close
Sanders,	Mrs	Room Setter	Nisbet's	Niddry's Wynd
Sanders,	Richard	Merchant	Armour's	North Foulis Close
Sanderson,	Mrs		Tod's	Horse Wynd West
Sandilands,	Jenet		Lawrie's	Blackfriar's Wynd
Sandilands,	Mark	Merchant	Lindsay's	West Bow Head
Sandilands,	Mrs	Ale Seller	McVey's	Milne Square
Sands,	Lady		Kinloch's	Kinloch's Close South
Sands,	William	Bookseller (Scots Magazine)		Parliament Close
Sandum,	Andrew	Fencing Master	Crawford's	Carruber's Close
Sauney,	William	Upholsterer	Innes's	Castlehill Head
Schaw,	Hendry	Chairmaster	Alves's	High Street at Borthwick's/Fishmarket
Schaw,	John	Upholsterer	Foulis's	Luckenbooths
Schaw,	Mrs		Schaw's	President's Close
Schaw,	Miss	Merchant	Lothian's	Warriston Close
Scirving,	John		Simpson's	Trunk Close
Scotland,	John	Skinner	Lindsay's	West Bow Head
Scotland,	John	Bookbinder	Laing's	West Bow Head
Scots Laboratory				University
Scots Magazine		Printed by Alexander Murray and James Cochrane Published by William Sands		
Scott,	Alexander	Merchant	Ramsay's	Luckenbooths
Scott,	Alexander	Merchant	Scott's	Cowgate Head North
Scott,	David	Spirit Merchant	Scott's	Fleshmarket Close Head
Scott,	David	Glover	Scott's	Fleshmarket Close Head
Scott,	David	*of Handelsope*		Fleshmarket Close Head
Scott,	Elizabeth	Merchant	Young's	Luckenbooths
Scott,	James	W.S.		High street above Bess Wynd
Scott,	James	Merchant	Scott's	West Bow Foot
Scott,	James	Sheriff's Officer	Sheil's	at Craig's Close
Scott,	James	Druggist	(Infirmary)	Robertson's Close
Scott,	John	*of Howden:* Writer	His Own	Brown's Land opposite Tolbooth

NAME		OCCUPATION	ADDRESS	
SCOTT,	John	Plumber	Fairholm's	Craig's Close
SCOTT,	John	Candlemaker	Nicol's	Pearson's Close
SCOTT,	Mary		Norrie's	Kinloch's Close North
SCOTT,	Mrs		Hamilton's	West Bow Foot
SCOTT,	Mrs	Minister's Widow	Rankin's	Milne's Square
SCOTT,	Mrs		Bull's	Cowgate South
SCOTT,	Mrs		Baird's	Hyndford's Close
SCOTT,	Mrs	*of Thirlstane*	Carnwath's	Niddry's Wynd
SCOTT,	Mrs		Cleghorn's	Horse Wynd
SCOTT,	Mrs		Stonehouse's	Fishmarket Close
SCOTT,	Mrs		Scott's	Cowgate
SCOTT,	Mistress		Laing's	James Court
SCOTT,	Mungo	Glazier	Callander's	Skinner's Close Head
SCOTT,	Peggy		Scott's	Fleshmarket Close Head
SCOTT,	Robert	Merchant	Biggar's	Swan's Close
SCOTT,	Thomas	Stabler	Wight's	Cowgate South
SCOTT,	Walter	Baxter	Murray's	Forrester's Wynd East
SCOTT,	Walter	*of Galashiels:* W.S.	Peter's	Horse Wynd East
SCOTT,	Walter	Linen Merchant	Heriot's Wark	Grassmarket Mid
SCOTT,	William	Merchant	Willson's	Paterson's Court
SCOTT,	William	Ale Seller	Weir's	Gosford's Close
SCOTT,	William	Merchant		Luckenbooths
SCOUGALL,	Christian		Scougall's	Advocate's Close
SCOUGALL & WAKE		Merchants	Scougall's	Advocate's Close
SCOUGALL,	Mrs	Widow	Brown's	Brownhills Land
SCRYMGEOUR,	Henry	W.S.		Kinloch's Close South
SCRYMGEOUR,	Hendry		Burn's	Libberton's Wynd
SEGAL,	James		Borthwick's	High Street at Borthwick's/Fishmarket
SELKIRK,	Mrs		Selkirk's	Cowgate North
SELKIRK,	Mistress		Robertson's	James Court
SELKIRK,	Robert	Merchant	Selkirk's	Cowgate North
SELKIRK,	Robert		Sinclair's	West Bow in Anderson's Land
SELKRIGG,	Robert		Lithgow's	Grassmarket West
SEMPLE,	Lord		Skinner's	Castlehill North
SEMPLE,	Mrs		Bruce's	Libberton's Wynd
SETON,	Christian	Ale Seller	Weir's	Gosford's Close
SETON,	Daniel	Merchant	Seton's	Lawnmarket at Roxburgh's Close
SETON,	George	Captain	Forbes's	High Street at Carruber's Close
SETON,	Sir Henry		Adams's	Foot of Kinloch's Close South
SETON,	James		Crockett's	West Bow Foot
SETON,	James	Merchant	Seton's	Warriston Close
SETON,	Lillie		Gordon's	Hyndford's Close
SETON,	Widow	Ale Seller	Mein's	Fleshmarket Close
SETON,	Mrs		Sandiland's	Forrester's Wynd East
SETON,	Miss		Home's	Gosford's Close
SETON,	Patrick	Merchant	Sinclair's	Blackfriar's Wynd
SEWRIGHT,	Mr		McLenan's	West Bow Mid.
SHANKS,	James	Spirit & Ale Seller	Young's	Candlemaker Row
SHARP,	John	Stabler	"White Hart Inn" Lithgow's	Grassmarket West
SHARP,	Mary	Lady	Butter's	Carruber's Close
SHEARER,	Archibald	Merchant	Crockett's	West Bow Foot
SHEARER,	Mrs		Deuchar's	Lawnmarket
SHIELS,	Archibald	Merchant	"Hand & Orange"	High Street at Back of Cross Well
SHIELS,	Alexander	Ale Seller	Shiel's	Covenant Close
SHIELS,	Micah	Cheesemonger	Bauld's	Gray's Close
SHIELS,	Mrs		Smith's	Skinner's Close
SHIELS,	Mr		Todd's	Castlehill North
SHEPHERD,	Mrs		Gardiner's	Argylle Square

NAME		OCCUPATION		ADDRESS
SHEWELTON,	Lord			Fishmarket Close
SHINBOW,	John	Wigmaker	Peter's	Horse Wynd
SHIRRIF,	Mrs		Wallace's	Borthwick's Close
SHORE,	John	Whip-maker	Fairholm's	West Bow Head
SIBBALD,	Thomas	Smith	Kerr's	Colledge Wynd
SIBBALD,	William	Taylor	Magdalen's	High Street above Tron
SIDESERF,	Mrs		Sideserf's	West Bow
SIEVEWRIGHT,	John		His Own	Cowgate Head North
SIGLUR,	George	Writer	Bowie's	Cowgate South
SIMPSON,	Charles	Furrier		
SIMPSON,	George	Glazier	Woodhouselie's	Anchor Close
SIMPSON,	James	Teacher	His Own	Bell's Wynd
SIMPSON,	Mrs	Ale Seller	Crawford's	Carruber's Close
SINCLAIR,	Alex.	Tailor	Laing's	World's End Close
SINCLAIR,	Angus	Ale Seller	Laing's	West Bow Head
SINCLAIR,	Archibald		Bell's	Forrester's Wynd
SINCLAIR,		Doctor	His Own	Trunk Close
SINCLAIR,	Euphan		Swinton's	Forrester's Wynd East
SINCLAIR,	Hendry		Middleton's	Trunk Close
SINCLAIR,	John	Writer	Pringle's	Old Post Office Close
SINCLAIR,	John		Smith's	Baillie Fyfe's Close Head
SINCLAIR,	John	Writer		Lawnmarket at Cullen's/Fisher's
SINCLAIR,	Mr		Handyside's	Trunk Close
SINCLAIR,	Mr		Bain & Jolly's	Cowgate North
SINCLAIR,	Mrs		Petrie's	Burnet's Close
SKED,	John	Vintner	Wood's	Luckenbooths
SKEEN,	Andrew	Weaver	Cleghorn's	Horse Wynd
SKEEN,	Catharine		Skeen's	Foulis Close South
SKELTON,	John	Ale Seller	Whitehead's	Mary King's Close
SMALLET,	James	of Bonhill: Advocate		Society
SMART,	George	Ale Seller	Young's	Kennedy's Close
SMART,	Mrs	Widow	Cleghorn's	Meal Market
SMEITON,	Alex.	Bookbinder	Brown's	Brown's Land opposite Tolbooth
SMEITON,	James	Wigmaker	Henderson's	High Street 1st below Blackfriar's
SMELLIE,	James	Merchant	His Own	President's Close
SMELLIE,	Mrs		Smellie's	West Bow in Anderson's Land
SMETHOLM,	Mistress		Smetholm's	Fountain Close
SMITH,	Alexander	Baxter	Riddle's	Royston's Close
SMITH,	Alexander	Wigmaker	Halyburton's	Grassmarket East
SMITH,	Charles		McLeod's	High Street at Smith's Land
SMITH,	Elizabeth	Ale Seller	Christie's	Borthwick's Close
SMITH,	Gilbert	Merchant	Crockate's	Bull's Close
SMITH,	George	Merchant	Spittle's	Hyndford's Close
SMITH,	James	Writer	Jack's	Covenant Close
SMITH,	James	Glover		Byre's Close
SMITH,	James	Skinner		Skinner's Close
SMITH,	James	Writer		Hyndford's Close
SMITH,	John	Ale Seller		Paterson's Court
SMITH,	John	Saddler/Ale Seller	Robertson's	High Street at Cantore's/Advocate's
SMITH,	John		Pencaitland's	Niddry's Wynd
SMITH,	John	Excise Officer	Wight's	New Stairs West Parliament Close
SMITH,	Margaret		Galloway's	Lawnmarket North
SMITH,	Micah		Bauld's	Gray's Close
SMITH,	Mrs		Penman's	Byre's Close
SMITH,	Mrs			Geddes Close
SMITH,	Mrs		Hogg's	Kennedy's Close
SMITH,	Mrs			Bess Wynd

NAME		OCCUPATION	ADDRESS	
Smith,	Mrs		Barclay's	Lawnmarket at Bank/Cullen's
Smith,	Mrs		Telfer's	West Bow Head
Smith,	Robert	Surgeon	Cleghorn's	New Stairs Foot Meal Market
Smith,	Thomas		Drummond's	Dickson's Close
Smith,	Thomas	Clerk		London Sun-Fire Insurance
Smith,	William	Merchant	Brand's	Castlehill South
Smith,	William	Merchant	Jameson's	Byre's Close
Smith,	William	Ale Seller	Kennedy's	Craig's Close
Somervail,	Andrew	Merchant	McKay's	Cap & Feather Close
Somervail,	Alexander	Port Surveyor	Black's	Fleshmarket Close
Somervail,	David	Merchant	Somervail's	Grassmarket Mid
Somervail,	Mr	Lint Merchant	Duncan's	Argylle Square
Somervail,	Nicol	Painter	His Own	Fleshmarket Close East
Somervail,	William	Skinner	Somervail's	Grassmarket Mid
Spalding,	Mrs		Sinclair's	Skinner's Close
Spark,	Hugh		Wardrop's	Cant's Close
Spark,	Patrick	Writer	Hallyburton's	Cowgate South
Speirs,	Mrs		Speir's	Lawnmarket North
Spence,	David	Writer: Secretary to the Bank of Scotland (*home*)	Thom's	Libberton's Wynd
Spence,	James	Clerk to Bank of Scotland (*home*)		Wardrope's Court
Spence,	James	Cordiner	Herring's	Grassmarket Mid
Spence,	Mr	Cordiner	Gray's	Grassmarket East
Spence,	Mrs	Ale Seller	Knox's	Lady Stair's Close
Spence,	William	Painter	Gowan's	Upper Baxter's Close
Spittle,	Mrs		Spittle's	Hyndford's Close
Spottiswood,	James			High Street at Syme's Land
Sprott,	John	Candlemaker	His Own	Blackfriar's Wynd
Staig,	John	Merchant		Blackfriar's Wynd
Staig,	Mrs		Dick's	Blackfriar's Wynd
Stair,	Lady		Mint	Gray's Close
Stamp Office			Warrender's	Parliament Close
Stark,	David	Weaver	New Lands	Dickson's Close
Steadman,	James	Vintner	Kennedy's	Craig's Close
Steel,	James	Merchant	Clelland's	Under Baxter's Close
Steel,	John	Watchmaker	Fairholm's	Allan's Close
Stenhope,	Mr		Telfer's	West Bow Head
Steuart,	Dr John	Professor of Natural Philosophy		University
Stevenson,	Alex.	Candlemaker	McMillan's	Stonelaw's Close
Stevenson,	Alexander	*of Montgreenan* W.S.	President's Stairs	Parliament Close
Stevenson,		Doctor	His Own	Royston's Close
Stevenson,	George	Wright	His Own	Kinloch's Close North
Stevenson,	George	Physician	Lauder's	Niddry's Wynd
Stevenson,		Professor	Kennedy's	Cant's Close
Stevenson,	James Rev.	Minister	Friershaw's	Grassmarket
Stevenson,	Mrs		Innes's	Cowgate South
Stevenson,	Roger	Merchant	Lumsden's	Robertson's Close
Stevenson,	Samuel	Merchant		Allan's Close
Stevenson,	William	Candlemaker	Sinclair's	Blackfriar's Wynd
Stewart & Scott		Merchants	Dean's	Don's Close
Stewart,	Alexander	Ale Seller	Blair's	Castlehill South
Stewart,	Alexander			Milne's Court
Stewart,	Alexander	Billiard Tables	Fairholm's	Allan's Close
Stewart,	Alexander			Todrick's Wynd
Stewart,	Alexander	Musician	Kennedy's	Marlin's Wynd
Stewart,	Alexander	W.S.	Scale Stairs	Old Assembly Close
Stewart,	Archibald	Merchant	Stewart's	West Bow Head
Stewart,	Archibald	Merchant	Stewart's	High Street at Baillie Fyfe's Close
Stewart,	Archibald	*of Torrance*; W.S.		Lawnmarket at Royston's Close

NAME		OCCUPATION		ADDRESS
Stewart,	Charles	Conservator at Campvere	Mitchell's	Lawnmarket at Libberton's Wynd
Stewart,	Daniel	Writer	Jack's	Covenant Close
Stewart,	Hugh	Manservant/Ale Seller	Gray's	Chamber's Close
Stewart,	James	Ale Seller	Robertson's	Peebles Wynd
Stewart,	James	Barber	Brown's	
Stewart,	James	Printer	Bruce's	Libberton's Wynd
Stewart,	James		Herring's	Grassmarket Mid
Stewart,	James	Merchant		James Court
Stewart,	James			Writer's Court
Stewart,	James			Brown's Land opposite Tolbooth
Stewart,	John	Cooper	Bell's	Geddes' Close
Stewart,	John	Musician	Davidson's	High Street at Carruber's Close
Stewart,	John	Manservant	Hart's	Carruber's Close
Stewart,	John	Merchant	Anderson's	Cowgate North
Stewart,	John	Wigmaker	Craig's	Grassmarket East
Stewart,	John	Bookseller		West Bow Foot
Stewart,	Sir John			Gray's Close
Stewart,	Kathrine	Ale Seller	Hamilton's	High Street at Halkerston's Wynd
Stewart,	Mathew	Professor of Math.	University	Colledge Wynd
Stewart,	Sir Michael	of Blackhall		Gray's Close
Stewart,	Mistress		Cleghorn's	Horse Wynd
Stewart,	Mrs		Syme's	Kinloch's Close North
Stewart,	Mrs	Widow	Erskine's	Netherbow
Stewart,	Mrs		Mein's	World's End Close Foot
Stewart,	Mrs		Jolly's	Burnet's Close
Stewart,	Mrs		Stewart's	Covenant Close
Stewart,	Mrs	Merchant	Petrie's	
Stewart,	Mrs		Wardrop's	Wardrop's Land
Stewart,	Mrs		Dewar's	West Bow Foot
Stewart,	Miss		Moffat's	West Bow Middle
Stewart,	Neil		Hunter's	Todrick's Wynd
Stewart,	Robert	Soldier	Bell's	High Street at North Foulis Close
Stewart,	Robert	Ale Seller	Bruce's	Libberton's Wynd
Stewart,	Robert	Meal Merchant	Muschet's	Grassmarket East
Stewart,	Thomas	Manservant	Winram's	Peebles Wynd
Stewart,	Walter		Thom's	Libberton's Wynd
Stewart,	William	Ale Seller	Orr's	Bell's Wynd
Stewart,	William	Chairmaster		Penston Letters' Land
Stirling,	Alex.	Merchant	Hutton's	Lawnmarket
Stirling,	Ann	Ale Seller		Wardrope's Court
Stirling,	James	Merchant (*shop*)	Stirling's	Luckenbooths
		(*home*)	Hellistob's	Cowgate opposite New Fishmarket Close
Stirling,	John	Teacher	Hart's	Carruber's Close
Stirling,	John	Merchant	Chalmer's	Lawnmarket at Forrester's/Libberton's
Stirling,	John	Room Setter		Bell's Wynd
Stirling,	Mrs		Dunbar's	Kinloch's Close North
Stirling,	Mrs	Druggist		Wardrope's Court
Stirling,	Miss	Mantua Maker	Wight's	Cowgate at Cant's/Dickson's
Stirling,	Misses		Dunbar's	Don's Close
Stobie,	John	Writer/Factor	Thom's	Libberton's Wynd
Stocks,	Christian		Selkirk's	Cowgate North
Stonebyres,	Lady		Blair's	Milne's Court
Stonehouse,	John	Merchant	Crockate's	Under Baxter's Close
Stonehouse,	Mrs		Stonehouse's	Covenant Close
Stormont,	Lady		Her Own	High Street at Smith's Land

NAME		OCCUPATION	ADDRESS	
Strachan,	John	Chairman	Moffat's	Peebles Wynd
Strachan,	Mrs		Neilsen's	West Bow Middle
Strachan,	Patrick	Cordiner	Strachan's	West Bow Middle
Strathnever,	Lady		Her Own	World's End Close
Straton,	Lady		Gavinlock's	Forrester's Wynd
Straton,	John	Surgeon	Carmichael's	Fleshmarket Close Head
Straton,	Mrs	Vintner	Stevenson's	Custom House Stairs Parliament Close
Straton,	Robert	Wright	Jameson's	Parliament Close
Strichen,	Lord			Cant's Close
Stuart,	of Edinglassie:	Teacher		Old Assembly Close
Stuart & Wallace		Goldsmiths		Advocate's Close Head
Sutherland,	Alex.	Merchant	Riddle's	Royston's Close
Sutherland,	Mrs		Dunbar's	Carrub er's Close
Sutherland,	William	Brewer	His Own	Gray's Close
Sutor,	John	Wright	Clelland's	Todrick's Wynd
Swan,	Mrs	Merchant	Hepburn's	Don's Close
Swan,	Robert	Ale Seller	Gray's	Dickson's Close
Swinton,	Margaret		Sandilands	Forrester's Wynd Head
Swinton,	William	Merchant	Young's	Blackfriar's Wynd
Sword,	Jean	Ale Seller	Grant's	Luckenbooths
Sword,	John	Merchant	Moubray's	Candlemaker Row North
Syme,	Andrew	Cooper	syme's	High Street at Niddry's Wynd
Syme,	Andrew	Merchant	McMillan's	Stonelaw's Close
Syme,	Alexander	Painter	Henderson's	Niddry's Wynd
Syme,	David	Furrier	Lauder's	Gosford's Close
Syme,	George	Slater	Lindsay's	Dickson's Close
Syme,	James	Taylor	Simpson's	Monteith's Close
Syme,	James	Slater	Syme's	High Street at Kennedy's Close
Syme,	John			Wardrope's Court
Syme,	Mrs		Smith's	Monteith's Close
Syme,	Mrs	Widow	Aitken's	Robertson's Close
Syme,	Mrs		Syme's	Lawnmarket at Forrester's/Libberton's
Syme,	Mrs		Hamilton's	West Bow Foot
Syme,	Robert	Vintner	Coffee House	Lawnmarket South
Syme,	William	Ale Seller	Aitken's	Robertson's Close
Symington,	James		Bull's	Cowgate South
Symington,	John	Baxter	Hogg's	Mary King's Close
Tait,	Alexander	Writer	Hay's in Anderson's 2nd Land	Friendly Insurance Co. West Bow
Tait,	James	Wright	Brown's	Forrester's Wynd Foot
Tait,	Mrs	Goldsmith	Seton's	Luckenbooths
Tait,	Mrs	Ale Seller	Chine's	Cowgate at Scott's Land
Tait,	Mrs	Widow	New Stairs Passage	Parliament Close
Taylor,		Doctor	Corbiston's	Kinloch's Close South
Taylor,	George	Factor/Writer		
Taylor,	James	of Pitcairlie: W.S.	Dickson's 2nd Land	Libberton's Wynd
Taylor,	Jean			Lyon's Close
Taylor,	Jean		Turnbull's	Cowgate Head
Taylor,	John	Merchant	Marjoribanks	Warriston Close
Taylor,	John	Merchant	Cummings	Fishmarket Close
Taylor,	John	Gentleman	Clunie's	Bull's Close
Taylor,	John		Mason's	Blackfriar's Wynd
Taylor,	Mr	Ale Seller	Taylor's	Baillie Fyfe's Close
Taylor,	Thomas		Crawford's	Colledge Wynd
Taylor,	William	Merchant	Pencaitland's	Cantore's Close
Taylor,	William	Goldsmith		Craig's Close
Taylor,	William	Writer	Gavinlock's	Forrester's Wynd
Telfer,	Miss		Shiell's	Monteith's Close Head
Telfer,	Mrs		Scheil's	Sandilands Close

NAME		OCCUPATION	ADDRESS	
Telfour,	James	Tailor	Crawford's	Halkerston's Wynd
Tennant,	Francis	Flesher	Black's	Fleshmarket Close
Tennoch,	William	Brewer	Heriot's Wark	Grassmarket Mid.
Thirlstane,	Lady		Watson's	High School Wynd
Thomas,	Godfrey	Bounty Hunter/ Maths. Teacher	"Duke's Head"	Anchor Close and at James McFarquhar Lodgings: High Street
Thomson,	Alex.	Ale Seller	Hope's	Monteith's Close
Thomson,	Alexander	Taylor	Stenhouse's	Marlin's Wynd
Thomson,	Alexander	Gunsmith	Wight's	Cowgate Head South
Thomson,	Andrew	Tobacconist	Grant's	Cullen's Close
Thomson,	Charles	Wigmaker	Hamilton's	High Street at Halkerston's Wynd
Thomson,	David		Myln's	Mary King's Close
Thomson,	David	Ale Seller	Mercer's	Custom House Stairs Parliament Close
Thomson,	Francis			Royston's Close
Thomson,	Gavin		Todd's	Horse Wynd West
Thomson,	James	Furrier	Thomson's	Grassmarket
Thomson,	James	Merchant		Milne Square
Thomson,	James	Wigmaker	Mein's	Covenant Close
Thomson,	James	Tobacconist	Heriot's	Cowgate Head South
Thomson,	James	Glover	Watson's	Cant's Close
Thomson,	Jean	Merchant	Garbiston's	High Street at 1st Below Tron
Thomson,	John	Musician	Orr's	Bell's Wynd
Thomson,	John		Baillie's	Grassmarket East
Thomson,	John		Alves's	Lawnmarket at Borthwick's/Fishmarket
Thomson,	Mrs		Nicol's	Geddes' Close
Thomson,	Mrs	Vintner	"Duke's Head"	Anchor Close
Thomson,	Mrs		Thomson's	Lawnmarket at Forrester's/Libberton's
Thomson,	Mrs		Scirving's	Good Town's Land
Thomson,	Mrs	Room Setter	Gray's	Grassmarket East
Thomson,	Mrs	Baxter	Anderson's	Grassmarket Mid
Thomson,	Miss	Merchant	Gibson's	Lady Stair's Close
Thomson,	Miss	Mantua Maker	Wilkie's	Lady Stair's Close
Thomson,	Miss		Syme's	Kinloch's Close North
Thomson,	Robert	Merchant	Veitch's	Cowgate Head North
Thomson,	Walter	Vintner	"Duke's Head"	Anchor Close
Thorburn,	Mrs		Mylne's	Peebles Wynd
Thores,	Mrs			Milne's Square
Thripland,	Sir Stewart			Fountain Close
Tillicoultry,	Lady		Cummings	Fishmarket Close East
Tod, Mutter & Co.		Seedsmen		High Street at back of Main Guard
Tod,	George	Cordiner	Anderson's	Grassmarket Mid
Tod,	Oliver	Merchant	Tod's	Advocate's Close
Tod,	Patrick	Merchant	Brigg's	Stonelaw's Close
Tod,	Thomas	Writer	Currie's	Castlehill South
Tod,	William jr.	Linen Merchant	S.E. Corner	Parliament Close
Tod,	William	Porter		Penston Letters' Land
Todd,	William		Tod's	Castlehill North
Torphichen,	Master of		New Stairs Foot	Parliament Close
Torrence,	Robert	Baxter	Hammermen's	Cowgate Head South
Toshock,	Andrew	Ale Seller	Callander's	Skinner's Close
Tough,	Alexander	Perfumer	Shearer's	Milne Square
Tough,	Andrew		Samuel's	Colledge Wynd
Trail,	John	Bookseller	Trail's	Don's Close
Trotter,	Archibald	Merchant	Milne's	Meal Market
Trotter,	John	Brewer	Ogilvie's	Ogilvie's Land
Trotter,	Mr			Libberton's Wynd
Trotter,	Mrs		Her Own	Chamber's Close

NAME		OCCUPATION	ADDRESS	
Trotter,	Mrs	Widow	Tod's	Horse Wynd West
Trotter,	Thomas	Merchant	Wallace's	West Bow Middle
Trotter,	Thomas jr.	Merchant	Lothian's	Gosford's Close
Trotter,	Thomas	Brewer	Taylor's	President's Close
Troupe,	Lady		Troupe's	James Court
Trustee's Office				Parliament Close
Tudhope,	Mrs		Somervail's	High Street at Kinloch's Close North
Turnbull,	Alex.	Wright	Campbell's	Bell's Wynd
Turnbull,	George	of Dalladies: W.S.	Bruce's (home)	Libberton's Wynd Old Post Office Stairs
Turnbull,	Jenet	Ale Seller	Gray's	Grassmarket East
Turnbull,	John	Baxter	Scheil's	Sandiland's Close
Turnbull,	Mr			Hyndford's Close
Turnbull,	Margaret	Vintner	Chalmer's	High Street at New Assembly Close
Turnbull,	Mrs	Room Setter	McGowan's	Grassmarket East
Tunnock,	William	Brewer	Young's	Grassmarket Mid.
Tweeddale,	Marquis of			Tweeddale's Court
Tyrie,	Alexander	Ale Seller	Ogilvie's	Milne's Court
Tyrie,	David		Kirktonholm's	Kennedy's Close
Tyrie,	John	Writer	His Own	Kinloch's Close South
Tytler,	William	of Woodhouselee: W.S.		Kinloch's Close North
Udny,	Alexander	Commissioner of Excise		Bull's Close at Milne's Square
Ure,	Mr	Goldsmiths	Ferguson's	Con's Close
Urquhart,	Barbara	Room Setter	Custom House Strs.	Parliament Close
Urquhart,	Kenneth		His Own	Lawnmarket North
Urquhart,	John	Cook	Watson's	Covenant Close
Urquhart,	Leonard	W.S.	Gavinlock's	Forrester's Wynd
Urquhart,	Mrs			Old Assembly Close
Vasey,	Agnes	Ale Seller	Gibson's	Custom House Stairs Parliament Close
Veitch,	James	Glazier	Halyburton's	Grassmarket East
Veitch,	James	Glazier		Covenant Close
Veitch,	Robert	Merchant	Cunningham's	Gosford's Close
Veitch,	Robert	Merchant	Tait's	Lawnmarket at Bank/Cullen's
Wachope,	Mistress		Douglas's	Milne's Court
Waddel,	David		Heriot's	Grassmarket Mid
Waddel,	Robert		McKay's	Cap & Feather Close
Wake,	Mrs	Merchant	Scougall's	Advocate's Close
Walker,	Adam		Williamson's	Fleshmarket Close
Walker,	Andrew	Merchant	Gray's	West Bow Middle
Walker,	John	Vintner	Montgomery's	Parliament Close
Walker,	John	Writer	Richardson's	Meal Market
Walker,	John	Stabler		High Street opposite Tron
Walker,	Mrs	Vintner	"Tavern"	Anchor Close
Walker,	Mrs		Brown's	Fleshmarket Close
Walker,	Mrs	Widow	Cochrane's	Lawnmarket at Forrester's/Libberton's
Walker,	Richard	Vintner	Penman's	Advocate's Close
Walker,	Robert	Surgeon	Walker's	Penston Letters' Land
Walker,	William	Writer	Walker's	Milne's Back Court
Walkingshaw,	Lady		Gavinlock's	Forrester's Wynd
Wall,	Alexander	Vintner	McGowan's	Luckenbooths
Wallace,	Archibald	Merchant	Cramond's	West Bow Middle
Wallace,	John	Surgeon	Wallace's	Under Baxter's Close
Wallace,	John	Ale Seller	Riddle's	Royston's Close
Wallace,	Robert		Edmonstone's	Lawnmarket South
Wallace,	Robert		Swinton's	Forrester's Wynd East
Wallace,	William			James Court

NAME		OCCUPATION	ADDRESS	
WALTER,	Robert	Surgeon	Surgeon's Hall	High School Yards
WARDEN,	George	Room Setter	Aitson's	Bell's Wynd
WARDEN,	John	Teacher	Garbiston's	High Street 1st below Tron
WARDEN,	Mrs	Sewing Mistress	Stewart's	Covenant Close
WARDEN,	Mr		Montgomery's	Niddry's Wynd
WARDREW,	Mrs		Dickson's	Cowgate Head South
WARDROPE,	Andrew	Merchant		Upper Baxter's Close
WARDROPE,	John		Campbell's	Grassmarket West
WARDROPE,	John	Merchant		Milne Square
WARDROPE,	Mary	Merchant	Bold's	Upper Baxter's Close
WARDROPE,	Mrs		Wardrope's	Wardrope's Court
WARDROPE,	Miss	Merchant	Lithgow's	Advocate's Close
WARRENDER,	Mistress		Cochran's	High Street at Smith's Land
WARROCK,	John	Taylor	His Own	New Stairs Foot Meal Market
WATKINS,	Adam	H.M. Printer	Mylne's	Castlehill South East Milne's Court
WATKINS,	Charles	Wigmaker	Andrew's	Dickson's Close
WATKINS,	Mr		Little's	Cullen's Close
WATSON,	Adam	Tanner	Hepburn's	Allan's Close
WATSON,	George	Painter	His Own	Mary King's Close
WATSON,	George			Marlin's Wynd
WATSON,	James	Underjanitor at College	Crawford's	Colledge Wynd
WATSON,	James	Dyer	Park's	Cowgate South
WATSON,	James	Candlemaker	Rutherford's	Lawnmarket at Libberton's Wynd
WATSON,	James	Stabler		Anchor Close
WATSON,	John	W.S.	His Own	Milne's Court
WATSON,	John	Vintner	Shiel's	Covenant Close
WATSON,	John	Poultryman	Rochead's	Marlin's Wynd
WATSON,	John	Poultryman	Ruddiman's	Marlin's Wynd
WATSON,	John		Mitchell's	Kennedy's Close
WATSON,	John	Slater	Millar's	Stonelaw's Close
WATSON,	John	Candlemaker	Thom's	Libberton's Wynd
WATSON,	Lilias		Moffat's	West Bow Middle
WATSON,	Mary		Petrie's	Cowgate at Fishmarket/Borthwick's
WATSON,	Mr		Warrender's	Niddry's Wynd
WATSON,	Mrs		Crockett's	West Bow Foot
WATSON,	Mrs		Jones'	Castlehill at Castle
WATSON,	Mrs	Widow	Curray's	Marlin's Wynd
WATSON,	Mrs	Poultrywoman	Johnstone's	Peebles Wynd
WATSON,	Mrs	Widow	Wright's	Con's Close
WATSON,	Mrs		Reoch's	President's Close
WATSON,	Robert jr.	Merchant	Justice's	Byre's Close
WATSON,	Thomas	Vintner	Henderson's	Wardrope's Court
WATSON,	William	Weaver	Oliphant's	Bull's Close
WATSON,	William	Ale Seller	Wardrop's	Dickson's Close
WATSON,	William	Excise Officer	Monro's	New Stairs Foot Parliament Close
WATSON,	William	Writer	Bell's	Castlehill
WATSON,	William	*of Pilmuir* W.S.		Covenant Close
WATT,	George		Mylne's	Castlehill South East
WATT,	James		Ramsay's	Trunk Close
WAUCHOPE,	Mr	*of Edmistone*	Campbell's Bldgs.	Argyll Square
WAUGH,	Gavin	Baxter		Blackfriar's Wynd
WAUGH,	James	Merchant	Willson's	Paterson's Court
WAUGH,	Mrs		Gray's	Milne Square
WEBSTER,	Alex.	Tolbooth Kirk	Currie's	Castlehill South
WEBSTER,	Elizabeth	Merchant	Hamilton's	Craig's Close
WEBSTER,	John	Candlemaker	Fairholm's	Craig's Close

NAME		OCCUPATION		ADDRESS	
WEBSTER,	Mrs		Bruce's	Craig's Close
WEDDERBURN,	Peter	Writer (Secretary to Excise)		Gray's Close
WEEMSON,	Mrs			Craig's Close
WEIR,	Miss		Burn's	Forrester's Wynd
WEIR,	Mrs		Peter's	Horse Wynd
WEIR,	William	Ale Seller	Mitchell's	Erskine's Land
WEIR,	William	Cordiner	Somervail's	Society
WELSH,	James	Goldsmith	Kid's	Warriston's Close
WELSH,	John	Goldsmith	Hamilton's	Milne's Court
WELSH,	Mrs	Widow	Anderson's	Cowgate South
WELSH,	Miss		Lerson's	Cowgate Head North
WEMYSS,	James	Jeweller	Ure's	Luckenbooths
WEMYSS,	Mrs		Wemyss'	Craig's Close
WEMYSS,	Mrs		Her Own	Halkerston's Wynd
WEMYSS,	Mr		His Own	
WEMYSS,	Mrs		Warrender's	Niddry's Wynd
WEMYSS,	Miss	Mantua Maker	Wemyss'	Penston Letters' Land
WEST,	John	of Customs	Lithgow's	Grassmarket Mid
WEST,	Morris	Com. of Customs	Romane's	Brown's Land opposite Tolbooth
WEST,	Mrs		Grant's	Trunk Close
WHITE,	Alexander	Writer	Mylne's	Milne Square
WHITE,	James	Wigmaker	Hunter's	Flint's Land Grassmarket South
WHITE,	James	Wigmaker		Lawnmarket at Old Assembly Close
WHITE,	John	Deputy Clerk of Session		Writer's Court
WHITE,	Mrs		Stewart's	Advocate's Close
WHITE,	Provost		Mylne's	Barringer's Close
WHITE,	Robert		New Land	Castlehill South
WHITE,	Robert	Doctor (jt. Prof. of Medicine)	Scale Stairs	Old Assembly Close
WHITE,	William	Wigmaker	Reid's	Cant's Close Foot
WHITEFOORD,	Allan	Merchant	His Own	Argylle Square
WHITEFOORD,	Sir John		Campbell's Bldgs.	Argylle Square
WHITEHILL,	Richard	Workman	Mitchelson's	Castlehill South East
WHITEROCK,	Lady		Crawford's	Colledge Wynd
WHITSUNDAY,	John	Cooper	Ferguson's	Cowgate Head South
WIGHT,	David	Baxter	Peter's	Horse Wynd
WIGHT,	George	Shoemaker		Cowgate South at Forrester's Wynd Foot
WIGHT,	James			Kinloch's Close North
WIGHT,	James	Dyer	Wight's	Cowgate South
WIGHT,	John	Dyer	Wight's	Society
WIGHT,	Robert	Merchant	Young's	James Court
WIGHT,	Robert	Baxter		Brown's Land opposite Tolbooth
WIGHT,	William	Baxter	Clerk's	Trunk Close
WIGHT,	William	Baxter	His Own	High Street at Barringer's Close
WIGHTMAN,	Elizabeth		Todd's	Castlehill North
WIGHTMAN,	Mr			Dickson's Close
WIGHTMAN,	Mrs		More's	Lawnmarket North
WIGHTMAN,	Miss	Boarding School	Innes's	Baillie Fyfe's Close
WILKIE,	James	Merchant		Luckenbooths
WILKIE,	Mrs		Reoch's	President's Close
WILKISON,	May		Her Own	Fountain Close
WILLIAM,	Mrs	*of Beckie*	Good's	Colledge Wynd
WILLIAMSON,	Alex.	Stabler	Hunter's	Candlemaker Row
WILLIAMSON,	Alexander	Ale Seller	Selkirk's	Grassmarket East
WILLIAMSON,	James	Flesher	Williamson's	Fleshmarket Close
WILLIAMSON,	Joseph	Advocate		Byre's Close
WILLIAMSON,	Robert	Merchant	Mitchell's	Fishmarket Close

NAME		OCCUPATION		ADDRESS
WILLIAMSON,	Mrs	Flesher	Williamson's	Fleshmarket Close
WILLIAMSON,	Mary			Advocate's Close
WILLIAMSON,	Walter	Writer	Williamson's	Skinner's Close
WILLIAMSON,	William	Poultryman	Kennedy's	Marlin's Wynd
WILLS,	Andrew	Wright	Dick's	Burnet's Close
WILLS,	Mr		Bull's	Cowgate South
WILLSON,	Alexander	Merchant	Willson's	Cowgate Head North
WILLSON,	Andrew	Waulker		Chamber's Close
WILLSON,	Daniel			Candlemaker Row
WILLSON,	George	Vintner	Spence's	Writer's Court
WILLSON,	George	Mason	Hunter's	Cant's Close Foot
WILLSON,	George	Indweller	Lumsden's	Marlin's Wynd
WILLSON,	James	Smith	His Own	Libberton's Wynd
WILLSON,	John	Merchant	Granger's	High Street 1st below Tron
WILLSON,	John	Bonnetmaker/Dyer	Tod's	Niddry's Wynd
WILLSON,	John	Bonnetmaker	Dickson's 2nd Land	Libberton's Wynd
WILLSON,	John	Writer	Admiralty Office	
WILLSON,	John	Flesher	Black's	Fleshmarket Close
WILLSON,	John		His Own	High School Yards
WILLSON,	Margaret		Pitcairn's	High Street at North Foulis Close
WILLSON,	May		Willson's	Paterson's Court
WILLSON,	Mrs	Tobacconist	Watson's	Mary King's Close
WILLSON,	Mrs		Mylne's	Milne Square
WILLSON,	Mrs	*of Bechie*	Good's	Colledge Wynd
WILLSON,	Mrs		Peter's	Horse Wynd
WILLSON,	Mrs			Marlin's Wynd
WILLSON,	Miss	Milliner	Willson's	Kinloch's Close South
WILLSON,	William	*of Howden* W.S.	His Own	Niddry's Wynd Head
WILLSON,	William	Cordiner	Anderson's	Cowgate North
WILLSON,	William	Flesher	Anderson's	Fishmarket Close West
WINGATE,	Robert		Cumming's	Fishmarket Close
WINTER,	George	Wigmaker	His Own	High Street at Baillie Fyfe's Close
WISHART,	Geroge, Rev.	Minister		New Assembly Close
WISHART,	Mrs			Colledge Wynd
WISHART,	William	D.D.: Principal of Univ.		University
WOOD,	James	Taylor	Gray's	Todrick's Wynd
WOOD,	James	Writer	New Stairs Foot	Cowgate North
WOOD,	John	Bookbinder	Somervail's	Society
WOOD,	Mrs		McCruther's	Stonelaw's Close
WOOD,	Mrs		Brownhill's	Cowgate North
WOOD,	Robert	Trunkmaker	Sheil's	Chamber's Close
WOOD,	William	Surgeon	Farquhar's	Advocate's Close
WOODS,	Mrs	Minister's Widow	Wood's	Brownhill's Land
WOODHALL,	Lady			Milne Square
WORDIE,	Walter			Bell's Wynd
WOTHERSPOON,	James	Weaver	His Own	New Assembly Close
WOTHERSPOON,	Mrs	Merchant	Sommervail's	Grassmarket Mid
WRIGHT,	Alexander		Weir's	Cowgate at Dickson's Close
WRIGHT,	Alexander		Morrison's	West Bow
WRIGHT,	Alexander	Pewterer	Hammermen's	Cowgate South
WRIGHT,	Charles	Bookseller	Grant's	Parliament Close
WRIGHT,	Daniel	Wright	Marshall's	Dickson's Close
WRIGHT,	David	Merchant	Wright's	Con's Close
WRIGHT,	David		Scott's	Cowgate North at Forrester's Wynd
WRIGHT,	David			Cowgate South at Robertson's Close
WRIGHT,	Duncan	Wright	Lawson's	Kinloch's Close South
WRIGHT,	Hendry	Manservant	Syme's	High Street at Niddry's Wynd

NAME		OCCUPATION	ADDRESS	
Wright,	James	Wright	Innes's	Meal Market
Wright,	James			President's Close
Wright,	John	Distiller	Wilkie's	Robertson's Close
Wright,	John	Merchant	Simpson's	Cant's Close Foot
Wright,	Mrs		Malloch's	Dickson's Close
Wright,	Mrs		Wright's	Con's Close
Wright,	Mrs		Johnstone's	Royston's Close
Wylie,	David	Vintner	Armour's	North Foulis Close
Wylie,	Robert	Ale Seller	Eagle's	High Street at Smith's Land
Yair,	John	Booksellers & Patent Medicines	Armour's (*home*) (*shop*)	James Court Parliament Close
Yetts,	John	Wright	Yett's	Dickson's Close
Young & Trotter		Upholsterers & Funeral Undertakers	"Pelican"	Byre's Close and Luckenbooths
Young, Trotter & Caddell:				
Young,	Alexander	Writer	Hallyburton's	Cowgate Head South
Young,	Catherine		Young's	Chamber's Close
Young,	Charles	Ale Seller	Mansfield's	Writer's Court
Young,	Charles			Anchor Close
Young,	George	Doctor	Young's	Paterson's Court
Young,	James	Ale Seller	Hamilton's	Grassmarket East
Young,	James	Bookbinder	Hammermen's	Cowgate Head South
Young,	James	Hair Merchant	Hamilton's	Grassmarket Mid.
Young,	John	Writer	Livingstone's	Lawnmarket at Upper Baxter's Close
Young,	John	Merchant	Bairfoot's	Peebles Wynd
Young,	John	Room Setter	Smeiton's	Stonelaw's Close
Young,	John	Horse Hirer	Mitchell's	Baillie's Land
Young,	John	Surgeon		James Court
Young,	Mr	Gauger	Paterson's	Grassmarket West
Young,	Mr	Midwifery Teacher	Murray's	Cowgate at Bain & Jolly's Land
			(*home*)	Paterson's Court
Young,	Mrs		Bell's	West Bow Middle
Young,	Mrs	Merchant	Young's	Penston Letters' Land
Young,	Mrs		Hope's	Monteith's Close
Young,	Mrs		Hunter's	Kinloch's Close South
Young,	Mrs		Jameson's	Borthwick's Close
Young,	Mrs		Brown's	Luckenbooths
Young,	Mrs		Ranie's	West Bow
Young,	Peter	Ale Seller	Stewart's	Candlemaker Row
Young,	Robert	Meal Seller	Mount's	Meal Market
Young,	Sarah	Teacher	Cramond's	West Bow Middle
Young,	Thomas	Surgeon	Tod's	James Court
Young,	William		Matheson's	Foulis Close South
Young,	William		Bull's	Cowgate South
Younger,	John	Merchant	Mitchell's	Baillie's Land
Yourstone,	James	Cutler	Hastie's	Borthwick's Close
Yourstone,	Mrs	Widow	McClelland's	Society
Yourstone,	Miss	Merchant	Willson's	Galloway's Close
Zeigler,	George	Glover	Hunter's	Mary King's Close

(b) RESIDENTS: CLOSE BY CLOSE

GRASSMARKET, North Side from West Port to West Bow
CRICHTON'S LAND
1 (12) David Ferrier — Stabler

PATERSON'S LAND
1 ( ) Robert Paterson — Brewer
2 (15) Samuel McCormack — Innkeeper
3   Mrs Kerr
       Mr Young — Gauger
       J. Ramage — Port Waiter
       Wm. Muir — Stabler
       J. Linton — Cowfeeder
       J. Orr — Stabler
       J. McPherson — Ale Seller
       J. Braidwood — Stabler

LITHGOW'S LAND
1 (36) J. Sharp — Stabler
2 (17) Robt. Selkrigg
   (17) John West of Customs
   (11) James Clark — Weaver
   (18) Thomas Dallas — Surgeon
3   John Dunbar — Skinner
       R. Hunter — Ale Seller
       G. Jack — Merchant
       Mrs Cleghorn — Cooper
       Mr George Robertson — Gauger
       Wm. Carmichael — Porter
       D. Carmichael
       T. Duncanson — Stabler
       D. Grahame — Merchant
       A. Galloway — Stabler

TRADES HOSPITAL LAND
1 (11) James Veitch — Glazier
   (10) Robert Barr — Stabler
3   A. Erskine — Smith
       Wm. Bruce, jr. — Merchant
       Mr Alston — Gauger
       G. Hastie — Ale Seller
       J. Young — Ale Seller
       D. Samuel
       D. Miller
       J. Alstone — Stabler
       A. McFarlane — Stabler
       T. Calder — Merchant
       J. McGivan
       J. Richardson — Merchant
       D. Campbell — Merchant
       Jenet McKinlay

GRASSMARKET, North East into West Bow
       Mr Carter — Gauger
       J. Dunbar — Stabler
       J. Thomson — Furrier
       J. Jackson
       P. Barrowman — Stabler
       W. Johnstone — Sheriff's Officer
       Mrs Hardy — Ale Seller
       Mrs Muirhead
       Wm. Aiton — Merchant
       J. Baillie — Coppersmith
       T. Mair — Merchant
       Mistress Corbet
       R. Forrester — Merchant
       A. Gibson — Cordiner

McKINLAY'S LAND
1 (11) Thos. Nicolson — Stabler
2 (10) Alex. Bruce — Merchant
2 (13) T. Bruce — Writer
   (12) J. Seton
3   D. Ross — Merchant
       Mrs Jardine — Merchant
       Wm. Bruce — Merchant
       J. Scott — Merchant

WEST BOW, left-hand side ascending into Lawnmarket
       J. Hempseed — Merchant
       Laird of Comiston

CROCKETT'S LAND
1 (24) Thos. Crockett — Merchant
2 (19) J. Grant — Merchant
   (10) Mrs Barclay
   (14) Ann Cunningham
   (19) Mrs Hepburn
3   D. Dowie — Merchant
       Mrs Watson
       R. McFarlane — Insurance Agent

VEITCH'S LAND
1 (10) And. Rankine — Coppersmith
   (11) Wm. Armstrong — Coppersmith
2 (12) Margaret Gibson
3   J. Lithgow — Merchant
       Mrs Hamilton — Seed Merchant
       G. Begbie — Smith
       T. Peddie — Ale Seller
       J. Finlay — Merchant
       J. Hunter — Apothecary
       Mr Samson
       Wm. Dewar — Merchant
       R. Mortimore — Glover

MORRISON'S LAND
1 (14) Margaret Murray
2 (12) Edward Rutherford — Writer
   (10) A. Wright
3   Mrs Reid — Merchant

MOFFAT'S LAND
1 (14) J. McMichan — Merchant
3   J. McKay — Coppersmith
       Miss Penman
       Miss Stewart
       Lilias Watson
       G. Murray — Cordiner
       R. Gilchrist — Cooper
       J. Bowie — Clerk
       P. Crawford — Merchant
       Lady Boghall
       Mr Drysdale — Cordiner
       Mrs Johnstone

FAIRHOLM'S LAND
1	(17)	Mr Fairholm	of Pilton
	(30)	Thos. Trotter	Merchant
2	(14)	Jas. Lindsay	Tobacconist
	(17)	Wm. Gustard, Reverend	Minister
3		A. Bruce	Merchant
		A. Henderson	Merchant
		John Pringle	Skinner
		Mrs Bake	Ale Seller
		Mrs Young	
		Mrs Lawrie	Minister's Widow

CRAMOND'S LAND
1	(14)	Mistress Maitland	
	(15)	Sarah Young	Teacher
	(13)	Arch. Wallace	Merchant
2	(12)	Robt. Murray	Skinner
		Mrs Strachan	
		P. Strachan	Cordiner
		A. Walker	Merchant

CLERK'S LAND (at Foot from Castlehill)
1	(12)	Deacon Robt. McMurray	Skinner
	(11)	Helen Montgomery	
2	(11)	Mrs Cochrane	

PROVOST STEWART'S LAND
2	(10)	John Paxton	Coachman
	(26)	Mrs Gordon	
3		Provost Archibald Stewart (1745)	Merchant

LINDSAY'S LAND
1	(13)	Mrs Lindsay	(Alex. Lindsay)
	(27)	John Scotland	Skinner
	(10)	Mark Sandilands	Merchant
2	(23)	Arch. Hamilton	of Dalserf
3		R. Napier	Ale Seller
		G. Falconer	Ale Seller
		G. Dunsmuir	Merchant
		C. Cruthers	
		Wm. Marshall	Writer

WEST BOW into Castlehill South, ascending

PATON'S LAND
1	(33)	J. Paton	Stationer
2	(29)	Gilbert Elliot Lord Minto, Lord of Session	
3		R. Whitehill	Labourer
		C. Blair	Goldsmith
		Mrs Blackwood	
		G. Watt	
		A. Watkins	H.M. Printer
		R. Allan	Baxter

KENNEDY'S LAND
1	(16)	Mrs Marion Kennedy	
	(12)	J. Forbes	Merchant
2	(44)	Earl of Dalkeith	

FOULIS'S LAND (Clerk's Head)
1	(13)	Wm. Douglas	
	(23)	Geo. Foulis	
	(18)	John Dawson	Cordiner
2	(46)	Charles Gordon Hamilton	
3		T. Moodie	
		J. Allan	Ale Seller
		H. Manuel	Writer
		Alex. Bower	Weaver
		Dr Mitchell	
		J. Brown	Weaver
		Mr Oliphant	Weaver
		Earl of Dumfries	

BRAND'S LAND
1	(14)	Dr John Boswall	
	(13)	Mrs Betty Kennedy	
2	(11)	Wm. Smith	Merchant
3		Mrs Blackwood	Merchant
		R. Nimmo	Stationer

CLERK'S LAND HEAD
2	(10)	Mrs Gillane	
	(10)	Jas. Allison	Hammerman
	(10)	Mr Nicoll	

CURRIE'S CLOSE
1	(44)	Wm. Hogg	Merchant
2	(36)	Alex. Webster	of Tolbooth Kirk

BAIRD'S LAND
1	(25)	Lord Haddington	
	(15)	Wm. Baird	of Brankston
	(15)	Sir Hugh Hamilton	

BLAIR'S LAND
1	(10)	Arch. Blair	Writer
	(22)	Lady Dirleton	
	(23)	Mr & Mrs Andrew Bonnar	Merchant
2	(17)	Mr David	Wright
		Mr Miller	
		Mrs Blackadder	
		Miss Drummond	
		Widow Reid	
		Mr Peters	Printer
		Wm. Barrowman	

LINDSAY'S NEW LAND
2	(10	A. Gairdner	
	(10)	T. Tod	
	(24)	R. White	
3		Mrs Watson	
		Wm. Sauney	Upholsterer
		Mrs Hepburn	

Castlehill North Side descending from Castle

RAMSAY'S LAND
2	(11)	Alan Ramsay	Bookseller

PIPE CLOSE
2	(15)	J. Millar	Tailor

MENZIE'S LAND
2	(12)	J. Menzies	Merchant

SKINNER'S LAND
- 2 (11) Mrs Lindsay
- (45) Lord Semple
- (24) Bertram of Nisbet

JOLLY'S LAND
- 2 (11) A. Nicolson — Mason
- (14) P. Jolly
- (13) Mrs Millar

TODD'S LAND
- 2 (25) Wm. Todd
- (16) Mr Shiell's
- (14) John Clelland — Merchant

NAIRN'S LAND
- 2 (10) Kenneth Gordon
- (13) Laurence Simon

CAMPBELLS LAND
- 2 (15) John Heslop
- (30) Miss McKay

BLYTH'S LAND
- 2 (12) Mrs Hay
- (15) John Irvine of Burleigh

DALRYMPLE'S LAND/MILNE'S BACK COURT
- 1 (19) John Forrest — Merchant
- 2 (10) Robert Orrock — Writer
- Robert Greig — Writer
- Mr Glass — Writer
- Wm. Walker — Writer
- Widow Arundale

MILNE'S COURT and fronting Lawnmarket to James Court
- 1 (13) Rebecca Wachope
- (16) Lady Stonebyres
- (14) James Mitchelson — Jeweller
- (12) Thomas Boyes — Writer
- (15) John Watson — Writer
- (13) Arch. Hamilton — Merchant
- (12) Alex. Denning — Stationer
- (12) Mrs Preston
- 2 (23) Adam Watkins — H.M. Printer
- (13) Arch. McCulloch
- (12) Pat. Cumming, Rev. — Minister, Old Kirk
- (14) Andrew Burnet — W.S.
- (17) John Hamilton — Cordiner
- (12) John Fraser
- (12) Patrick Lindsay — Merchant
- (12) John Dundas
- (10) Rev. John Glen — Minister, College Kirk
- (13) John Hallyburton
- (11) Rev. Geo. Logan — Minister, College Kirk
- 3 P. McAulay
- Mrs Braidfoot
- Mrs Christian McDougal
- Wm. Ross — Writer, Clerk to SPCK
- Mrs Forbes
- John Welsh — Goldsmith

- Malcolm Ogilvie — Merchant
- Elizabeth Nimmo
- Mrs Murray
- Alex. Stewart
- Alex. Tyrie — Ale Seller
- Miss Robertson — Merchant
- Mrs Naismith — Merchant
- Wm. Dunbar — Barber

LAWNMARKET North Side and into James Court
- 1 (11) Mrs Frances Grant
- (10) Wm. McG(h)ie
- (16) Mr de Lamotte — Dancing Master
- (11) Chas. Cheyne — Merchant
- 1 (13) John Young — Writer
- 2 (13) Arch. Campbell — W.S
- (13) Arch. Murray
- (18) Alex. Goldie of Ryes — W.S.
- (15) Geo. Cunningham — Surgeon
- (19) Alex. McMillan — W.S.
- (14) Montgomery of Langshaw
- (12) Robt. Blackwood — Merchant
- (11) Alex. Gray
- (23) Wm. Alstone — W.S.
- (12) Thos. Buchan
- (14) Jas. Stewart of Drumsheugh — W.S.
- (12) Thos. Baillie of Polkemmet — W.S.
- (10) Wm. Gordon — Bookseller
- (14) Andrew Alves — W.S.
- (12) Andrew McDougall
- (12) Pat. Halden — H.M. Solicitor
- (10) Wm. Wallace
- 3 John McIntosh — Staymaker
- Wm. Hamilton — Stationer
- Lady Troupe
- John Yair — Bookseller
- Mrs Scott
- Stephen Govan — Glazier
- David Grahame — Barber
- Thos. Mitchell — Jeweller
- Jas. Lindsay — Tobacconist
- Angus Sinclair — Ale Seller
- John Scotland — Bookbinder
- Mrs Allan
- Malcolm McLean
- Eliz. Davidson
- Wm. Crooks — Baxter
- Lady Carlowrie
- Baillie John Dunbar
- Geo. Paterson — Merchant
- Robt. Wight — Merchant
- Geo. Boid — Merchant
- Jas. Fowler — Ale Seller
- Wm. Mitchell — Merchant
- Robt. Donaldson — Glover
- Mistress Selkirk
- W. Gordon — Bookseller
- Wm. McGhie — Writer
- Geo. Pitcairn — Merchant
- John Duff — Hair Merchant
- Alex. Martine — Herald
- John Brand
- Robt. Jameson — Merchant
- Mrs McGregor — Vintner
- Thomas Young — Surgeon

2nd BOUND: East on Lawnmarket North from Gladstone's Land to head of Craig's Close

GLADSTONE'S LAND

1	(13)	Mrs J. Robertson	Milliner
	(13)	Mrs Margt. Reid	Merchant
2	(16)	Dr Hamilton	
3		Alex. Noble	Candlemaker
		Miss Pillans	Merchant
		Neil Ezat	Ale Seller
		A. Munro of Coull	Treasurer, Heriot's Trust
		A. Begg	Merchant
		Mrs Hunter	
		Miss Henderson	Merchant
		Miss Inglish	Merchant
		Miss Brown	Merchant

LADY STAIR'S CLOSE

1	(12)	Andrew Home	Accomptant
	(14)	isobel Knox	
	(18)	Lady Dalrymple	
2	(14)	Boswell of Balminto	
	(27)	Hugh Forbes	Advocate
3		Robert Greenlees	Merchant
		Mrs Fisher	
		Geo. Brymer	Merchant, Staymaker
		Miss Thomson	Merchant
		Miss Mason	Merchant, Ale Seller
		Duncan McDonald	Druggist
		Andrew Murray	Wigmaker
		Andrew Kinneir	Pewterer
		Wm. Hepburn	Surgeon
		Mrs Anderson	
		Miss Thomson	Mantua Maker
		Mrs Robertson	
		Jas. Grierson	Merchant
		Mr Fisher	Servant
		Mrs Anderson	
		Mrs Gibb	
		John Rippath	
		Mr Brown	
		Mrs Spence	
		Mrs Maxwell	

UPPER BAXTER'S CLOSE

2	(15)	Rich. Norrie	
	(14)	Jas. Lothian	Skinner
	(10)	Chas. Craig	Merchant
	(10)	Andrew Wardrope	Merchant
	(10)	Mrs Robertson	
3		Widow Anderson	
		John Barclay	Skinner
		Mary Wardrope	Merchant
		Mrs Campbell	
		Mrs Couper	Upholsterer
		Mrs Bruce	
		Mrs Russell	
		Wm. Dundas	
		Adam Murray	Baxter
		Margaret Currie	
		Mrs Ramsay	Room Setter
		Hendry Anderson	Cordiner
		Wm. Spence	Painter

WARDROPE'S COURT

1	(15)	Mr Henderson of Liston	
	(17)	Jas. Spence	of the Bank
	(10)	Deacon Hendry Hardie	Baxter
2	(14)	Ann Stirling	Ale Seller
	(16)	George Cunningham	
	(17)	John Syme	
	(17)	John Philp	Auditor in Exchequer
	(17)	Geo. Clark	Merchant
	(11)	Robt. Gray	
3		Hugh Inglis	Wright
		Thos. Watson	Vintner
		Jas. Robb	
		Wm. McCulloch	Merchant
		Alex. Ritchie	Merchant
		Jas. McKain	Merchant
		Edward Inglis	Druggist
		George Drummond	White Iron smith
		Lady Kinnaldie	
		Robt. Noble	Merchant
		Wm. Buchan	Ale Seller
		Mrs Wardrope	
		Mrs Campbell	
		Mrs Rutherford	
		Wm. Gallatly	Merchant
		Mrs Brown	Merchant
		Thos. McGrogan	Merchant
		John McLure	Writing Master
		McMichon & Stewart	French Masters
		Geo. Reid	Ale Seller
		John Smith	Ale Seller

PATERSON'S COURT

1	(10)	Robt. Lithgow	Merchant
	(11)	Lady Wm. Hay	
	(15)	Dr James Lind	
	(19)	Dr George Young	
	(14)	May Wilson	
	(10)	James Waugh	Merchants
2	(20)	James Hay	
	(17)	Andrew Hunter	
	(17)	Thos. Miller	
	(17)	Lady Glasgow	
	(13)	Mrs Finlayson	
	(11)	John Houston	Writer
	(12)	Robt. Campbell	
	(14)	Wm. Loch	
3		Wm. Scott	Merchant
		Walter Hogg & Co.	Merchants
		Wm. Baillie	Wright
		Mrs Bogle	
		John Dalgleish	Watchmaker
		Mrs Boswall	
		Robt. Boyd	Merchant
		Mrs McDougall	
		Mrs Wightman	
		John More	Merchant & Co.
		Mrs Gardiner	Merchants

UNDER BAXTER'S CLOSE

1	(12)	Mrs Robertson	
	(17)	John Mein	Slater
	(14)	Jas. Purvies	W.S.

UNDER BAXTER'S CLOSE—Continued

2	(10)	Robt. Brown	Tailor
	(10)	Amelia Hall	
	(11)	John Grieve	
	(11)	Walter Ruddiman's Printing House	
3		Thos. Hedderwick	Baxter
		Mrs Gilles	
		Alex. Naughtone	
		John Fish	Merchant
		Charles Malcolm	
		Robt. Allan & Others	Baxters
		John Middlemist & Others	
		Thos. Hill	Tanner
		Isobell Fisher	Ale Seller
		John Wallace	Surgeon
		Jas. Steel	Merchant
		John Stonehouse	Merchant
		Alex Cumming	Cook
		Mrs Menzies	Merchant
		Mrs Forrest	
		Mrs Burnett	
		Mrs Greenlees	

GALLOWAY'S CLOSE

1	(18)	John Brown	
	(10)	Patrick Drummond	Seed Merchant
	(11)	George Begbie	Baxter
	(10)	Alexander Bell	Wigmaker
3		George Lothian	Merchant
		Jas. Neilsen	Ale Seller
		Mrs Ewing	Room Setter
		Francis Jaffrey	Wigmaker
		Robt. Dewar	Writing Master
		Margaret Smith	
		James Brodie	Surgeon
		James Paterson	Tailor
		Miss Yourstone	Merchant
		Robt. Johnstone	Merchant
		Jas. Kidd	Merchant
		Mrs Speirs	
		Wm. Dowie	
		Messrs Bartram & Williamson	Linen Merchants
		Robert Cuddie	Ale Seller
		Gill Baillie	Glazier
		Chas. Bruce	Glazier

PENSTON LETTER'S LAND

1	(18)	Mrs Young	Merchant
	(17)	Robt. Walker	Surgeon
2	(11)	Wm. Stewart	Chairmaster
	(12)	Wm. Tod	Porter
2	(19)	Thos. Murdoch	
3		Miss Wemyss	Mantua Maker
		John Bryson	Merchant

GOUDILOCK'S LAND (Gavinlock's)

2	(12)	Edward Lothian	Goldsmith
	(13)	Wm. Garden	
	(10)	Mrs Ogston	Room Setter
	(11)	Mr Thomson	
3		Arch. Douglas	Merchant
		Mrs Dunsmuir	Merchant
		Alex. Stirling	Merchant
		John Fettes	Merchant
		Mrs Kirkland	Merchant
		Messrs Baillie & Seton	Merchants
		Chas. Lesslie	Merchant
		Robt. Frogg	
		Kenneth Urquhart	

BROWN'S LAND (opposite Tolbooth)

1	(10)	Alex. Henderson	Wintner
	(12)	George Nicoll	Merchant
	(14)	Alex. Smeiton	Bookbinder
	(10)	Jas. Brown	Bookseller
2	(13)	Laurence Oliphant	Goldsmith
	(13)	Alex. Menzies	Wigmaker
	(17)	Jas. Stewart	Barber

BYRE'S CLOSE

1	(17)	Peter Clelland	Vintner
	(18)	Dougal Gedd	Goldsmith
	(14)	George Richardson	Writer
2	(14)	Mrs Erskine of Carnock	
	(24)	Joseph Williamson	Advocate
	(22)	George Brown of Colston	
	(10)	Robt. Russell	Merchant
	(10)	Jas. Smith	Glover
3		Mrs Borthwick	
		Thos. Michie	Ale Seller
		Young & Trotter	Upholsterers
		Alex. Hogg	Merchant
		J. McKain	Merchant
		John Grieve	Merchant
		Patrick Robertson	Ale Seller
		Jean Johnstone	Merchant
		Thos. Paton	Merchant
		Robert Watson jr.	Merchant
		Wm. Smith	Merchant
		Thos. Johnstone	
		Mrs Ramsay	
		John More	Bookbinder
		Wm. Clapperton	Merchant
		John Black	Merchant
		Francis Marshall	Merchant
		Burns & Finlayson	Merchants
		Mrs Smith	
		Wm. Taylor	Merchant

CANTORE'S CLOSE

1	(47)	Mrs Mansfield	(Jas. Mansfield & Co.)
	(29)	Jas. Russel	
	(11)	Wm. Murray	Haberdasher

ADVOCATE'S CLOSE & LORD KAIME'S NEW LAND on High Street

1	(17)	Lady Blair Drummond	
	(10)	Wm. Wood	Surgeon
	(19)	Patrick Bowie	Merchant
	(33)	Richard Walker	Vintner
	(10)	Mrs Scougall & Mrs Wake	Merchants
	(12)	Chas. Butter	Merchant, Wright
	(10)	Mary Angus	Merchant
	(19)	Robt. Barclay	Tailor
2	(10)	John Forrester	
	(27)	Lord Kaimes	
	(10)	John Smith	Saddler, Ale Seller
	(17)	John Davidson	
	(17)	Mary Williamson	
	(39)	Wm. Grant	Lord Advocate

ADVOCATE'S CLOSE & LORD KAIMES NEW LAND—Continued

3	Miss Wardrope	Merchant
	Mrs Kay	Merchant
	Oliver Tod	Merchant
	Mr Anderson	Writer
	Dr Porterfield	
	Robt. Russell	Merchant
	Geo. Livingstone	Vintner
	Edward Caithness	Merchant
	Mrs White	
	Arch. McCoull	Merchant
	John Edman	
	Cochrane & Hamilton	Merchant

ROXBURGH'S CLOSE with Don's Close

1 (11)	Alex. Hepburn	Merchant
(15)	Lady Riccarton	
2 (10)	Margaret McDougall	
(16)	Thos. Kinneir	Shipping Agent
(19)	Jas. Farquhar	Merchant
(22)	Daniel Seton	Merchant
(24)	Jas. Ferguson	
(17)	Robt. Menzies of Coultraws	W.S.
(21)	John Kenny	
(32)	John Sicadd	
3	Arch. Bowie	Merchant
	Stewart & Scott	Merchant
	Arch. Campbell	Merchant
	Arch. Mouatt	Merchant
	David Home	Merchant
	Arch. Angus	Merchant
	Mr Howboise	Vintner
	Fanny Gardener	Vintner
	Mistress Stirling	
	John Trail	Stationer
	Mrs Murray	
	Ludovic Duncan	
	Mrs Swan	Merchant

WARRISTON'S CLOSE

1 (13)	James Welsh	Merchant
(19)	Baillie Jas. Seton	
2 (14)	John Orr	Baxter
		Room Setter
(14)	Mrs McPhail	
(15)	Wm. Richardson	Farrier
3	Miss Murray & Kidd	Merchants
	George Nairn	
	Betty Hunter	
	Mrs Brown	
	Peter Falconer	
	Mrs Reid	
	John Nicoll	Wright
	John Mitchell	Bookbinder
	Ralph Dundas	Merchant
	John Taylor	Merchant
	Callander & Hamiltone	Merchants
	Robt. Kinneir	Merchant
	Miss Husband & Bogg	Merchants
	Miss Rannie & Wood	Merchants
	Miss Schaw	Merchant
	Mrs Guthrie	Room Setter
	Dr Hay	

	Robert McIntosh	Writer
	James Baillie	Merchant
	Andrew Jameson	Merchant
	Wm. Smith	Baxter
	Mrs Murray	

WRITER'S COURT

1 (23)	Alex. Lesslie	Vintner
(32)	Geo. Wilson	Vintner
(14)	Wm. Aiton	Goldsmith
(14)	Gabriel Napier	Writer
2 (13)	Duncan McPherson	
(12)	James Stewart	
(11)	James Burnet	W.S.
	Lord Monboddo	
(13)	Alex. Cunningham of Lathrisk, W.S.	
(12)	John Carmichael	
(10)	Chas. Young	Ale Seller
(12)	Ann McClachlane	
(10)	John White	Deputy Clerk of Session
3	Mr Brymer	Merchant
	Robt. Brown	Furrier
	Jas. Brown & Co.	
	Patrick Arthur	Merchant, British Coffee House
	Mrs Hill	Merchant
	Dunbar & McGhie	Merchants
	Gilbert Gow	Vintner
	Robert Clark	Vintner
	Mrs Brown	

MARY KING'S CLOSE

1 (15)	Walter Aiton	Glover
(12)	Ann Cockburn	
2 (11)	Jas. Burns	
(12)	Jas. Lesslie	Writer
(19)	George Zeigler	Glover
(15)	Adam Barclay	
3	John Orr	Wigmaker
	Robt. Brown	Tailor
	Jas. Robertson	Merchant
	John Maben	
	Mrs Dougall	
	Peter McNaughton	
	Mr Couper	Journeyman Weaver
	Jas. Hogg	Merchant
	Mrs Wilson	Tobacconist
	John Fyfe	Writer
	Alex. Henderson	Cordiner
	David Thomson	
	Wm. Reid	Chairman
	Patrick Murray	Merchant
	Geo. Watson	Painter
	John Gray	Cordiner
	John Skelton	Ale Seller
	Patrick Mylne	Ale Seller
	Mr Robertson	Gentleman
	Andrew Bell	Engraver

HIGH STREET NORTH from Mary King's to Pearson's Close

3	Wm. Johnstone	Wigmaker
	J. Symington	Baxter

HIGH STREET NORTH—Continued

	Jas. Balfour	Coffee House
	John Millar	Caddie
	John Oswald	Coffee House
	Wm. Brymer	
	Jas. Hutton	Merchant

PEARSON'S CLOSE to Allan's Close

1	(12)	Robert Fleming	Printer, Edinburgh Evening Courant
2	(10)	John Ingles	Merchant
3		John Braid	Glover
		John Buchanan	Printer
		Mrs Dickson	
		Mr Johnstone	
		Alex. Moodie	Wright
		John Clark	Glazier
		Mr Sanders	Printer
		Mr Harley	Tailor

HIGH STREET

John Loch	Coffee House (Laigh Coffee House)
Elizabeth Webster	Merchant

ALLAN'S CLOSE

2	(18)	John Mellies	Flesher, Ale Seller
	(10)	James Kerr	Goldsmith
	(15)	John Robertson	
3		John Binnie	Distiller
		John Scott	Candlemaker
		Mrs Renton	Merchant
		Elizabeth Duncan	
		John Shore	
		John Steel	Watchmaker
		Sam. Stevenson	Merchant
		Alex. Stewart	Billiard Tables
		Wm. Hill	Letter Carrier
		Arch. Hunter	Vintner
		Mrs Chalmers	
		John Malice	Ale Seller
		David Paterson	Merchant
		John Jameson	Merchant
		Wm. & Andrew Petries	
		John Muir	Ale Seller
		Adam Watson	Tanner
		Mrs Knox snr.	

3rd BOUND from Craig's Close to Barringer's Close

CRAIG'S CLOSE

1	(23)	Adam Fairholme & Co.	Merchants
	(32)	Mrs Wemyss	
	(12)	Mrs Riddle	
	(12)	Jas. Steadman	Vintner
	(14)	Alex. Murray	Printer, Scots Magazine
	(16)	John Scott	Plumber
	(16)	Wm. Cheyne	Printer
2	(10)	Wm. Mosman	Merchant
	(12)	Arch. Ingles of Auchendinny	
	(13)	Roderick McLeod of Sunbank, W.S.	
	(18)	Mrs Andrews	
	(21)	Lady Rochead	

(22)	Alex. Brown	Upholsterer
(22)	Francis Farquharson	Accomptant
(29)	Wm. Taylor	Goldsmith
(13)	Hugh Campbell	Grocer/Ale Seller
3	Wm. Smith	Bookseller
	Baillie David Inglis	Linen Merchant
	Mrs McVey	Printer's Relict
	John Webster	Candlemaker
	Jas. Herriot	Wright
	David Nevay	Merchant
	Jas. Cochrane & Co.	Printers, Scots Magazine
	John Learmonth & Others	
	Mrs Rutherfoord	Ale Seller

HIGH STREET below Craig's Close

2	(18)	Mrs Ogle	Exchange Coffee House
3		Nicol McIntyre	
		Jas. Hutchison	Merchant
		John Black	Ale Seller
		Mrs Sanders	Vintner
		Thos. Purdie	Merchant
		John Moir	Merchant
		Jas. Mitchell	Goldsmith

OLD POST OFFICE CLOSE

1	(14)	Jas. Cargill	Merchant
	(11)	Thos. More	Vintner
	(13)	Robt. Pringle	Merchant
2	(14)	John Balfour	Bookseller
	(14)	John Cargill	
3		David Wylie	Vintner
		Capt. Campbell of Finnab	
		John Hutton	Brushmaker
		Patrick McKellar	Writing Master
		John Sinclair	Writer
		Colin Robertson	Wigmaker

HIGH STREET opposite Cross

3	Hamilton & Balfour	Stationers
	Jas. Scott	Sheriff's Officer
	Thos. Henderson	Merchant
	Widow Brown	Ale Seller

ANCHOR CLOSE

1	(24)	Walter Thomson	Vintner, Duke's Head Tavern
	(24)	Richard Johnstone	Vintner
1	(12)	Helen Anderson	Room Setter
	(17)	Wm. Dallas	Wright
2	(17)	John McFarlane	Writer
	(10	James Watson	Stabler
	(13)	Wm. Hendry	
	( )	Wm. Budge	W.S.
	(12)	Barbara Cowan	
	(16)	Charles Young	
3		Duncan McPherson	Room Setter
		Robt. Hamilton	Merchant
		George Simpson	
		John Baillie	Bookseller

SWAN'S CLOSE/GEDDES CLOSE

1	(14)	Lady Powfowlis	
	(10)	Alex. Hay	Wright

SWAN'S CLOSE/GEDDES CLOSE—*Continued*

2 (14)	Robert Reid	W.S.
(14)	Mrs Thomson	
(14)	Lord Drummore	Lord of Session
(13)	Mrs Smith	
3	John Stewart	Cooper
	David Marshall	Porter
	Mr Lowrie	Schoolmaster
	Wm. Geddes	Poulterer
	Arbuthnot & Scott	Merchants
	Mrs Ross	Ale Seller
	John Clarkson	Baxter
	Robert Drummond & Co.	Printers
	Chas. Espline	Merchant
	Jas. Gowan	Wigmaker
	Robert Scott	Merchant
	Wm. Fowles	Ale Seller

HIGH STREET at North Foulis Close

1 (14)	Mrs Brown	Watchmaker
2 (14)	Mrs Glass	
(16)	Mrs Montgomerie	
(12)	Mrs Johnstone	Milliner
3	Catharine Millar	Merchant
	Jenet Lowrie	
	James Gillespie	Merchant
	Thos. Millar	
	Alex. Dick	Vintner
	Mrs Thomson	
	Mrs Webster	
	John Fenwick	Chairman
	Margaret Wilson	
	Robert Stewart	Soldier
	Wm. McIntosh	Ale Seller
	St Christopher's Sugar House	
	David Doig	Merchant

NEW BANK CLOSE (Ship Tavern Close)

1 (47)	The Royal Bank of Scotland	
3	Thomas Cumming	Flesher
	Mrs Drummond	Ale Seller

HIGH STREET, Bank Close to Lyon's Close

3	John Brown	Ironmonger
	Elizabeth Davidson	Merchant
	Duncan McLean	Ale Seller

LYON'S CLOSE

2 (15)	Jean Taylor	
(12)	Mrs Gachan	
(18)	Isobel Ross	Ale Seller
3	Mrs Cumming	Room Setter
	Robert Fraser	Room Setter
	Wm. Ballantyne	Printer
	Mrs Edgar	
	Wm. Morrison	Hatter
	Colin Campbell	Merchant

JACKSON'S CLOSE

1 (23)	Katharine Ramsay	Milliner
(12)	David Greig	Vintner
(33)	Andrew Chalmers	Writer
(14)	Arch. Richardson	Bookbinder
2 (15)	Wm. Forbes	
3	Mrs Dawson	
	Lady Arnprier	

	Wm. Dempster	Goldsmith
	Richard Sanders	Merchant
	John McGrigor	Billiard Tables

FLESHMARKET CLOSE

1 (13)	Hugh Penman	Goldsmith
(11)	Lady Galstone	
(12)	David Scott	Merchant
(21)	James Rae	Surgeon
(17)	Mrs Freebairn	
(11)	Nicol Somervail	Painter
2 (12)	Andrew Greig	Flesher
(18)	Michael Hugh	
(11)	Miss Peggy Scott	
(12)	Thomas Mathew	
(24)	Mrs Gibson	
(18)	Thomas Clarkson	Baxter
(12)	Thomas Betts	
(17)	Thomas Dick	
3	John Straton	Surgeon
	Widow Lawson	
	Mrs Walker	
	Francis Tennant	Flesher
	Alex. Somervail	Port Surveyor
	Widow Clerk	
	John Willson	Flesher
	Patrick Burns	Sheriff's Officer
	Allan McLean	Flesher
	George Malice	Flesher
	Mrs Williamson	Flesher
	Nicol Brown	Flesher
	Jas. Williamson	Flesher
	Mrs Balderstone	
	Adam Walker	
	Thos. Robertson	Flesher
	Mrs Main	
	John Aitken	Stationer
	Mrs Campbell	
	Chas. Robertson	Flesher
	Widow Seton	Ale Seller
	Robert Kinloch	Glover
	Jas. McGibbon	Merchant
	Arch. Campbell	Ale Seller
	Mrs Laing	Merchant
	Thos. Lamb	Gardner
	Charles Craig	Tobacconist
	Malcolm Brown	Saddler
	Captain Pringle	
	Mrs Annicus	
	Jas. Moodie	Tailor
	David Gilchrist	Flesher

BULL'S CLOSE

1 (14)	Alex. Oram	Writer
(14)	Lady Falconer of Mountaine	
(14)	Mrs Murray	Room Setter
(19)	Mrs Maitland	Room Setter
(14)	David Auchinleck	Vintner
(10)	Barbara Forrester	Room Setter
2 (14)	Alex. Nairn	Advocate
(14)	Gibson of Cliftonhall	
(12)	Wm. Mercer	Apothecary
(43)	Lord Milton	Lord Justice Clerk
(28)	Campbell of Monse	
1 (18)	Janet Cowan	Room Setter
(10)	Commissioner Udny	

BULL'S CLOSE—Continued

3	Gilbert Smith	Merchant
	George Clark	Merchant
	Wm. Watson	Weaver
	Alex. Dickson	Glazier
	Andrew Deuchar	Writer
	Mr Forbes	Teacher
	Geo. Hamilton	Tailor
	Alex. Ross	Ale Seller
	Jas. Hardy	Wright
	Paul Husband	Merchant
	John Taylor	Gentleman
	Mrs Morrison	Ale Seller

MILNE'S SQUARE and BULL'S CLOSE EAST

1	(13)	Robert Arbuthnot	Merchant
	(12)	Lady Balmerino	
	(22)	Alex. Arbuthnot	Merchant
	(15)	David Lyon	Vintner
	(10)	Alex. Clark	Ale Seller/ Glover
	(31)	Robert Baillie	Merchant
	(10)	Misses Colquhoun	
2	(24)	Jas. Cumming	
	(12)	Jas. Grahame	
	(21)	Lady Woodhall	
	(12)	Patrick Manderston	Merchant
	(22)	Lord Dun	
	(12)	John Fowles	
	(18)	Captain Clark	Merchant
	(17)	James Thomson	Merchant
	(10)	John Wardrope	Merchant
	(23)	Mrs Main	Room Setter
	(11)	Andrew Somervail	
3		John Kennedy	Surgeon
		John Drummond	Chairman
		David Law	Ale Seller
		Archibald Hart	Merchant
		Mrs Christie	
		Patrick Cowie	Ale Seller
		James Rochead	Distiller
		Widow Marshall	
		Alex. Tough	pefumer
		Thos. Clelland	Saddler
		Mrs Waugh	
		Gilbert Auchinleck	Cutler
		Mrs McIntosh	Merchant
		Christopher Alexander	Vintner
		Wm. Forbes	Room Setter
		Patrick Brown	Ale Seller
		Jas. McFarlane	Wigmaker
		Maitland Bannatyne	Merchant
		David Scott	Glover
		Mrs Sandilands	Ale Seller
		Mrs Scott	Minister's widow
		Wm. Brown	Valet
		Wm. Anderson	Ale Seller
		Wm. Hill	Clerk
		James Robertson	Poulterer
		Alex. White	Writer
		Mrs Wilson	
		Robert Greig	Merchant

CAP & FEATHER CLOSE and HALKERSTON'S WYND

1	(11)	Mrs Learmonth	
	(14)	Charles Thomson	Wigmaker
	(20)	Mrs Boggie	
	(35)	Walter Foggo	Wigmaker
	(12)	Wm. Lawson	Teacher
2	(10)	Mrs McCalla	
	(10)	John Jameson	Lodging House
	(12)	Mrs Cumming	Boarding School
	(22)	Robt. Grant of Ruthrie	W.S.
	(10)	John Murdoch	Teacher
	(26)	Robert Hamilton	Minister
	(26)	Mrs Stirling	
3		Mr Bartram	Teacher
		Walter Montgomerie	Valet
		Robert Waddel	
		Alex. McIntosh	Writer
		George Penman	Cordiner
		Geo. Boswall	Saddler
		John McIlwreath	Staymaker
		Mrs Gray	Merchant
		Kathrine Stewart	
		David Grierson	
		John Halley	
		Patrick Christie	
		Mrs Brown & Son	Watchmakers
		David Caithness	Cook
		Thos. McCulloch	
		Jas. Telfour	Tailor
		Mrs Wemyss	
		Lady Minto	
		Mistress Dow	
		Mr Bartram of Nisbet	
		Robt. Andrew	
		Wm. Reoch	Wright

KINLOCH'S CLOSE

1	(19)	John Patullo	Bookseller
	(19)	James Norrie	Painter
2	(10)	Robert Andrew	
	(10)	Mr Rattray	
	(14)	Wm. Tytler of Woodhouse-lee	W.S
3		Jas. Bonsie	Valet
		Wm. Ormiston	Valet
		Miss Mary Scott	
		Laurence Brown	Wigmaker
		Mrs Norrie	
		John McCoull	Shoemaker
		Mrs Herriot	
		John McGlashan	Merchant
		Isobell Fotheringham	Merchant
		Lady Craigentinny	

CARRUBER'S CLOSE and High Street North to Baillie Fyfe's Close

1	(14)	Alex. Robertson	Merchant
	(24)	Lady Houston	
	(14)	George Bailey of Hamilton	
	(18)	Alex Robertson of Parson's Green	W.S.
	(12)	George Penman	Cordiner
	(10)	John Downie	Dancing Master
	(17)	Mrs Piper	Milliner
	(25)	Lady Dundonald	
2	(14)	Charles Butter	Merchant/Wright
	(18)	David Anderson	Waulker
	(37)	Lady Blantyre	

CARRUBER'S CLOSE—Continued

	(12)	William Ramsay	Banker
	(13)	Miss B. Ferguson	
	(19)	Wm. McG(h)ie	Merchant
	(18)	Jas. Grahame	W.S.
	(35)	Robt. Dundas of Arniston	
	(30)	Mrs Maitland	Room Setter
3		Lady Mary Sharp	
		Wm. auld	Wright
		McCulloch & Tod	Merchants
		Andrew Sandum	Fencing Master
		Mrs Simpson	Ale Seller
		Captain George Seton	
		John Fraser	Ale Seller
		Wm. Purvis	Ale Seller
		Jeremiah McCulloch	Coachman
		John Callander	Glover
		John Whitehead	
		Wm. Davidson	Valet
		Thos. Donald	Smith
		Mrs Ann Elphingstone	
		David Beat	Writing Master
		Jenet Callander	
		John Milne	Founder
		Daniel Mack	Ale Seller
		John Stewart	Musician
		Alex. Campbell	Valet
		James Ronaldson	Baxter
		Robt. Marjoribanks	
		Mrs Forbes of Knapernie	
		Thos. Robertson	Writer
		Mrs Gullane	
		John Herriot	Candlemaker
		John Reoch	Musician
		John Stirling	Teacher
		John Stewart	Valet
		Lady Pumpherston	
		Mrs Binning	
		Mrs Tudhope	
		Helen Balfour	Merchant
		Miss McGlashan	
		George Beasey	Buckle-maker
		Mrs Stirling	
		Nathan Porteous	Glover
		John Moubray	Hair Merchant
		Mrs Betty Monteith	
		Mrs Norrie	
		Mrs Sutherland	

BAILIE FYFE'S CLOSE

1	(23)	Miss Wightman	Boarding School
2	(30)	Archibald Hart	
	(28)	Mrs Johnstone	
3		John McIntosh	Merchant
		Wm. Anderson	
		James Cameron	
		Daniel Ross	Upholsterer
		Mrs Taylor	
		Colin Haiggs	Lint Dresser
		Robert Murray	Valet
		Wm. Barclay	Optician
		Chas. Craigie	Merchant
		John Hill	Skinner

SMITH'S LAND at High Street; head of Bailie Fyfe's

1	(14)	Lady Ednum	

	(12)	George Boswall	Writer
	(12)	Mrs Warrender	
	(13)	Archibald Stewart	Merchant
	(22)	Charles Smith	
	(10)	Col. Wm. Murray	
	(13)	Archibald Eagle	Seed Merchant
	(23)	Lady Stormont	
2	(12)	John Mathie	Weaver
	(12)	James Nisbet	
	(11)	John Sinclair	
	(12)	Ladies Douglas	
	(11)	Peter McKellar	
3		Robert Wylie	Ale Seller
		Mrs Kennedy of Kilkingie	
		Ladies of March	
		John Balfour	Stationer
		George Purdie	Merchant, Druggist

HIGH STREET to Barringer's Close

	George Winter	Wigmaker
	Jenet Batchelor	
	David Clark	Wigmaker
	Mrs Craw	
	Thomas Mathie	Valet
	Mrs Crockate	Minister's Widow

BARRINGER'S CLOSE

1	( )	Lady Auchterfardel	
2	(10)	Wm. Hutton	
	(20)	David Kennedy	Advocate
3		John Alexander	Limner
		Provost White	
		Wm. Wight	Baxter
		Wm. Gardiner	Candlemaker

FOURTH BOUNDS: from Chamber's Close to Old Netherbow

North Side of High Side

1	(19)	Robert Norrie	Painter
	(11)	John Murray	Merchant, Glassgrinder
2	(25)	John Milne	Founder
	(15)	Andrew Wilson	Waulker
	(11)	Hugh McKay	
	(10)	John Cross	
3		Adam Anderson	Wigmaker
		Robert Wood	Trunk maker
		Mrs Trotter	
		Countess of Kincardine	
		Robert Couden	Wright
		Mrs Ravenscroft	
		Mrs Catherine Young	
		Wm. Black	Wright
		Jas. Gordon	Saddler
		Stephen Ronaldson	Cordiner
		Jas. Nicoll	Trunk-maker
		Lady Danwick	
		Robert Blyth	Trunk-maker
		Lady Ruthven	
		Mrs Clelland	
		Hugh Stewart	Valet
		Mr Johnstone	Surgeon
		Wm. Moore	

HIGH STREET from Chamber's Close to Sandiland's Close

3	Robert Morrison	Wigmaker

HIGH STREET—*Continued*

	Mrs McKenzie	
	Mr Garden	Wright
	John Turnbull	Baxter
	Mrs Telfer	
	Mrs Hay	

SANDILAND'S CLOSE

2	(13)	Richard Lake	Merchant
	(14)	Mrs Chaipland	
3		Ronald Cameron	
		David Kinnaird	

MONTEITH'S CLOSE

1	(11)	Mrs Drummond (Professor	Drummond)
	( )	Mrs Cockburn	(Thos. Cockburn, Writer)
	(12)	Mrs Murray	
	(13)	James Syme	Tailor
2	(12)	Ludovic Grant	
	(56)	Robert Pringle	
	(12)	John Anthonius	Wright
3		Mrs Marjoribanks	
		Lady Pitcarly	
		Daniel McCulloch	
		Mrs Syme	
		John Clarkson	Merchant
		David Baillie	Writer

TRUNK CLOSE to Old Netherbow

1	(11)	Mrs Hope	
	(11)	Dr Sinclair	
	(10)	Jas. Aitkenhead	Merchant
	(11)	Dr Elliot	
	(10)	Wm. Wight	
	(23)	Jas. Auchinleck	Hammermen
2	(16)	Archibald Govan	
	(40)	Baron Maule	
3		David Hill	
		John Christie	Merchant
		Jonathan Jones	Ale Seller
		Wm. Russell	Clerk
		Jas. Anderson	Goldsmith
		Mrs Johnstone	
		George Lawson	Upholsterer
		Mrs Cockburn	
		Mrs Mirrie	
		Alex Thomson	Merchant
		David Finlay	Wright
		Lady Dalziel	
		Mr McIntosh	Writer
		Mrs Young	
		Thos. Jameson	Glover
		Wm. Mylne	Mason
		John Carnegie	Merchant
		Margaret Gilles	
		Elizabeth Gibb	
		David Millar	
		Wm. Moffat	Merchant
		Mrs McGuffock	
		John Donaldson	Gilder
		Mr Alexander	Merchant
		Robert Philip	
		Jas. Caddel	Upholsterer
		Jas. Hutchison	
		Thos. Calder	

Benjamin Millar	Merchant
Hugh Dallas	Merchant
Charles Lammond	
Mrs Bennet	
Isobell Leitch	Ale Seller
James Watt	
James Miles	
Adam Anderson	Pewterer
John Bell	Baxter
Mrs Mitchell	
Lord Kirkcudbright	
Mr Clark	Mason
Mrs Down	
Mrs West	
George Lamb	Wright
John Medina	Limner
Mr Christie	Cordiner
Widow Forbes	
Alexander Imrie	
Mrs Cossenot	
Mrs McLagan	
John Neilsen	Glass Grinder
John Scirving	

FIFTH BOUNDS from Netherbow Port, south-east to Kinloch's Close and Hellistob's Land

ERSKINE'S LAND

1	(14)	Widow Stewart	
3		Robert Carmichael	
		Thomas Jarvie	Merchant
		Wm. Weir	Ale Seller
		Thos. Grant	Brewer

WORLD'S END CLOSE

1	(19)	Lady Strathnever	
2	(10)	Mr Falconer	
	(11)	Mrs Johnston	
	(13)	Lady Katherine Lindsay	
	(18)	Mr McDougall	
3		John Mitchell	
		George Lauder	Surgeon
		Mrs Cairns	
		Mrs Jean Law	
		Captain Home	
		Mr Ogilvie of Coul	
		Alexander Sinclair	Tailor

TWEEDDALE COURT

2	(56)	Marquis of Tweeddale	
	(10)	Mr Hay	
	(12)	Mrs Plenderleith	
	(12)	Mr McKenzie	
	(11)	Mrs Drummond	

FOUNTAIN CLOSE

1	(11)	May Wilkiston	
	(23)	Dr Dundas	
2	(12)	Mrs Gordon	
	(10)	Sir Steuart Thripland	
	( )	John Johnstone	
3		Mrs Dallas	
		Mrs Henderson	Merchant
		Jas. Clark	Grocer
		Jas. Fettes	Porter
		Lady Dunning	

HIGH STREET at Fountain Close to Foulis Close

3 Miss Smetholm
   Mrs Douglas
   Mr Mirrie
   Mrs Stewart
   Miss Robertson
   Elspit Baverly
   Mrs Home
   Dr Horseburgh
   Mrs Gordon
   Mrs Murray

FOULIS CLOSE

1 (15) Lady Orbiston
   (13) Chas. Congleton   Surgeon
   (14) Mrs Alexander Hay
   (12) Captain Ogilvie
   (13) Andrew Marjoribanks   Merchant
   (15) Mrs Marjoribanks
   ( ) John Cochrane of Ravelridge
   (28) Martin Eccles   Surgeon
   (15) Mrs Ronalds
   (14) Mr Rattray   Surgeon
2 (13) Mrs Skeen
   (14) Mr Patullo   Merchant
   (15) Sir Robert Morton
   ( ) Wm. Harper
3   Gilbert Robertson   Merchant
         William Young
         Mrs Chalmers
         Mrs Drysdale
         Hendry Gibson   Flesher
         James Ramsay   Merchant
         Ann Gordon
         Mr Pale   Cobbler
         Wm. Herriot   Gunsmith

HYNDFOORD'S CLOSE

1 (12) James Millar   Painter
   (12) Mrs Scott
   (14) Mrs Ross   Ale Seller
2 (54) Lord Milton   Lord Justice Clerk
   (11) Thomas Dundas
   (10) James Smith   Writer
   (12) Mr Turnbull
3   Mrs Hamilton
         Andrew Raeburn   Wright
         Wm. Michie   Merchant
         George Smith   Merchant
         Mrs Spittal
         Mrs Lillie Seton

GRAY'S CLOSE

1 (15) Wm. Richardson
2 (28) James Naismith   Writer
   (14) Mrs Clark
   (20) Peter Wedderburn   Secretary to Excise
   (14) Mrs McEwan   Ale Seller
   (17) Sir Michael Stewart of Blackhall
   (16) Sir John Stewart
3   Mrs Lesslie
         Lady Mary Hamilton
         Micah Smith
         Micah Shiels   Cheesemonger
         Mrs Houston

         Lady Maxwell
         Mr Taylor
         Wm. Inglis
         Lady Humbie

HIGH STREET at Easton's Land

1 (15) Wm. Sutherland   Brewer
2 (14) Mr Hallyburton

SKINNER'S CLOSE

1 (13) M. Picque   Dancing Master
   (13) Sir James Cockburn
   (14) Mr McVey   Skinner
   (13) Lady Auchenbowie
   (13) Mrs Spalding
   (14) John Jameson
2 (13) Gordon Patrick
   (14) Mr Beatt jr.
   (15) Dr Kinneir
   (12) Mr Elphingston
   (12) James Smith   Skinner
3   Lady Dunlop
         Walter Williamson   Writer
         Mrs Douglas
         Alex. Clark   Stabler/Ale Seller
         Robt. Ramsay   Tailor
         James Allan   Wright
         Mrs Shiels
         John Ronaldson   Merchant
         Widow Bell
         Mrs Ireland   Merchant
         James Nicoll   Trunk maker
         Andrew Toshock   Ale Seller
         Mungo Scott   Glazier
         Mrs Loch
         Mrs Oliphant

MURDOCH'S CLOSE

1 (12) Mrs Moncrieff
   (12) Mrs Buchanan
2 (12) Mrs Armstrong
3   Miss Durham
         Miss Fleming
         Peter Angus   Ale Seller
         Lady Caithness
         Mrs Halyday
         Wm. Hodge   Baxter
         Mrs Christian Cochrane
         Jas. Inglis   Merchant
         Mrs Reid

TODRICK'S WYND

1 (12) John Moubray   Wright
   (12) Jas. Murray   Merchant
2 (11) John Robertson   Writer
   (10) Alex. Stewart
   (26) Mrs Gibson
   (14) Mrs McFarlane
3   Mrs Ramsay
         John Sutor   Wright
         Mr McCulloch
         Francis Finlay   Goldsmith
         Mrs Hamilton
         Neil Stewart

TODRICK'S WYND—Continued
- Mrs Hay
- Andrew Buchanan
- Dr Martine

BLACKFRIAR'S WYND
1. (13) John Sprott — Candlemaker
   - (15) John Davidson — Merchant
   - (10) Lady Balgowan
   - (28) Lady Lovatt
   - (26) James Marjoribanks
   - (11) Sir Walter Montgomerie
2. (33) Baron Clark
   - (14) Gavin Waugh — Baxter
   - (15) John Hay
   - (17) Mr Barclay
   - (12) Lady Inverary
3. Jas. Reoch — Procurator
   - Jas. Cranstone — Shopkeeper
   - John Montgomery — Wright
   - Mrs Jean Innes
   - Thomas Smith — Clerk
   - William McCulloch
   - Mr Drummond of Hawthorndean
   - Mr Adamson
   - Wm. Barr
   - John Drummond
   - John Philip — Valet
   - George Christie — Baxter
   - Jenet Sandilands
   - John Manners — Dyster
   - James Paterson of Kirkton — Advocate
   - Mrs Craw — Room Setter
   - John Taylor
   - Mrs Forbes
   - Mrs Baillie
   - Mr Blair of Excise
   - Alex. Dallas — Silk Dyer
   - Alex. Crinzin
   - David Riddoch
   - Donald McDonald — Merchant
   - Mrs Irvine
   - Wm. Stevenson
   - James Johnstone
   - Patrick Seton — Merchant
   - Mrs Christie
   - David Berrey — Cobbler
   - James Gair
   - Mrs Cockburn
   - David Brown — Ale Seller
   - Wm. Swinton — Merchant
   - David Bonnar
   - Hugh Hamilton
   - John Anderson — Grocer
   - Charles Cunningham — Baxter
   - John Houston — Valet
   - John McNab — Merchant
   - Mrs Johnstone
   - James Smeiton — Wigmaker
   - Mrs Staig
   - Mr Marshall — Ale Seller
   - Walter Johnstone
   - Alex. Moubray — Wigmaker
   - Mr Edgar

CANT'S CLOSE
1. (15) Professor Stevenson — Schoolmaster
   - (13) Mrs Oswald
2. (15) Dr Martin
   - (26) Mr Murray — Druggist
   - (27) Lord Strichen
   - (10) Mr Glendinning
   - (10) Thos. Clarkson
   - (29) Mme. Le Blanc — Boarding School
   - (22) Ronald Crawford of Restalrig — W.S.
   - (13) Miss Geddes
   - (14) John Kennedy — Surgeon
   - (13) James Lawrence
3. James Thomson — Glover
   - Daniel Fraser — Footman
   - Hugh Spark
   - John Park — Shoemaker
   - Mrs Fleming
   - Adolphus Hay
   - Mr Hamilton of Gilderscleugh
   - Mr Henderson
   - Miss Chatto
   - Mrs Ronaldson
   - Alex. Middleton
   - Miss Stirling — Mantua Maker
   - Robert Anderson — Taylor
   - Alex. Wright
   - Gordon's Barley Office
   - Mrs McDonald

DICKSON'S CLOSE
1. (14) David Aitkenhead — Surgeon
   - (14) Countess of Balcarres
   - (18) George Buchan — Writer
   - (15) Mr Guild — Writer
   - (18) John Yetts — Wright
   - (13) Thomas Hay — Baxter
2. (10) Mrs Murray — at "The Mermaid"
   - (13) Mr Douglas
   - (16) Provost George Drummond — Excise
   - (13) Mr Wightman
   - (19) Mrs Blair
   - (10) Mr Jackson — W.S.
3. Thomas Fordice — Writer
   - Mrs Garroch
   - Mrs Bain
   - Wm. Watson — Ale Seller
   - Robt. Swan — Ale Seller
   - Mr Rose — Painter
   - Mrs Cochrane
   - Chas. Watkins — Wigmaker
   - Wm. Dunbar — W.S.
   - Mrs Chatto
   - Hugh Fraser
   - Mr Hogg — Schoolmaster
   - David Stark — Weaver
   - George Syme — Slater
   - Daniel Wright
   - Mrs Cairns
   - Francis Kemptie — Merchant
   - Mrs Wright
   - James Aitkenhead — Cordiner

KINLOCH'S CLOSE
1 (14) Mrs Halden
  (16) James Hunter — Wright
  (17) David Robertson — Smith
  (17) Lady Kello
  (19) Lady Pitcairn
  (10) Jas. Montgomery — (Mrs Montgomery, Milliner)
  (15) Dr Taylor
  (12) Helen Glass — Mantua Maker
  (14) Mrs Mill — Midwife
  (12) John Tyrie — Writer
  (14) Mr Inglis — Surgeon
2 (12) Jas. Wright
  (19) Mrs Wilson
  (17) Gilbert Lawrie
  (13) Dr Porterfield
  (14) Mrs Henderson
  (15) Henry Scrymgeour — W.S
3   Robert Brown — Furrier
       Mrs Rollo
       Charles Ross — Merchant
       Mrs Betty McDougall
       Mr Muirhead
       Master of Elphingston
       Lady Sands
       Mrs Law
       John Douglas — Armourer
       Duncan Wright
       John Peacock — Glazier
       Mrs Ogilvie
       Mr Reid — Schoolmaster
       Dr Ferguson
       Mrs Young
       Wm. Fraser — Valet

From foot of Cant's/Kinloch's Closes to Cowgate Port
COWGATE North Side
3   William Balderstone — Wheelwright
       Charles Mayelstone — Apothecary
       Wm. Robertson — Valet
       George Willson
1 (14) Charles Mack — Mason
3   George Hogg — Brewer
       Dr Plummer
       Mrs Crawford
       Mrs Murray
       Mrs Harvey
       John Ferguson
       Wm. Balfour — Smith
       D. McLachlane — Cordiner
       Wm. White — Wigmaker
       Thos. Baillie — Wright
       James Ballantyne — Wheelwright
       Mrs Cameron
       James Angus — Wright
       Duncan Robertson — Valet
       John Wright — Merchant

HAWTHORNDEN'S LAND
2 (13) Thomas Lawson
  (16) Mrs Moubray

BROWNHILLS LAND
1 (14) George Arbuthnot — Merchant

  (14) Mrs Wood — Minister's Widow
2 (13) Mr McKenzie
  (14) Mr Kinloch
3   James Kennedy — Horse Hirer
       Wm. Crawford — Valet
       Widow Scougall
       Andrew Dall
       Captain Pringle

BAIN & JOLLY'S LAND
1 (11) Richard Lothian — Writer
  (14) Mr Young — Midwifery Tutor
2 (11) Mr Sinclair
  (14) Mr McPherson
3   Mrs Hay
       Mrs Mathie
       Wm. Moffat — Room Setter
       Mrs Robertson — Room Setter
       Mrs Kidd

From Cowgate Port on Cowgate South going west at Bull's Land
3   Mr Brown — Gauger
       Mrs McNat
       Mrs Cuthbertson
       Mr Wills
       Mrs Perrie

HIGH SCHOOL YARDS
1 (19) Baillie John Wilson
2 (12) Alex. Wright
  (16) Mrs Brown of Carseleath
3   James Symington
       James Alexander — Dyer
       Wm. Young
       Mrs Scott
       Charles Lawson
       Mrs McPherson
       John Finlayson — Instrument Maker
       Lady Thirlestane

SURGEON'S HALL
East
  (14) Lady Henderson
West
  (29) Sir Peter Hacket

INFIRMARY
Easter Pavilion
1 (12) John Lees — Teacher
3   Wm. McDowall — Merchant
       Mrs Kerr
Main Building
1 (56) Lady Haddington
2 (16) Lady Campbell
  (15) Lady Marjoribanks
3   James Scott — Druggist
       Gavin Hamilton & Co. — Merchants
Wester Pavilion
2 (16) Magdalen Keir

ROBERTSON'S CLOSE
1 (23) Sir John Inglis

ROBERTSON'S CLOSE—Continued
	(27)	Lady Seton	
2	(41)	Charles Sinclair	
	(24)	James Rochead	
	(40)	David Wright	
3		Mr Ross	Flesher
		Robert Gray	Writer
		Wm. Syme	Ale Seller
		Widow Syme	
		Lady Polkemmet	
		Mr Pitcairn	
		Andrew McArra	
		George Aitken	Smith
		Jenet Cumming	
		Mr Loch	

ADAM'S LAND
1	(46)	John Adams	Architect
	(25)	Lady Baird	
2	(25)	John Dickie jr.	
	(34)	James Lesslie	
3		Alexander Boswall	Painter
		Walter Colville	Baxter

PLAINSTONE CLOSE/SCOTT'S LAND
1	(11)	Wm. Haiggs	Baxter
	(11)	Betty Dundas	
3		Lady Montgomery	
		Widow Brown	
		Mrs Murray	
		Mr McFarlane	Schoolmaster
		George Chalmers	Writer

HELLISTOB'S LAND
1	(14)	Janet Murray	
2	(15)	Lady Kintore	
	(19)	Andrew Mouatt	
	(10)	James Hamilton	
	(19)	James Stirling	Fishmonger
	(14)	Mrs Alison	

SIXTH BOUND from Niddry's Wynd to Horse Wynd

NIDDRY'S WYND
at Warrender's Court:
1	(15)	Mrs Wemyss	
	(13)	Mrs Murray	
	(21)	Wm. Wilson of Howden	Writer
2	(13)	Mr Watson	
3		Betty Elder	Ale Seller
		Mrs Sanders	Room Setter
		Hugh Fraser	Ale Seller
		David Great	China Mender
		John Gordon	
		John Baird	Ale Seller
		Langton Oliphant's Daughters	
		Denis Foy	Silk dyer
		George Bairnsfather	Plumber
		Isobell McDougall	Ale Seller

at Carnwath's Court:
1	(32)	Mr Lockhart, George of Carnwath	
	(14)	Mrs Robertson	
2	(30)	Scott of Thirlestane	
3		George Stevenson	Physician
		John Grieve	Valet
		Sir David Cunningham	

		John Hay	Writer
		Robt. Douglas	Writer
		Wm. Greig	Valet
		Lady Mary Crichtone	
		John Lamb	Wright

at Montgomery's Land
2	(10)	Thos. Cockburn	
	(10)	John Warden	Teacher
	(13)	Thos. Brodie	W.S.

at Pencaitland's Land
2	(13)	Mr Ross	
	(12)	John Smith	
	(24)	George Innes	

at Smith's Land
1	(16)	Wm. Dow	Merchant
	(17)	Lady Glassie	
	(17)	Mrs Fairholm	
2	(15)	Lady Murray	
	(19)	John Belches of Innermay	
	(21)	Robt. Pringle	
	(19)	George Inglis	
	(18)	Commissary Clerk	
3		Lady Bomana	
		John Willson	Silk Dyer
		Andrew Robertson	Ale Seller
		Mrs Henderson	
		Alex. Syme	Painter
		Mrs Campbell	
		Duncan Buchan	Valet

HIGH STREET at Tron Kirk (above Niddry's Wynd)
3		Andrew Syme	Cooper
		Hendry Wright	Valet
		Thomas Lawrie	Valet
		Wm. Ronalds	Ale Seller
		Jean Thomson	Merchant
		John Willson	Merchant
		Andrew Douglas	Merchant
		Patrick Henderson	Merchant

MARLIN'S WYND
1	(19)	Mrs McGill	
	(19)	Mrs Grahame	
	(14)	Wm. Williamson	Poultryman
2	(14)	Mrs Campbell of Arbuckle	
	(10)	John Dingwall	
	(19)	Erskine of Carnock	
	(15)	William Millar	Bookseller
	(12)	Mrs Blackwood	
	(19)	George Watson	
	(13)	James Mitchell	
	(18)	Mrs Wilson	
	(14)	Alex. Millar	Painter
	(15)	Robert Craw	Brewer
3		George Willson	Indweller
		Widow Watson	
		John Watson	Poultryman
		Widow Clelland	
		John Watson	Poultryman
		Mrs Johnstone	Poultrywoman
		Alex. Stewart	Musician
		John Elder	Shoemaker
		Mrs Peat	
		Alex Thomson	Tailor
		John Black	Poultryman

OLD POST HOUSE STAIRS at foot of Marlin's Wynd
2 (11) WM. FRAZER jr.
   (11) WALTER COSSOR — Excise and Writing Master
   (11) MRS CONGALTON

PEEBLES WYND
at Cummings Land:
2 (11) MRS BAXTER
at Craigleith Court:
1 (12) GEORGE HOME — Baxter
2 (37) THOMAS HAY — Baxter
   (12) ALEX. MANNERS — Merchant
   (12) AGNES LIDDELL
3   THOMAS NIMMO
   WIDOW HERRIOT — Ale Seller
   MRS WATSON — Poultrywoman
   JOHN STRACHAN — Chairman
   CATHERINE COVENTRY
   JAS. MURRAY — Candlemaker
   JOHN ROBERTSON
   JOHN MORRISON — Wigmaker, Ale Seller

   MRS THORBURN
   THOMAS STEWART — Valet
   MRS AUCHINLECK — Milliner
   MRS AITKMAN
   JOHN YOUNG — Merchant
   JOHN CAMPBELL — Ale Seller
   MRS LAWRIE
   DONALD MCNIVEN
   ANDREW MCNEILL
   JOHN ROBERTSON — Chairman
   THOS. MCKAY — Ale Seller
   MR ANDERSON — Teacher
   MRS HORNER — Pastry Cook
   JAS. STEWART — Ale Seller
   ANDREW HARDY — Baxter

KENNEDY'S CLOSE
1 (12) GEORGE DUGUID
   (13) ARCHIBALD INGLIS — Pewterer
   (19) JOHN DICK snr.
2 (13) WM. ELLIOT — Writer
   (20) DAVID AUCHINLECK
   (13) MISS MAUNDERSON
3   WM. MYRTLE — Baxter
   DAVID BROWN
   MR PRINGLE OF CRIGHTONE
   ANDREW ALLAN — Merchant
   MRS LUMSDEN
   MRS DONALDSON
   MRS GALLOWAY — Cork Cutter
   MRS SMITH
   JOHN MCKENZIE — Cork Cutter
   WIDOW BELL
   ALEX. PRINGLE — Wright
   JOHN WATSON
   JAMES MCKELTOPE — Merchant
   WM. HAY OF CHESTERFIELD

HIGH STREET at Syme's and Magdalen's Lands
(head of Kennedy's and Stonelaw's)
2 (12) JAMES SYME — Slater
   (14) JAMES SPOTTISWOOD

   (24) JOHN DALRYMPLE — Merchant
   (11) WM. CHEAP — Linen Merchant
   (18) WILLIAM AIKMAN — Merchant
   (14) WM. SIBBALD — Tailor
3   DAVID TYRIE
   JOHN LEGET
   GEORGE SMART — Ale Seller
   JOHN POLSON — Ale Seller
   MISS GEDDES — Milliner
   JAS. RONALDSON — Glazier
   MR LANCASHIRE — Coachmaker
   ALEX. BRUCE — Surgeon
   MISS MUTTER — Milliner
   MISS MCRABBIE — Milliner
   MRS HAY

STONELAW'S CLOSE
1 (10) GRIZELL FOWLES
   (10) ROBT. MCDUFF — Goldsmith
   (15) JAMES KAY — Wright
2 (14) JOHN WATSON — Slater
   (12) JOHN MORE
   (14) ALEX. HUNTER — Merchant
   (10) JOHN YOUNG — Room Setter
   (10) WILLIAM HILL — Merchant
   (10) MRS CAIRNS
   (10) JOHN QUESNOT — French Teacher
3   WM. KELTIE — Merchant
   ALEX. ROSS — Ale Seller
   MRS CLELLAND
   JOHN ROBERTSON — Vintner
   ROBT. GAIRNS — Waiter
   ROBT. LINDSAY
   MR HAMILTON — Teacher
   MR MURRAY — Valet
   ANDREW MCLAREN
   MISSES HARRISON & DAVISON
   THOS. GOURLIE — Weaver
   DONALD MCDONALD
   MRS WOOD
   MRS CUNNINGHAM — Teacher
   ANDREW SYME — Merchant
   ALEX. STEVENSON — Candlemaker
   JAS. NISBET — Wheelwright

HIGH STREET at Wilkie's Land, Black Turnpike and Todd's Land
at Wilkie's
2 (11) ELIONORA MUTTER — Ale Seller
   (10) JOHN NAISMITH — Chairmaster
   (11) MISS HALYDAY
   (15) JOHN DUFF
at Black Turnpike
2 (16) ALEX. NISBET — Surgeon
at Todd's Land
   (12) THOMAS MUTTER
   (10) JAMES MCGIBBON

NEW ASSEMBLY CLOSE
1 (21) DR MCFARLANE
   (19) MARGARET TURNBULL — Vintner
2 (26) GEORGE WISHART — Rev., Minister
3   MR MCDERMOTT — Ale Seller
   JOHN DRYSDALE — Cordiner
   ROBERT LOCH

NEW ASSEMBLY CLOSE—Continued

Jas. Morrison	Glover
Robert Gedd	Dyer
George Nicoll	Cordiner
James Wotherspoon	Weaver

BELL'S WYND including Chalmer's Land, Campbell's Land and Naismith's Land

1	(12) James Simpson	Teacher
	(10) John Hay	Wigmaker
	(19) Alex. Burtone	Glazier
	(13) Mrs Kelso	Milliner
	(14) Alex. Turnbull	Wright
2	(15) Walter Wordie	
	(14) John Campbell	Tailor
	(17) Mrs Naismith	
3	John Fyfe	Merchant
	James Geddes	Watchmaker
	Martin Carfrae	Wright
	Mrs Bain	Washer
	Wm. Grant	
	Mr Elliott	
	Wm. Cowan	
	John Brownlie	
	George Warden	Room Setter
	John Johns	Valet
	Mr Cowie	Chairmaster
	John Thomson	Musician
	Wm. Stewart	Ale Seller

CLAMSHELL TURNPIKE AND AINSLIE'S LAND
at Clamshell Turnpike

1	(19) Mrs Dallas	
2	(17) Robert Dewar	Writing School
3	Mrs McKechnie	Merchant (Old Stage Coach Office)
	Robert Anna	Merchant
	Mistress Aikman	Milliner
	Miss McKay	
	John Gibson	Auctioneer

at Ainslie's Land

2	(15) Wm. Burnet	Merchant
	(14) Mrs Ainslie	
3	Wm. Nicoll	Watchmaker

BURNET'S CLOSE & Jolly's Land

1	(14) Andrew Petrie	
2	(13) Mrs Lindsay	
3	Mrs Stewart	Merchant
	Alex. Douglas	Wright
	Wm. McLean	Ale Seller

at Jolly's Land

1	(11) David Lindsay	
	(15) Thomas Reid	Chairman
3	Wm. Finlay	Glassgrinder
	James McGlashan	Ale Seller
	John Monro	Ale Seller
	Patrick Mathison	Ale Seller

COVENANT CLOSE

1	(25) Archibald Shiells	Merchants
	(18) James Cleghorn	Baxter
	(12) Richard McKenzie	Vintner
	(23) Lady Northesk	
	(18) Margaret McKenzie	

	(17) John Osburn	Merchant
2	(18) Wm. Watson of Pilmuir	W.S.
	(23) Dr Porterfield	
	(19) James Veitch	Glazier
	(16) Walter Ainslie	Shipping Agent
	(20) McQueen, Robert	Lord Braxfield
	(15) Betty Harries	
3	Wm. Burnet	Merchant
	Alex. Hutton	Ale Seller
	John Watson	Vintner
	James Thomson	Wigmaker
	Mary Espline	
	Mrs Warden	Sewing Mistress
	Mrs Stewart	
	Lady Billie (murdered at Eyemouth Aug. 1751)	
	Mr Home	
	John Riddock	Valet
	David Montgomery	Manservant
	Jas. Carmichael	Ale Seller
	Alex. Innes	Writer
	John Urquhart	Cook
	Colin Alison	Wright

CON'S CLOSE AND RIDDEL'S LAND

1	(10) John Herriot	Cordiner
	(12) John Stonehouse	
2	(11) Wm. Aitken	Wright
3	Misses Ross & Paton	Merchants
	James Allan	Merchant
	Mr Pringle	Valet
	Wm. Bowman	Tailor
	John Ferguson	Merchant
	Mrs Wright	
	David Wright	Merchant
	Wm. Ferguson	
	Robert Home	Wright
	Widow Watson	
	Widow Birnie	
	John Nicolson	Valet
	Deacon Ure	Goldsmith

OLD ASSEMBLY CLOSE

2	(10) Mrs Urquhart	
	(20) John Ross	
	(19) James Hay	W.S.
	(31) Dr Plummer	
	(19) David Anderson	W.S.
	(19) David Moncrieff	W.S., Secretary to Exchequer
	(18) James Pringle	
	(23) Wm. Robertson	Writer
	(19) David Bruce	
	(20) Alex. Stewart	W.S
	(15) Dr Robert White	joint Professor of Medicine
	(14) Florence Harvey	
	(19) Christian Anderson	
	(17) Elizabeth Forrest	
	(10) James White	
	(14) Mrs Loch	

BORTHWICK'S CLOSE

1	(14) Archibald Punton	
2	(14) Dr Farquharson	
	(12) Mrs Oliphant	
	(32) George Pringle	Furrier

BORTHWICK'S CLOSE—Continued

3	JAMES LYON	Merchant
	THOS. ADAMSON	Tailor
	ELIZABETH SMITH	Ale Seller
	PATRICK CHRISTIE	Printer
	ROBERT GEDD	Dyer
	JOHN BROWN	Cork Cutter
	GEORGE MARTIN	Ale Seller
	DAVID CAMPBELL	Ale Seller
	SIMON LAWRENCE	Ale Seller

COWGATE, at foot of Borthwick's/Old Assembly Closes

3	JAMES DICK	Brewer
	MISS JOHNSTONE	
	DEACON ROBERT JAMESON	Mason
	MRS YOUNG	
	MRS ANDERSON	
	MRS SHIRRIFF	
	ALEX. MYLES	Brewer
	MRS HAMILTON	

COWGATE SOUTH
at Hastie's

2 (10)	JAMES YOURSTONE	Cutler
(10)	GEORGE ADAMSON	Druggist

LABORATORY

(15)	JOHN HAY	Baxter
(14)	MRS CHEESLIE	

COLLEDGE & WYND

(29)	PROFESSOR GOLDIE	
(14)	MR HUNTER	
(14)	MR ROBERTSON	
(14)	GEORGE STEWART	
(15)	MATHEW STEWART	Professor of Mathematics
(32)	MRS WISHART	
(16)	MR CROCKETT	

COLLEDGE WYND
South end

(10)	BETTY COCHRANE	
(28)	MR DAWSON	Professor of Hebrew
3	DAVID BOWIE	Mason

at Good's Land

1 (17)	ANDREW GOOD	Wright
2 (12)	ALEX. MEALS	

at Crawfoord's Road

2 (15)	ROBERT HAMILTON	W.S.

in the Wynd

3	JOHN RAE	Teacher
	CHARLES CAMPBELL	Gauger
	MRS HOUSTON	
	MRS CUNNINGHAM	
	MRS WILLIAM OF BECKIE	
	PATRICK KERR	
	JENET CRAWFORD	
	DUNCAN CAMPBELL	Painter
3	ANDREW INNES	Wright

at Samuel's Land

2 (14)	THOS. SIBBALD	Smith
(11)	ANDREW TOUGH	
3	LADY WHITEROCK	

	JAMES WATSON	Underjanitor in College
	JAMES JAMESON	Ale Seller
	ALEX. NISBET	Weaver
	THOMAS TAYLOR	

HORSE WYND

2 (35)	DR CLARK	
(33)	LORD MINTO (Gilbert Elliot)	
(42)	LORD GALLOWAY	
(10)	JAMES CRASS	
(17)	JOHN OLD	
3	ADAM KEIR	Baxter
	DONALD GRANT	
	MISTRESS STEWART	
	ALEXANDER BRIGGS	Merchant
	MRS BELL	
	MRS LAUDER	
	WIDOW GREIG	
	ANDREW SKEEN	Weaver
	JAMES BUTTER	
	JOHN FORBES	Ale Seller
	MRS SCOTT	
	MRS FOGGO	
	JOHN TROTTER	Brewer
	ROBERT LEES	Ale Seller
	JOHN MACK	Mason
	ROBERT FINLAY	Brewer
	MISS BOYD	
	CAPTAIN JOHNSTONE	
	ROBERT SAMUELS	
	JOHN GORDON	Stabler
	MISS FARQUHARSON	
	MISSES BALDERSTONE	Milliners
	MR KENDALL	Slater
	WM. MCCARTER	

at Todd's Land

2 (10)	GAVIN THOMSON	
(11)	MRS RANKIN	

at Peter's Land

1 (30)	ALEX. PETERS	Wright
(12)	MR SCOTT OF GALASHIELS	
2 (52)	JOHN MCKENZIE	
3	WM. LAING	Factor
	DAVID WIGHT	Baxter
	MRS BALFOUR	
	JOHN CAMPBELL	Valet
	JOHN SHINBOW	Wigmaker
	ARCHIBALD HOLLANDS	
	MRS HILL	
	MRS WILLSON	
	ROBERT FIDDES	
	JOHN MCDONALD	
	MRS WEIR	
	MRS CAMPBELL	
	MRS JOHNSTONE	
	WM. GORDON	Litster
	THOS. MITCHELL	
	JOHN CHARLES	
	JOHN RICHMONT	Teacher

SEVENTH BOUND from Fishmarket Close to Lawnmarket
at head of Gosford's Close

HIGH STREET south to east of Fishmarket Close

3	MRS GRAY	Vintner

HIGH STREET—Continued

Mrs Symers	
Hector McPhail	Vintner
John Thomson	Vintner
Hendry Schaw	Chairmaster
Lady Coulteraws	
Florence Harvey	Merchant
Robert Pringle	Merchant
James Reoch	Ale Seller
James Segal	

FISHMARKET CLOSE, including Cumming's and Anderson's Lands

1	(12)	Lady Tillicoultry	
	(25)	Lumsden, Robertson & Co.	Merchants
	(19)	Wm. Keir	Baxter
	(11)	Misses Hallyburton	
2	(11)	John Taylor	Merchant
	(19)	Lord Shewelton	
	(19)	Thomas Belches	Sheriff Clerk Depute
	(12)	Mrs Hutton	
	(19)	Wm. Wilson	Flesher

at Anderson's Land

3	Widow Welsh	
	Archibald Punton	Baxter
	Robert Kennedy	Cooper
	Alexander Lyle	Chairmaster
	Wm. Barclay	Wright
	Edward Bell	Smith
	James Forbes	Merchant
	Mr Williamson	Merchant
	Andrew Millar	Wheelwright
	Mrs Burton	

at Cumming's Land

3	Robert Wingate	
	John Orrock	
	Isobell Michison	
	David Nevay	Merchant
	John Reid	Valet
	Thos. Richie	Glazier
	John Goldman	Turner
	Wm. Rutherford	Hair Merchant
	John Dow	
	James Gilmore	
	Thos. Robertson	Tailor
	Alex. Givan	Glover
	Alex Noble	Hair Merchant
	Wm. Davie	Goldsmith
	Mrs Scott	

COWGATE at Foot of Fishmarket Close

George Siglur	Writer
Robert Bowie	
Mary Hutton	
James Watson	Dyer
Mrs Stevenson	
Dr Baird	
Mrs Ellis	
Mrs Farquharson	
John Milligan	Merchant
Mr Brown	

HIGH STREET from Fishmarket Close to Parliament Close

3	Jas. McDougall	Merchant
	Jas. Hogg	Merchant
	Widow Aitken	Ale Seller
	John Skeed	Vintner

PARLIAMENT CLOSE
at Custom House Stairs

1	(46)	Custom House	
	(13)	Mrs Rannie	Room Setter
	(14)	Barbara Urquhart	Room Setter
	(14)	Dr Rutherford	
	(12)	Patrick Blair	John's Coffee House
2	(12)	Charles Inglis	
	(13)	Alexander Boswall	Advocate
	(12)	Wm. Forbes	
	(14)	Keith Alexander	
	(23)	James Balfour	Merchant
3		John Douglas	Surgeon
		James Baird	Ale Seller
		Agnes Vasey	Ale Seller
		David Thomson	Ale Seller
		Alex. McKenzie	Vintner
		Mrs Straton	Vintner
		Ebenezer Oliphant	Goldsmith
		Robert Straton	
		Wm. Gordon	Stationer
		Charles Wright	Stationer

at President's Stairs

1	(14)	Thomas Dundas	Merchant
	(12)	Wm. Cumming	Cordiner
2	(34)	John Hope	Merchant
	(32)	James Coutts	Merchant
	(14)	Alex. Stevenson of Mountgreenan	W.S.
	(14)	Lady Penelope Crichtone	
	(18)	Wm. Frazer	W.S.
	(17)	Lord John Drummond	
	(25)	Thos. Fordyce	
3		Michael Hue	Gilder
		Gideon Crawford	Stationer
		Clerk, Stevenson & Co.	Merchants
		John Ross	Stationer
		Mrs McKenzie	Vintner

at Post Office Stairs

1	(16)	Post Office	
	(17)	Lauchlane Hunter	Stationer
2	(17)	David Grahame	
	(19)	Andrew Lumsden	
	(18)	James Kay	
3		Frances Chartries	Gentleman
		Coutts Trotter & Co.	

at Exchange Stairs

2	(18)	William Dempster	Goldsmith

in the Close

1	(18)	Stamp Office	
	(19)	Thomas Ruddiman	Printer
2	(14)	Trustees Office	

at New Stairs, including Campbell's Land & Meal Market

1	(12)	Hugh Grahame	Writer
	(23)	Robert Dundas	Merchant
	(21)	Robert Dick	Writer
	(17)	Robert Smith	Surgeon
	(11)	William Watson	Excise Office
	(22)	Professor Charles McKay	
2	(11)	Insurance Office	
	(18)	Archibald Angus	Merchant
	(13)	Charles Robertson	Professor

PARLIAMENT CLOSE—*Continued*

(11)	Walter Goodale	Printer, Caledonian Mercury
(24)	John Hamilton	
(17)	Master of Torphichen	
(14)	James Wood	Writer
(40)	Alex. Lockhart of Craighouse	
3	Thos. Kinneir	Merchant
	Robert Gibb	Vintner
	Mr Rattray	
	George Hay	Printer
	Miss McNeill	
	Heirs of Mrs Littlejohn	
	John Warrock	Tailor
	Alex. Gillespie	Ale Seller
	Jas. Brymer	Ale Seller
	Widow Smart	
	John Mouatt	Ale Seller
	James Ramage	Meal Seller
	Mr Binnie	Cobbler
	James Wright	Wright
	Alex. Innes	Merchant
	Walter Ruddiman	Printer
	Mrs Cochrane	
	Mrs Marjoribanks	
	Mrs Ross	
	Robert Duncan	Trunkmaker
	Alex. Aitchison	Ale Seller
	Andrew Chapman	Meal Seller
	Duncan Buchan	
	Miss Duff	Merchant

LUCKENBOOTHS in High Street, from front of St Giles to Tolbooth at north-west corner of Parliament Close

2	(28)	John Schaw	
3		Robert Low	Goldsmith
		James Wemyss	Jeweller
		Alex. Aitchison	Jeweller
		John Clark	Jeweller
		Patrick Robertson	Jeweller
		Andrew Gibb	Ale Seller
		James Gilliland	Jeweller
		Kerr & Dempster	Jeweller
		Alex. Donaldson	Stationer
		Thomas Rannie	Merchant
		Alex. Wall	Vintner
		Wm. Hutton	Merchant
		Alex. Scott	
		Jean Sword	
		Mistress Blackwood	
		Isobel Aikman	Milliner, Ale Seller
		Reid & Chalmers	Merchants
		Anna Muschet & Co.	
		Angus Davie	Merchant
		Claud Inglis	Merchant (Linen)
		Alex. Edmonstone	Merchant
		Margaret Aikman	Milliner, Ale Seller
		Alex. Purvis	Merchant
		Mathew McAlister	Merchant
		Miss Barclay	
		Thos. Dundas & Co.	Merchants
		James Allan	Merchant
		McCoull & Watson	Merchants
		Wm. Baillie	Merchant
		Mrs Tait	Goldsmith

	Wm. Douglas	Merchant
	Wm. Cumming	Cordiner
	Brown & Hepburn	
	Jas. McKenzie	Goldsmith

BROWN'S LAND opposite Tolbooth (Lawnmarket South)

3	James Brown	Glover
	Alex. Menzies	Wigmaker
	Robert Wight	Baxter
	Charles King	Ale Seller
	James Stewart	Barber
	Alex. Leith	
	Jas. Ireland	Ale Seller
	Hugh Paterson	Tailor
	Mrs Elliott	
	Miss Balfour	
	James Anderson	Valet

LAWNMARKET at Bess Wynd
at McGowan's Land

2	(36)	Crawford of Jordanhill	W.S.
	(17)	John McGowan	W.S.
	(12)	William Millar	Ale Seller

BESS WYND

1	(10)	James Scott of Howden	W.S.
2	(13)	Mrs Smith	
	(22)	Mrs Inglis	
	(10)	William Brown	
	(13)	Crookbone	
	(14)	John Home	
3		Mrs Abercrombie	
		Morris West of Customs	
		George Livingstone	

LAWNMARKET

1	(26)	Charles Little	Lawnmarket Coffee House
2	(13)	Robert Syme	Vintner
3		William Dun	Merchant
		George Cunningham	Porter
		Haddington Warehouse	

FORRESTER'S WYND, including Swinton's Land, Sandiland's Land, Douglas Lane, Burn's Land, Gavinlock's Land, Foulis Land and Deuchar's Land
at Swinton's Land

1	(10)	David Boswall	Glazier
	(14)	Robert Wallace	
	(19)	Mrs Euphan Sinclair	
2	(12)	John Bryson	
	(14)	John Rutherford	Milliner
	(14)	John Russell	W.S
3		Mrs Shearer	
		Mrs Buchan	
		Mr Bruce	Printer
		Walter Scott	Baxter
		Thomas Murray	Baxter

at Sandiland's Land

1	(14)	Mrs Margaret Swinton	
2	)10)	Hugh Robertson	
3		James Aitchison	Merchant
		Mrs Seton	
		Thos. Paton	Bookbinder
		James Ogilvie	

FORRESTER'S WYND—*Continued*

THOS. MARTINE	Merchant
DAVID MILLAR	Ale Seller
JAMES TAIT	Wright
MRS CHRISTIE	
HUGH MOSMAN	Writer
MRS BROWN	
MRS MITCHELL	
MRS ROBERTSON	
MRS DONALDSON	
SAMUEL MCCORMACK	in Excise
MRS EDGAR	
MRS CUMMING	
DAVID WRIGHT	
WM. MITCHELL	Ale Seller
MRS CRAICH	
MRS BRUCE	
MRS GORDON	
MR MONRO	Cordiner
MRS HEPBURN	
WM. CHALMERS	Tailor
MRS GRAY	
THOMAS LEISHMAN	
ALEX. KELTIE	

at Douglas Lane

2 (12) MRS KERR
3   ALEX. HERRON — Cordiner
     MRS ABERNETHY
     EDWARD BURD
     DAVID ALSTONE — Glazier
     MRS RANNIE

at Burn's Land

1 (10) JAMES BURNS — Wright
  (12) MRS PRINGLE
2 (13) LADY JARDIN
  (12) MISS WEIR
3   THOMAS FORTUNE — Tanner
     MRS KELLIE
     ANDREW DOUGLAS
     ANDREW FORREST — Waulker
     MISS MONTGOMERY
     JOHN HOME — Schoolmaster

at Gavinlock's Land

1 (15) MR MCKENZIE
2 (14) LEONARD URQUHART — W.S.
  (14) EBENEZER OLIPHANT — Goldsmith
  (14) LADY WALKINGSHAW
  (14) MRS GRAHAME
  (14) JOHN GRANT
  (14) ROBERT BRUCE
  (14) DR MCKENZIE
  (17) JOHN GORDON
  (14) MRS GRANT
3   MRS YOUNG
     GEORGE RIGG — Merchant
     JAMES RONALDSON — Baxter
     MRS BARCLAY
     MRS MURRAY
     MISS BELCHES
     ARCHIBALD SINCLAIR
     ALEX. BAVERIDGE
     JOHN CRAWFORD — Ale Seller
     LADY STRATON
     JOHN HALLYBURTON — Merchant
     LADY PENELOPE CRICHTONE
     WILLIAM TAYLOR — Writer

at Foulis Land

2 (15) CHARLES JOHNSTON — Druggist

at Deuchar's Land

2 (15) MRS BLAND

LAWNMARKET, between Forrester's Wynd and Libberton's Wynd

1 (10) LADY DUNSTAFFNAGE
  (13) ANDREW DICKIE — Watchmaker
  (13) LADY ROTHIEMAY
  (11) LADY CAVERS KERR
  (16) BAILLIE HUGH HATHORN — Merchant
  (14) MRS ALLAN
2 (18) MR LOVEBONE
  (10) MRS THOMSON
  (10) JOHN CHISHOLM
3   JOHN PERRIE
     WIDOW WALKER
     MCCULLOCH & TOD — Merchants
     JOHN STIRLING — Merchant
     MISS HUNTER
     ROBERT MITCHELHILL — Merchant
     MISS GRAHAME
     MRS COCHRANE
     CHARLES DICKSON — Goldsmith
     JAMES WATSON — Candlemaker
     WIDOW LYLE

LIBBERTON'S WYND, including Bruce's Land, Thom's Land and Dickson's 2nd Land

1 (17) LORD BELHAVEN
2 (13) ARCHIBALD BOWIE — Shipping Agent
  (13) JOHN NISBET — Merchant
  (13) MR TROTTER
  (12) MESSRS GORDON & IRVINE
3   LADY PITFOUR HAY
     MRS ROBERTSON
     MR DRYSDALE — Excise Officer
     THOS. CLEMENT — Cordiner
     ROBERT STEWART — Ale Seller
     JOHN GORDON
     JAMES STEWART — Printer
     MRS BRAND
     RICHARD NEWTON
     LADY HENRIETTA CAMPBELL
     JAMES RUSSELL
     JAMES WILSON — Smith

at Bruce's Land

1 (23) MRS SEMPLE
2 (18) MRS GEDD
  (19) GEORGE TURNBULL OF DALLADIES — W.S.
  (19) LADY CHARTRIES
  (19) CHARLES GUTHRIE — Writer
3   FRANCIS MCKENZIE — Ale Seller
     PETER CUTHBERTSON
     MRS BLAND
     CHARLES STEWART — Conservator at Campvere
     JOHN MAXWELL

at Dickson's 2nd Land

1 (11) MRS STEWART
2 (10) JOHN WILLSON — Bonnetmaker
  (35) JOHN PRINGLE — W.S.
  (11) JAMES TAYLOR OF PITCAIRLIE — W.S.
  (12) JOHN MANUEL

LIBBERTON'S WYND—*Continued*
3   Mrs Burns
       Pennie Babie
       Dr McKenzie
       Mrs Finlay
       Mrs Beech

at Thom's Land
1 (29) Alex. Monro   Surgeon
  (11) Thomas Trotter jr.   Merchant
2 (11) John Stobie   Writer/Factor
  (28) Mr Grant
  (11) Walter Stewart
  (20) John Watson   Candlemaker
  (18) James Hallyburton   W.S.
  (13) George Pitcairn   Merchant
  (18) David Spence   Writer, Secretary
                              to Bank of Scotland

at Wardrop's Land and Burn's Land
2 (11) James Baillie
  (13) William Baillie
  (19) Mrs Fergus
  (11) Miss Finlay
  (13) Hendry Scrymgeour
  (13) Dr McKenzie
  (11) Martin Lindsay

GOSFORD'S CLOSE
2 (11) Mrs Murray
  (18) Lady Hall
  (30) Ronald Dunbar   W.S.
  (11) James Dalgleish   Merchant
A
3   John Hardy   Baxter
       Christian Seton   Ale Seller
       Mrs Bogle
       Mrs Mitchell   Merchant
       Robert Veitch   Merchant
       Wm. Scott   Ale Seller
       Walter Hogg   Merchant
       Lady Dean
       Mrs Couper
       Lady Anchorfield
       Alex. Fyfe   Ale Seller
       Mrs Hunter & Lauder
       John Bruce   Printer
       Anna Ronaldson   Merchant
       Mrs Lauder   Merchant
       David Syme   Merchant
       James Baveridge   Merchant
2 (17) James Gartshore
  (15) Mrs Douglas
  (14) Lady Nisbet
  (13) Alex. Donaldson

SEVENTH NEW WALL (7nw) BOUND covering south side of Cowgate from President's Close to Society

PRESIDENT'S CLOSE including Taylor's Land, Comiston's Land, Mirtle's Land and Ogilvie's Land
1 (15) Thos. Trotter   Brewer
  (12) Mary Lockhart
  (13) Lady Cavers Kerr
  (12) Andrew Lowrie   Precentor at New Kirk
  (12) Thomas Mirtle
2 (30) Alex. Kincaid   Bookseller
  (10) James Wright
  (10) Thos. Grahame   Brewer
  (14) Henry Bunkle
3   James Dow   Merchant
       James Smellie   Merchant
       Colin Campbell   Bookbinder
       John Hogg   Cork Cutter
       Harry McKenzie
       John Bell   Stabler
       Richard Pollock   Baxter
       Mrs Reid
       Mrs Reoch
       Mrs Wilkie
       Miss Lothian
       Mrs Watson
       Mr Nisbet   Manufacturer
       Hector Pillans   Baxter
       James Penny
       Mr Kerr   Writer
       Miss Lind
       Robert Dewar   Glazier
       David Oram   Writer
       Mrs Lyon
       Thos. Dunlop
       Wm. Cock   Cordiner
       Mrs Schaw
       Mrs Pringle
       Mrs Lawson
       George Mackie   Merchant
       Wm. Gardiner   Dyer
                              Bonnetmaker
       Alex. Davidson   Cordiner
       John Aitken
       Widow Ferguson

ARGYLLE SQUARE including Campbell's Buildings and Brewery
1 (18) Alex. Campbell   Brewer
  (29) Alan Whiteford   Merchant
  (22) Sir John Whiteford
2 (25) Thomas Hope   Brewer
  (10) James Baveridge   Merchant
  (10) Thos. Martin   Merchant
  (34) John Russell jr.
  (24) James Carmichael
  (45) Wauchope of Edminston
  (24) John Hepburn
3   George Millar
       George Campbell   Wright, Factor
       Thos. Drysdale   Stabler
       Wm. Arnistone   Bookbinder
       Mrs Hathorn
       Thos. Elphingstone
       Mr Somervail   Lint Merchant
       Mrs Shepherd

SOCIETY
       James Baxter   Meal Seller
       James Gilbert   Ale Seller
       Widow Yourstone
       Mrs Lyle
       Alex. Martin
       Wm. Reid   Tailor
       Mrs Downie
       Wm. Lowrie   Cutler
       Robt. Noble   Cordiner

SOCIETY—Continued

	Samuel Grahame	Bookbinder
	Mr Reid	Merchant
	Mr Gibson	Slater
	Jas. Meggat	Bookbinder
	Mr Purdie	Merchant
	Grahame, Samuel & John	Bookbinders
	Mrs Grahame	Wigmaker

at Sommervell's Land including Duncan's Land

1	(12)	John Wood	Bookbinder
	(12)	George Cowan	Wright
2	(11)	Wm. Ormiston	Coppersmith
3		Wm. Weir	Cordiner
		Mrs Braidwood	Candlemaker
		John Moir	Merchant
		James McKain	
		Thos. Murray	Skinner
		John Carnegie	Merchant
		Mrs Hamilton	
		John Wight	Dyer
		Wm. Callander	Ale Seller

Society including Scott's Close and Good Town's Land

1	(15)	Jean Cleghorn	Brewer
	(18)	Gavin Hamilton	Merchant
	(10)	Mrs Finlayson	
2	(21)	James Smallet of Bonhill	Advocate
	(11)	P. Lawson	Weaver
	(10)	D. Alves	
	(12)	Robt. Auld	
	(14)	John Brand	
3		John Ramage	Merchant
		James Drummond	
		Mrs Thomson	
		Widow Robertson	
		Alex. Leishman	Lint Dresser
		Mrs Dalgleish	

at Candlemaker Row East in Chalmer's Land

1	(32)	Wm. Chalmers	Merchant
	(10)	John Reid	Printer
3		John Biggar	Merchant

EIGHT BOUND, from Bank Close to the West Port

BANK CLOSE

1	(36)	Bank of Scotland	
2	(18)	Dr McKenzie	
3		Drummond & Austin	Surgeons
		George More	Merchant
		James Fyfe	

LAWNMARKET: Bank Close to Cullen's Close

1	(28)	Alex. Finlayson	Underlerk of Session
	(22)	Geo. Chalmers	Merchant
2	(24)		Post Office
	(19)	James Armour	W.S.
3		James Lorimer	W.S.
		John Craig	Clerk to Presbytery of Edinburgh
		George Home	Baxter
		Robert Veitch	Merchant
		Mrs Smith	
		Mrs Jackson	
		Lady Jean Napier	

CULLEN'S CLOSE

1	(13)	Francis Brodie	Wright

	(14)	Lady Liberton	
	(12)	Mrs Crichton	
2	(24)	John More	
	(22)	Mr Falconer	
	(11)	Wm. Gordon	Ale Seller
	(11)	James Rankine	Wright
3		Mr Watkins	
		Mrs Ann Gilmour	
		Mr McQueen	Schoolmaster
		Andrew Thomson	Tobacconist
		Lady Cunningham	
		Charles Howison	Wright
		Mr McKay	Ale Seller

LAWNMARKET at Fisher's Land

2	(14)	John Sinclair	Writer
	(18)	Charles Binning (Lord Binning)	Advocate
	(17)	John Callander	Merchant
	(27)	Robert Craigie	Lord President, Lords of Session
	(21)	John Davidson	Factor
	(24)	Adam Drummond	Surgeon
	(23)	Craigie of Kilgriston	
	(20)	Thomas Gibson	W.S.
	(11)	Lawrence Craigie	W.S.
3		Wm. Mein	Merchant
		Wm. Gray	Sootie Man
		John Neilsen	Ale Seller
		Alex. Duncan	Druggist
		Andrew Anderson	Merchant
		Jean Duncan	

ROYSTON'S CLOSE

	(24)	R. Stevenson	Doctor
2	(32)	Wm. Alexander	Merchant
	(35)	John Carmichael	Merchant
	(12)	Lady Philipshaugh	
3		Alex. Sutherland	Merchant
		Lady Henderson	
		Dr Fowles	
		George Riddle	Wright
		Alex. Smith	Baxter
		John Wallace	Ale Seller
		John Gordon	Merchant

LAWNMARKET: Royston's Close into West Bow East

1	(16)	Mrs McGill of Rankeillor	
2	(24)	Lord Haining	
	(24)	Archibald Stewart of Torrance	W.S.
	(16)	Mr Maxwell	
	(13)	George Chalmers	
3		Mrs Katie Hepburn	
		Andrew Cockburn	White Iron Smith
		Alex. Edmonstone	Merchant
		Mrs Wright	
		Deacon John Craig	Cordiner
		David Ogilvie	Ale Seller
		George Monro	
		Widow Anderson	

at Anderson's Close, including Anderson's first and second lands

1	(12)	Mr Burnet of Barns	
	(14)	Alexander Tait	Friendly Fire Insurance Co.

LAWNMARKET—Continued
	(14)	Mrs Erskine	
2	(18)	James Dundas	
	(13)	Mrs Elphinstone	
	(10)	Mr Marishall	
	(14)	Robt. McFarlane	Insurance Agent
	(15)	Mrs Monro	
3		Alex. Anderson	Coppersmith
		Wm. Willson	Cordiner
		John Stewart	Merchant
		Mrs Ramsay	
		Mrs Ferguson	
		Mr Brown	Writer
		Robert Selkirk	Merchant
		Robert Cleugh	Merchant
		Miss Paton	
		Mrs Smellie	
		Mr Eason	Gauger

at Sideserf's Land
1	(11)	James Forrester	(Writer)
2	(12)	Mrs Sideserf	
	(14)	Miss Bland	
3		John Mill	
		James Ferguson	Coppersmith
		John Dalgleish	Skinner
		John Adam	

GRASSMARKET East End into Cowgate (North)
at Ranie's Land
1	(11)	Andrew Hamilton	Merchant
2	(11)	Mrs Young	
3		Mrs Murray	
		Andrew Rannie	Merchant
		David Cunningham	Baxter
		Mr Hamilton	Merchant
		Lady Killiecranky	

at Dewar's Land
1	(11)	Mrs Stewart	
2	(11)	Mr Forrest of Comiston	
	(11)	Mr Wallace	
3		Wm. McConachie	Linen Merchant
		Lady Comiston	

COWGATE HEAD, north side heading east
at Stark's Land
2	(10)	James Craig	
3		Mr Hunter	Pewterer
		John Stewart	Wigmaker
		Thomas Herriote	Ale Seller
		Mrs Gardiner	
		Jenet Turnbull	
		John Hamilton	Cordiner
		Widow Bennet	
		George McLean	
		Miss Welsh	
		Jean Taylor	
		Thos. Murray	Baxter
		Alex. Willson	Merchant
		Robert Anderson	Merchant
		John Kidd	Merchant

at back of Anderson's Close in MacLenan's Land
1	(16)	Dr Murray	
	(16)	Mrs Kidd	
	(14)	John Sievewright esq.	
	(16)	James Dewar of Vogrie	
	(16)	Andrew Hay	

2	(14)	Mr Murray of Cringelly	
	(17)	David Inglis	
	(19)	Alex. Chalmers	Writer
3		Robert Thomson	Merchant
		John Allan	Baxter
		David Murray	Stabler
		Wm. Grahame	Saddler
		Mr Mitchell	Cordiner
		John Bell	Stabler
		Mr Dick	Hair Merchant

at Scott's Land
1	(19)	Alexander Scott	
	(14)	William Neilsen	Merchant
2	(10)	John Nisbet	
	(17)	Walter Begbie	
3		Mrs Tait	Ale Seller
		Mathew Brown	Merchant
		Charles Begbie	Stabler

at Baillie's Land
1	(14)	Lady Murray of Broughton	
	(15)	Mrs Ferguson	
2	(14)	John Thomson	
3		John Younger	Merchant
		John Young	Horse Hirer

at foot of Royston's Close
Mrs Geddes	
Mrs Cheeslie (Selkrig)	
Robert Selkirk	Merchant
Christian Stocks	
John McNiven	Merchant
Mrs Law	
Lady Braehead	
Mrs Mollison	
Mrs Cochrane	
Mistress Hay	
Alex. Harley	Merchant
John Martin	

COWGATE HEAD South Side heading west from entry at The Excise Office
at Hallyburton's Land
2	(14)	Patrick Spark	
	(13)	Alex. McConachie	
	(14)	Alex. Young	Writer
3		James White	Wigmaker
		John Cleghorn	
		Baillie James Flint	Merchant
		John Whitsunday	Cooper
		Jas. Gordon	
		Jas. Thomson	Tobacconist
		Peter Cobzier	in Excise
		Wm. Begg	Gauger

at Merchant's Entry and Hammermen's Land [Magdalen Chapel]

WIGHT'S LAND
1	(103)	Excise Office	
	(16)	Alex. Alison	
2	(11)	James Wight	Dyer
	(10)	Alex. Elliot	Baxter
	(11)	William Gray	Printer
	(11)	Thomas Scott	
3		Robert Torrence	Baxter
		James Robertson	Waiter
		James Young	Bookbinder
		Widow Ross	
		John Robertson	

WIGHT'S LAND—Continued

	Mrs Margaret Osburn	
	David Lesslie	Meal Seller
	Mr Gray	Ale Seller
	Charles Banks	Stabler
	Mrs Crawford	
	Alex. Thomson	Gunsmith
	Lady Harwood	
	Samuel Ramsay	Stabler
	Mrs Wardrew	
	James Grahame	Confectioner
	Margaret Lochere	
	David Murray	Merchant
	John Sword	Merchant
	Agnes Lithgow	Sells Grass
	Jerome Butter	Druggist
	Charles Lawrence	
	James Shanks	Spirit Seller
	Charles Hamilton	Stabler

CANDLEMAKER ROW, West

1	(19)	James Boggie	Stabler
	(19)	Thomas Gifford	Smith
3		Jas. Murray	Ale Seller
		Mrs Murray	
		Mary Robertson	
		Charles Campbell	Horse Hirer
		Alex. McGrigor	
		John Rattray	
		Margaret Nicoll	Ale Seller
		Thomas Fraser	
		Mrs Rankine	

at Stewart's Land

1	(17)	Mrs Coulter	Pewterer
3		Peter Young	Ale Seller
		Mrs Dick	
		Thos. Anderson	Saddler
		Mr Nimmo	Lint Dresser
		Jas. Martin's children	
		John Dale	Wigmaker
		Andrew Hutton jr.	Brewer
		Alex. Williamson	Stabler
		Robert Stewart	Meal Merchant
		Jean Neilsen	
		Mr Drummond	of Excise
		John Grahame	Printer
3		Thos. Irvine	Stabler
		Mrs Thomson	Room Setter
		James Russell	Merchant
		Patrick Fyfe	Stabler
		James McNeill	Distiller
		Thos. Lethem	Smith
		Wm. Dickson	Dyer
		Alex. Williamson	
		Mrs Grant or David Bruce	
		Thomas Cumming	Dyer
		James Gardiner	Smith
		Mr Spence	Cordiner

GRASSMARKET SOUTH going west

		Mrs Thomson	Baxter
		David Farras	
		John Lawrie	Flesher
		George Tod	Cordiner
		Alex Anderson	Coppersmith
		Mr Cranstone of Dewar	
		James Stewart	
		Adam Anderson	Candlemaker
		Dr James Russell	
		James Spence	

at Hay's Land

1	(11)	Robert Montgomery	Brewer
3		Mr McPherson	
		Mrs Porteous	Mantua Maker

FLINT'S LAND to Heriot's Bridge at back of Muse Well

1	(14)	Thomas Goldie	Carrier
	(12)	William Tunnock	Brewer
2	(15)	James Flint	
	(14)	David Waddel	
	(27)	George Douglas	Farmer
	(18)	James Stevenson	Minister
	(10)	Wm. Chalmers	Writer
3		Mrs Wotherspoon	Merchant
		Convener Somervail	Skinner
		Mr Copeland	Writer
		Mrs Gairns	

at Hamilton's Land

1	(11)	William Rannie	Stabler
	(20)	William Hamilton	Merchant Brewer
3		James Young	Hair Merchant
		Andrew Johnstone	Stabler
		David Somervail	Merchant

at Bruce's Land

1	(15)	Archibald Campbell	Brewer
2	(16)	Mrs Gibson	
3		Mrs Bruce	
		James Kirkland	Merchant
		Robert Bruntone	Merchant

at Thomson's Land

2	(12)	Walter Murray	
3		Charles Fisher	Merchant
		James Gibson	
		William Black	Stabler

at Cleghorn's Land

1	(14)	Bartholomew Bell	Brewer
	(11)	Adam Cleghorn	Merchant
	(11)	John Bowie	Stabler
	(11)	Charles Brown	Stabler
3		Mrs Lethem	Baxter
		Robert Keltie	Merchant
		James Ewart	Accomptant
		Mr Cairns	Flesher
		Mrs Piper	

at Campbell's Land

1	(10)	Hugh Francis	
	(10)	John Wardrop	

TRADE DIRECTORY

(a) A-Z

(b) Apprentices and Masters

TRADE DIRECTORY

(a) A-Z

ACCOMPTANTS	: see Writers	JEWELLERS	: see Goldsmiths
ADVOCATES	: ,, ,,		
ALE SELLERS	:	LIMNERS	: see Painters
APOTHECARIES	: see Druggists	LINT DRESSERS	: see Waulkers
ARMOURERS	: see Smiths	LODGING HOUSES	:
Auction and Sale Rooms	:		
		MANTUA MAKERS	: see Milliners
BARBERS	: see Wigmakers	MANUFACTURERS	: see Wrights
BAXTERS	:	MASONS	: see Wrights
BILLIARD TABLES	: See Wrights	MEAL SELLERS	:
BONNETMAKERS	:	MERCHANTS:	
BOOKBINDERS	: see Booksellers	MIDWIVES	: see Doctors
BOOKSELLERS	:	MILLINERS	:
BREWERS	:	MUSICAL INSTRUMENTS: see Musicians	
BRUSHMAKERS	: see Wrights	MUSICIANS	:
BUCKLEMAKERS	: ,, ,,		
		OPTICIANS	:
CANDLEMAKERS	:		
CARRIERS	: see Stablers	PAINTERS	:
CHAIR MEN	:	PEWTERERS	: see Hammermen
CLERKS	: see Writers	PLUMBERS	: see Wrights
COACHMAKERS	: see Wrights	PORTERS	: see Stablers
COBBLERS	: see Cordiners	POULTRYMEN	: see Fleshers
COFFEE HOUSES	:	PRINTERS	: see Booksellers
COOPERS	: see Brewers		
COPPERSMITHS	: see Hammermen	ROOMSETTERS	: see Lodging Houses
CORDINERS	:	SADDLERS	:
CORK CUTTERS	: see Brewers	SEEDSMEN	:
COWFEEDERS	: see Stablers	SERVANTS	:
CUSTOMS	: see Excise	SHOEMAKERS	: see Cordiners
CUTLERS	: see Hammermen	SKINNERS	:
		SMITHS	:
DISTILLERS	: see Brewers	SPIRIT MERCHANTS	: see Vintners
DOCTORS:		STABLERS	:
DRUGGISTS	:	STATIONERS	: see Booksellers
DYERS	:	SURGEONS	: see Doctors
ENGRAVERS	: see Wrights	TAVERNS	: see Vintners
EXCISE	:	TAYLORS	:
		TEACHERS	:
FARRIERS	: see Stablers	TOBACCONISTS	:
FLESHERS	:	TRUNK MAKERS	:
FRUITERERS	:	TURNERS	:
FUNERAL UNDERTAKERS: see Upholsterers			
FURRIERS	: see Skinners	UNIVERSITY	:
		UPHOLSTERERS	:
GILDERS	: see Wrights		
GLAZIERS	: see Wrights	VINTNERS	:
GLOVERS	: see Skinners		
GOLDSMITHS	:	WATCHMAKERS	:
GRASS SELLERS	:see Stablers	WAULKERS	:
GROCERS	:	WEAVERS	: see Websters
GUNSMITHS	: see Smiths	WEBSTERS	:
		WHEELWRIGHTS	: see Wrights
HABERDASHERS	: see Milliners	WHIPMAKERS	: see Wrights
HAMMERMEN	:	WIGMAKERS	:
HATTERS	: see Waulkers	WRIGHTS :	
HORSE HIRERS	: see Stablers	WRITERS	:
HOSIERS	: see Milliners		

85

ALE SELLERS

Aikman,	Isobel	Milliner	**Hutton,**	Alexander	
Aikman,	Margaret	Milliner	**Hutton,**	Mary	Grocer
Aitchison,	Alexander		**Ireland,**	James	
Aitken,	Mrs		**Jameson,**	James	
Allan,	James		**Jameson,**	Robert	
Anderson,	William		**Jones,**	Jonathan	
Angus,	Peter		**King,**	Charles	
Baird,	James		**Law,**	David	
Baird,	John		**Lawrence,**	Simon	
Bake,	Mrs		**Lees,**	Robert	
Balfour,	Mrs	Grocer	**Leitch,**	Isobel	Grocer
Barr,	Robert	Stabler	**Linton,**	John	Cowfeeder
Boggie,	James	Stabler	**McCarter,**	Mr	Excise
Brown,	David		**McCulloch,**	Wm.	Grocer
Brown,	Patrick		**McFarlane,**	And.	Stabler
Brown,	Widow		**McGlashan,**	James	
Brymer,	James		**McGrigor,**	Hugh	
Buchan,	Andrew	Gentleman's Servant	**McIntosh,**	John	Grocer
			McIntosh,	John	Staymaker
Callander,	William		**McIntosh,**	William	
Campbell,	Archibald		**McKay,**	Mr	
Campbell,	David		**McKat,**	Thomas	
Campbell,	Duncan	Dyester	**McKenzie,**	Francis	
Campbell,	Hugh	Grocer	**McClean,**	Duncan	
Campbell,	John		**McClean,**	William	
Carmichael,	James		**McPherson,**	John	Grocer
Clark,	Alexander		**Mack,**	Daniel	
Clark,	Alexander	Stabler	**Marshall,**	Mr	
Clark,	David	Wigmaker	**Martin,**	George	
Cleghorn,	Mrs	Brewer	**Mason,**	Miss	
Cowie,	Patrick		**Mathison,**	Patrick	
Cranstone,	James	Grocer	**Mellis,**	John	Flesher
Crawford,	John		**Michie,**	Thomas	
Cuddie,	Robert		**Millar,**	David	
Douglas,	Robert		**Millar,**	William	
Drummond,	Mrs		**Mitchel,**	William	
Elder,	Betty		**Monro,**	John	
Ezat,	Neil		**Morrison,**	John	Wigmaker
Falconer,	George		**Morrison,**	Mrs	Grocer
Fisher,	Isobel		**Mouatt,**	John	Cowfeeder
Forbes,	John		**Muir,**	John	
Fotheringham,	Isobel	Merchant	**Muir,**	William	Stabler
Fowler,	James		**Murray,**	James	
Fowles,	William		**Mutter,**	Elionora	Grocer
Fraser,	Hugh		**Mylne,**	Patrick	
Fraser,	John		**Mylne,**	William	
Fyfe,	Alexander		**Napier,**	Robert	
Galloway,	Alex.	Stabler	**Neilsen,**	James	
Gardiner,	Fanny	Vintner	**Neilsen,**	John	
Garroch,	John		**Nicoll,**	Margaret	Grocer
Gibb,	Andrew		**Nimmo,**	James	
Gilbert,	James	Cowfeeder	**Ogilvie,**	David	Grocer
Goldie,	Thomas	Carrier	**Paul,**	Alexander	Stabler
Gordon,	William		**Peddie,**	Thomas	
Gray,	Mr		**Polson,**	John	
Hackney,	David		**Purvis,**	William	
Hardie,	Mrs		**Reid,**	William	
Hastie,	George		**Reoch,**	James	
Henderson,	Miss	Merchant	**Robertson,**	Andrew	
Herriot,	Mrs		**Robertson,**	Patrick	
Herriot,	Thomas		**Ronalds,**	William	
Howboise,	Mr	Vintner	**Ronaldson,**	Anna	Grocer
Hunter,	Robert		**Ross,**	Alexander	

ALE SELLERS—Continued

Ross,	Mrs	
Rutherford,	Mrs	
Sandilands,	Mrs	
Scott,	William	
Seton,	Christian	Grocer
Shanks,	James	Spirit Merchant
Shiels,	Alexander	
Simpson,	Mrs	Grocer
Sinclair,	Angus	
Skelton,	John	
Smart,	George	
Smith,	John	Saddler
Spence,	Mrs	Grocer
Stewart,	Alexander	Grocer
Stewart,	Hugh	Gentleman's Servant
Stewart,	James	
Stewart,	Kathrine	Grocer
Stewart,	Robert	
Stewart,	William	
Stirling,	Anne	Grocer
Swan,	Robert	
Sword,	Jean	Grocer
Syme,	William	
Tait,	Mrs	Grocer
Taylor,	Mrs	
Thomson,	Alex.	Grocer
Thomson,	David	
Toshock,	Andrew	
Turnbull,	Jenet	
Tyrie,	Alexander	
Vasey,	Agnes	
Wallace,	John	
Watson,	William	
Weir,	William	
Williamson,	Alex.	
Wylie,	Robert	
Young,	Charles	
Young,	James	
Young,	Peter	

AUCTION AND SALE ROOMS

Auction Rooms

Lawnmarket in Old Bank Close : James Miller's
High Street opposite Crown-well : Mr Gibson's
Hunter's Hall above Forrester's Wynd
Merchiston's Land below Blackfriar's : "Golden Fan"
Writer's Court North

Sale Rooms

Carruber's Close in Butter's Land
High : North Side opposite Tolbooth
Street : "at the sign of The Pelican."
: Back of the Cross-well.
: Second entry in Bull's Close.
: First Laigh Shop above Cap and Feather Close.
: Mary King's Close; second Turnpike down Close.
West Bow Foot; North Side
"at the sign of the Red Lion."

BAXTERS

Allan,	John	
Allan,	Robert	
Allan,	Robert	
Begbie,	George	
Bell,	John	Constable
Boyd,	Alexander	
Brown,	David	
Clarkson,	John	
Clarkson,	Thomas	
Clarkson,	Thomas	
Cleghorn,	James	
Colville,	Walter	
Craig,	James	
Crawford,	Alex.	
Crooks,	William	
Cunningham,	Chas.	
Cunningham,	David	
Elliott,	Alexander	
Haiggs,	William	
Hardie,	Andrew	Constable
Hardie,	Henry	Deacon
Hay,	Thomas	
Hedderwick,	Thos.	
Hodge,	William	
Home,	George	
Home,	George jr.	
Keir,	Adam	
Keir,	William	Deacon
Lethem,	Mrs	
Murray,	Adam	Constable
Murray,	Thomas	
Murray,	Thomas	
Nicoll,	John	
Orr,	Mr	Lodging House
Pillans,	Hector	
Punton,	Archibald	
Ronaldson,	James	
Ronaldson,	John	
Scott,	Walter	Constable
Smith,	Alexander	
Symington,	John	
Thomson,	Mrs	
Turnbull,	John	
Waugh,	Gavin	
Wight,	David	
Wight,	Robert	Deacon
Wight,	William	
Wight,	William	

BONNETMAKERS

Brandon,	Charles	
Cumming,	Thomas	
Duncan,	Henry	
Gardiner,	William	
Willson,	John	Dyer
Willson,	John	

BOOKBINDERS: See Booksellers

BOOKSELLERS
Including BOOKBINDERS, PRINTERS, STATIONERS

Aitken,	John	Stationer
Arnistone,	William	Bookbinder
Baillie,	John	Bookbinder
Baillie,	John	
Balfour,	John	Stationer
Balfour,	John	
Ballantyne,	William	Printer
Brown,	James	
Brown,	Mrs	
Buchanan,	John	Printer
Campbell,	Colin	Bookbinder
Cheyne,	William	Printer
Cochrane, James & Co.	Printers	
Crawford,	Gideon	
Davidson,	James	Printer
Dinning,	Alexander	Stationer
Donaldson,	Alex.	Stationer
Drummond & Co.		
Fleming,	George	Printers &
Fleming,	Robert	Publishers
Gordon,	William	
Gordon,	William	
Grahame,	John	Printer
Grahame,	Samuel	Bookbinder
Gray,	William	Printer
Hamilton & Balfour		
Hamilton,	William	
Hay,	George	Printer
Hunter,	Lauchlan	
Kincaid,	Alexander	
Kincaid & Donaldson		
Meggat,	James	Bookbinder
Millar,	David	Printer
Miller,	William	
More,	John	Bookbinder
Murray,	Alexander	Printer
Nimmo,	Richard	Stationer
Orr,	John	
Paton,	John	
Paton,	Thomas	Bookbinder
Peters,	Mr	Printer
Richardson,	Arch.	Bookbinder
Ross,	John	Stationer
Ruddiman, Bros.	Print. & Publish.	
Sanders,	Mr	Printer
Sands,	William	
Scotland,	John	Bookbinder
Smeiton,	Alex.	Bookbinder
Stewart,	James	Printer
Stewart,	John	
Trail,	John	
Watkins,	Adam	Printer to H.M.
Wood,	John	Bookbinder
Wright,	Charles	
Yair,	John	
Young,	James	Bookbinder

BREWERS
Including COOPERS, CORKCUTTERS & DISTILLERS

Bell,	Bartholomew	
Bell,	Messrs	
Binnie,	John	
Brown,	John	Cork Cutter
Bruce,	Mr	
Campbell,	Alex.	
Campbell,	Arch.	
Cleghorn,	Mrs	Ale Seller
Craw,	James	
Dick,	James	
Finlay,	Robert	
Galloway,	Mrs	Cork Cutter
Gilchrist,	Robt.	Cooper
Hamilton,	Wm.	Baillie
Hogg,	George	
Hogg,	John	Cork Cutter
Hope,	Thomas	
Hutton,	Andrew jr.	
Kennedy,	Robert	Cooper
McKenzie,	John	Cork Cutter
McNeill,	James	Distiller
Montgomery,	Robt.	Baillie
Myles,	Alexander	
Paterson,	Robert	
Rochead,	James	Baillie: Distiller
Stewart,	John	Cooper
Sutherland,	Wm.	
Syme,	Andrew	
Trotter,	John	
Trotter,	Thomas	
Tunnock,	William	
Whitsunday,	John	Cooper
Wright,	John	Distiller

CANDLEMAKERS

Anderson,	Adam
Braidwood,	Mrs
Braidwood,	Wm.
Gardiner,	William
Herriot,	John
Murray,	James
Noble,	Alexander
Scott,	John
Sprott,	John
Stevenson,	Alex
Watson,	James
Webster,	John

CARRIERS; See Stablers

CHAIRMEN

Cowie,	Mr
Drummond,	John
Fenwick,	John

CHAIRMEN—*Continued*

Lyle,	Alexander
Reid,	Thomas
Thomas,	William
Robertson,	John
Schaw,	Henry
Strachan,	John

CLERKS	: See Writers
COACHMAKERS	: See Wrights
COBBLERS	: See Cordiners
COFFEE HOUSES	: See Vintners
COOPERS	: See Brewers
COPPERSMITHS	: See Hammerman

CORDINERS
Including: COBBLERS, SHOEMAKERS

Aitkenhead,	Jas.	
Anderson,	Hendry	
Berry,	David	Cobbler
Binnie,	Mr	Cobbler
Callander,	Andrew	
Christie,	Mr	
Clement,	Thomas	
Cock,	William	
Cumming,	William	
Davidson,	Alex.	
Dawson,	John	
Dick,	Mrs Thos.	
Drysdale,	Joseph	
Drysdale,	Mr	
Elder,	John	Shoemaker
Gibson,	Archibald	†.15.10.52
Gray,	John	
Hamilton,	John	
Hamilton,	John	
Hart,	Orlando	
Herriot,	John	
Herron,	Alexander	
McClachlane,	Duncan	
MCoull,	John	
Maitland,	Obrian	Shoemaker
Mitchell,	Mr	
Monro,	Mr	
Murray,	George	
Nicoll,	George	
Noble,	Robert	
Pale,	Mr	Cobbler
Park,	John	Shoemaker
Penman,	George	
Ronaldson,	Steph.	
Spence,	Mr	
Strachan,	Patrick	
Tod,	George	
Weir,	William	
Wight,	George	Shoemaker

CORK CUTTERS	: See Brewers
COWFEEDERS	: See Stablers
CUSTOMS	: See Excise
CUTLERS	: See Hammermen
DISTILLERS	: See Brewers

DOCTORS
Including MIDWIVES & SURGEONS

Austin,	Adam	
Baird,	Dr	
Boswell,	John	
Brodie,	James	Surgeon
Bruce,	Alexander	Surgeon
Bruce,	Alexander	Surgeon
Chalmers,	William	Surgeon
Congleton,	Charles	Surgeon
Cunningham,	George	Surgeon
Dallas,	Thomas	Surgeon
Douglas,	John	Surgeon
Drummond & Austain		Surgeons
Dundas,	Dr	
Eccles,	Martin	Surgeon
Elliot,	Dr	
Farquharson,	Walter	
Ferguson,	Dr	
Fowles,	Dr	
Hamilton,	Dr	
Hay,	Dr	
Horseburgh,	Wm.	
Johnstone,	Mr	Surgeon
Kennedy,	John	Surgeon
Kinneir,	Dr	
Lauder,	George	Surgeon
Lind,	James	
McFarlane,	Dr	
McKenzie,	Dr	
Martin,	Dr	
Mill,	Mrs	Midwife
Mitchel,	Dr	
Monro,	Alexander	Surgeon
Murray,	Dr	
Ogilvie,	Mrs	Midwife
Plummer,	Dr	
Porterfield,	Dr	
Rae,	James	Surgeon
Rattray,	John	Surgeon
Russell,	Francis	Surgeon
Russell,	James	Surgeon
Russell,	James	Surgeon
Rutherford,	John	
Sinclair,	Dr	
Smith,	Robert	Surgeon
Smith,	Robert	Surgeon
Smith,	William	
Stevenson,	Dr	
Stevenson,	George	Physician
Sraton,	John	Surgeon
Taylor,	Dr	
Walker,	Robert	Surgeon
Wallace,	John	Surgeon

DOCTORS—Continued

WALTER,	Robert	Surgeon
WHITE,	Robert	
WOOD,	William	Surgeon
YOUNG,	George	
YOUNG,	John	Surgeon
YOUNG,	Mr	Midwifery Teacher
YOUNG,	Thomas	Surgeon

DRUGGISTS
Including APOTHECARIES

BULLER,	Jerome	
DUNCAN,	Alexander	
HUNTER,	John	Apothecary
INGLIS,	Edward	
JOHNSTONE,	Chas.	
LAWRIE,	Gilbert	Councillor
MACDONALD,	Duncan	
MERCER,	William	Apothecary
MURRAY,	John	
PURDIE,	George	
SCOTT,	James	
STIRLING,	Mrs	

DYERS

ALEXANDER,	James	
CAMPBELL,	Duncan	Ale Seller
DALLAS,	Alexander	
DICKSON,	William	
FOY,	Dennis	
GEDD,	Robert	
GEDD,	Robert	
GORDON,	James	
WATSON,	James	
WIGHT,	James	
WIGHT,	John	
WILLSON,	John	Bonnetmaker

EXCISE
Including CUSTOMS

ALSTONE,	Mr	Gauger
BEGG,	William	Gauger
BLAIR,	Mr	
BROWN,	Mr	Gauger
CAMPBELL,	Charles	Gauger
COBZIER,	Peter	
COSSOR,	Walter	Deputy Comptroller
DRUMMOND,	George	Commissioner
DRUMMOND,	Mr	
DRYSDALE,	Mr	
EASON,	James	Gauger
COWIE,	Mr	Waiter
GAIRNS,	Robert	Waiter
MCCARTER,	Mr	Ale Seller: Gauger
MCCORMACK,	Sam.	
RAMAGE,	John	Port Waiter
ROBERTSON,	Mr	Gauger
SMITH,	John	
SOMERVAIL,	Alex.	Port Surveyor
UDNY,	Alexander	Commissioner
WATSON,	William	
WEDDERBURN,	Peter	Customs Commissioner
YOUNG,	Mr	Gauger
ROBERTSON,	James	Waiter

FISHMONGERS

GODSMAN,	John
RITCHIE,	George

FLESHERS
Including POULTRYMEN

BLACK,	John	Poultryman
BROWN,	Nicol	
CAIRNS,	Mr	
CUMMING,	Thomas	
GEDDES,	William	Poultryman
GIBSON,	Hendry	
GILCHRIST,	David	
GREIG,	Andrew	
GILCHRIST,	John	
GREIG,	Andrew	
GREIG,	John	
JOHSTONE,	Mrs	
MCLEAN,	Allan	
MELLIS,	George	
MELLIS,	John	Ale Seller
ROBERTSON,	Charles	
ROBERTSON,	James	Poultryman
ROBERTSON,	Thomas	
ROSS,	Mr	
SQUIRE,	James	
SQUIRE,	John	
TENNANT,	Francis	
WATSON,	John	Poultryman
WATSON,	John	Poultryman
WATSON,	Mrs	Poultry-woman
WILLIAMSON,	James	
WILLIAMSON,	Mrs	
WILLSON,	John	

FRUITERERS

CRAWFORD,	John

FUNERAL UNDERTAKERS	: See Upholsterers
FURRIERS	: See Skinners
GILDERS	: See Wrights
GLAZIERS	: See Wrights
GLOVERS	: See Skinners

GOLDSMITHS
Including JEWELLERS

Aitchison,	Alex.	Jeweller
Ayton,	William	
Blair,	Charles	
Clark,	John	Jeweller
Dave,	William	
Dempster,	William	
Finlay,	Francis	
Gedd,	Dougal	
Gilchrist,	William	
Gilliland,	James	Jeweller
Gordon,	Robert	
Kerr Dempster		Jewellers
Lothian,	Edward	
Low,	Robert	
McDuff,	Robert	
McKenzie,	James	
Mitcell,	Thomas	Jeweller
Mitchelson,	James	
Murray,	Patrick jr.	
Oliphant,	Ebenezer	
Penman,	Hugh	
Robertson,	Patrick	Jeweller
Stuart & Wallace		
Tait,	Mrs	
Taylor,	William	
Ure,	Deacon	
Welsh,	James	
Welsh,	John	
Wemyss,	James	Jeweller

GRASS SELLERS: See Stablers

GROCERS

Anderson,	John	
Balfour,	Mrs	Ale Seller
Baverly,	Elspet	
Campbell,	Hugh	Ale Seller
Clark,	James	
Cranstone,	James	Ale Seller
Douglas,	Andrew	
Hutton,	Mary	Ale Seller
Leitch,	Isobel	Ale Seller
McCulloch,	William	Ale Seller
McEwan,	Mrs	Ale Seller
McHardie,	John	
McIntosh,	John	Ale Seller
McKechnie,	Jas.	
McKechnie,	Alex.	Vintner
McMichan,	John	
McPherson,	John	Ale Seller
Mayelstone,	Chas.	
Morrison,	Mrs	Ale Seller
Mutter,	Elionora	Ale seller
Nicoll,	Margaret	Ale Seller
Ogilvie,	David	Ale Seller
Paterson,	David	
Rigg,	George	
Ronaldson,	Anna	Ale seller
Seton,	Christian	Ale Seller
Simpson,	Mrs	Ale Seller
Spence,	Mrs	Ale Seller
Stewart,	Alex.	Ale seller
Stewart,	Kathrine	Ale Seller
Stirling,	Ann	Ale Seller
Sword,	Jean	Ale Seller
Tait,	Mrs	Ale Seller
Thomson,	Alexander	

HABERDASHERS: See Milliners

HAMMERMEN
Including: COPPERSMITHS, CUTLERS, PEWTERERS

Anderson,	Adam	
Armstrong,	William	Coppersmith
Auchenleck,	Gilbert	Cutler
Auchenleck,	James	
Baillie,	John	Coppersmith
Cockburn,	Andrew	
Coulter,	Mrs	Pewterer
Drummond,	George	White-Iron Smith
Ferguson,	James	Coppersmith
Gardiner,	James	
Gifford,	Thomas	
Hunter,	Mr	Pewterer
Inglis,	Archibld	Pewterer
Kinneir,	Andrew	Pewterer
Lawrie,	William	Cutler
McKay,	James	Coppersmith
Miln,	John	
Rankine,	Andrew	Coppersmith
Simpson,	Thomas	
Yourstone,	James	Cutler

HATTERS	: See Waulkers
HORSE HIRERS	: See Stablers
HOSIERS	: See Milliners
JEWELLERS	: See Goldsmiths
LIMNERS	: See Painters
LINT DRESSERS	: See Waulkers

LODGING HOUSES (Room Setters)

Anderson,	Mrs
Cowan,	Mrs
Craw,	Mrs
Cumming,	Mrs
Ewing,	Mrs
Forbes,	William
Forrester,	Barbara
Fraser,	Robert
Greenlees,	Mrs
Guthrie,	Mrs
Hay,	Mrs
Jameson,	John
McPherson,	Duncan
Maitland,	Mrs

LODGING HOUSES—Continued

Moffat,	William	
Murray,	Mrs	
Ogston,	Mrs	
Orr,	Mr	Baxter
Ramsay,	Mrs	
Rannie,	Mrs	
Robertson,	Mrs	
Sanders,	Mrs	
Stirling,	John	
Turnbull,	Mrs	
Urquhart,	Barbara	
Warden,	George	
Young,	John	

MANTUA MAKERS	: See Milliners
MASONS	: See Wrights

MEAL SELLERS

Baxter,	James
Chapman,	Andrew
Lesslie,	David
Ramage,	James
Stewart,	Robert
Young,	Robert

MERCHANTS

Aikman,	Mr
Aitchison,	James
Aitkenhead,	James
Aiton,	William
Alexander,	Mr
Alexander,	William
Alison,	Alexander
Alison,	Andrew
Allan,	Andrew
Allan,	James
Allan,	James
Allan,	Robert
Anderson,	Andrew
Anderson,	Helen
Anderson,	Robert
Angus,	Archibald
Angus,	Archibald
Angus,	David
Angus,	Mary
Arbuthnot,	Scot
Arbuthnot,	Alexander
Arbuthnot,	George
Arbuthnot,	Robert
Arbuthnot,	Robert
Bailie, & Seton & Houston	
Baillie,	James
Baillie,	James
Baillie,	Robert
Baillie,	William
Baird,	David
Balfour,	Helen
Balfour,	James
Bannatyne,	Maitland
Barclay,	Miss
Bartram & Williamson	
Baveridge,	James
Begg,	Allan
Biggar,	John
Black,	John
Blackwood,	Robert
Boid,	George
Bonnar,	Andrew
Boswall,	David
Bowie,	Archibald
Bowie,	Patrick
Boyd,	Robert
Brand,	John
Brown & Hepburn	
Brown, James & Co	
Brown,	Mathew
Brown,	Mrs & Son
Brown,	Miss
Brown,	Robert
Brown,	William
Bruce,	Alexander
Bruce,	William
Bruce,	William jr.
Bruntone,	Robert
Bryson,	John
Buchan,	Andrew
Burd,	Edward
Burnet,	William
Burns & Finlayson	
Butter,	Charles
Cairns,	Mrs
Caithness,	Edward
Calder,	Thomas
Callander & Hamilton	
Campbell,	Archibald
Campbell,	Colin
Campbell,	Duncan
Cargill,	James
Carmichael,	John
Carnegie,	John
Carnegie,	John
Chalmers,	William
Cheap,	William
Cheyne,	Charles
Chisholm,	John
Christie,	John
Clapperton,	William
Clark,	George
Clark,	George
Clarkson,	John
Cleghorn & Livingston	
Cleghorn,	Adam
Clerk, Stevenson & Co.	
Cleugh,	Robert
Cochrane & Hamilton	
Coutts, Trotter & Co.	
Coutts,	James
Coutts,	John
Craig,	Charles
Crawford,	Peter
Crichton, Patrick & Co.	
Crichton,	Patrick

MERCHANTS—Continued

CROCKETT,	Thomas
CUMMING,	William
DALGLEISH,	James
DALRYMPLE,	John
DAVIDSON,	Elizabeth
DAVIDSON,	John
DAVIE,	Angus
DEWAR,	William
DICK,	Mr
DOIG,	David
DOUGLAS,	Andrew
DOUGLAS,	Archibald
DOUGLAS,	William
DOWIE,	David
DRUMMOND,	Patrick
DUFF,	John
DUFF,	Miss
DUN,	William
DUNBAR,	George
DUNDAS, THOMAS & CO.	
DUNDAS,	Thomas
DUNSMUIR,	George
DUNSMUIR,	John
DUNSMUIR,	Mrs
EAGLE,	Archibald
EDMONSTONE,	Alexander
ESPLINE,	Charles
FAIRHOLM, ADAM & CO.	
FAIRHOLM,	Adam
FAIRHOLM,	Thomas
FARQUHAR,	James
FERGUSON,	John
FETTES,	John
FIFE,	James
FIFE,	John
FINLAY,	John
FINLAYSON,	Duncan
FISH,	John
FISHER,	Charles
FLINT,	James
FORDYCE,	John
FORREST,	John
FORRESTER,	Robert
FORTHERINGHAM,	Isobell
FYFE,	James
GALLATLY,	William
GARDINER,	Mrs
GILLESPIE,	James
GORDON,	John
GOVAN,	Stephen
GRAHAME,	David
GRAHAME,	David
GRANT,	Alexander
GRANT,	James
GRAY,	George
GRAY,	Mrs
GREENLEES,	Robert
GREIG,	Robert
GREIRSON,	James
GRIEVE,	John
HALLYBURTON,	John
HAMILTON & BRUCE	
HAMILTON,	Mr
HAMILTON,	Mrs
HAMILTON,	Robert
HARLEY,	Alexander
HART,	Archibald
HARVEY,	Florence
HATHORN,	Hugh
HEMPSEED,	John
HENDERSON,	Mrs
HENDERSON,	Patrick
HEPBURN,	Alexander
HILL,	Mrs
HOGG,	Alexander
HOGG,	James
HOGG,	James
HOGG,	Walter
HOGG,	William
HOME,	David
HOPE,	John
HUNTER,	Alexander
HUSBAND,	Paul
HUTCHISON,	James
HUTTON,	William
HUTTON,	William
INGLIS,	Claud
INGLIS,	David
INGLISH,	Miss
IRELAND,	Mrs
JACK,	George
JAMESON,	Andrew
JAMESON,	John
JARDINE,	Mrs
JARVIE,	Thomas
JOHNSTONE,	Jean
JOHNSTONE,	Robert
JOHNSTONE,	Thomas
KAY,	Mrs
KELTIE,	Robert
KELTIE,	William
KEMPTIE,	Francis
KIDD,	James
KIDD,	John
KINNEIR,	Robert
KINNEIR,	Thomas
KIRKLAND,	James
KIRKLAND,	Mrs
LAING,	Mrs
LAUDER,	Mrs
LAWRENCE,	Simon
LEARMONTH,	Alexander
LESSLIE,	Charles
LINDSAY,	Alexander
LITHGOW,	James
LITHGOW,	Robert
LORIMER,	James
LOTHIAN,	John
LUMSDEN & ROBERTSON	
MCALISTER,	Mathew
MCCONACHIE,	William
MCCOULL & WATSON	
MCCOULL,	Archibald
MCCULLOCH & TOD	
MCCULLOCH,	William
MCDOUGALL,	James
MCDOUGALL,	James
MCDOWALL,	William

MERCHANTS—*Continued*

McGhie,	William
McGibbon,	James
McGlashan,	John
McGlashan,	Miss
McGrogan,	Thomas
McHardie,	John
McIntosh,	Mrs
McKain,	John
MKcKain,	James
McKechnie,	William
McKeltope,	James
McNab,	John
McNiven,	John
Mackie,	George
Mair,	Thomas
Manderson,	Patrick
Manners,	Alexander
Majoribanks,	Andrew
Marshall,	Francis
Martin,	John
Martin,	Thomas
Masson,	James
Mein,	William
Menzies,	Mrs
Michie,	William
Millar,	Benjamin
Millar,	Catherine
Millar,	George
Milligan,	John
Milroy,	James
Mitchell,	Anna
Mitchell,	William
Mitchellhill,	Robert
Moir,	John
Moir,	John
More,	George
More, John & Co.	
Mosman,	John
Moubray,	John
Murray,	James
Murray, Miss & Kidd	
Murray,	Patrick
Naismith,	Mrs
Nevay,	David
Nevay,	David
Nicoll,	George
Nisbet,	John
Noble,	Alexander
Noble,	Robert
Ogilvie,	Malcolm
Osburn,	John
Paterson,	David
Paterson,	George
Paton,	Thomas
Patullo,	John
Pillans,	Miss
Pitcairn,	George
Pitcairn,	George
Pringle,	Robert
Purdie,	Mr
Pringle,	Robert
Purdie,	Thomas
Purvis,	Alexander
Ramage,	John
Ramsay,	James
Rannie,	Andrew
Rannie, Miss & Wood	
Rannie,	Thomas
Reid & Chalmers	
Reid,	Mr
Reid,	Mrs
Reid,	Mrs
Renton,	Mrs
Richardson,	John
Ritchie,	Alexander
Robert,	Anna
Robertson,	Alexander
Robertson,	Alexander
Robertson,	Gilbert
Robertson,	James
Robertson,	Miss
Ronaldson,	John
Ross,	Charles
Ross,	Daniel
Ross, Miss & Paton	
Ross,	Patrick
Russell,	James
Russell,	Robert
Rutherford,	Samuel
Sanders,	Richard
Sandilands,	Mark
Schaw,	Miss
Scott,	Alexander
Scott,	Alexander
Scott,	David
Scott,	Elizabeth
Scott,	James
Scott,	Robert
Scott,	Walter
Scott,	William
Scott,	William
Scougall & Wake	
Selkirk,	Robert
Seton,	James
Seton,	Patrick
Shearer,	Archibald
Shiels,	Archibald
Smellie,	James
Smith,	Gilbert
Smith,	George
Smith,	William
Smith,	William
Somervail,	Andrew
Somervail,	Andrew
Somervail,	David
Somervail,	Mr
Staig,	John
Steel,	James
Stevenson,	Roger
Stewart & Scott	
Stewart,	Archibald
Stewart,	Archibald
Stewart,	James
Stewart,	John
Stewart,	Mrs
Stewart,	Robert
Stirling,	Alexander
Stirling,	James

MERCHANTS—Continued

Stirling,	John	
Stonehouse,	John	
Sutherland,	Alexander	
Swan,	Mrs	
Sword,	John	
Syme,	Andrew	
Taylor,	John	
Taylor,	John	
Taylor,	William	
Thomson,	James	
Thomson,	Jean	
Thomson,	Jean	
Thomson,	Miss	
Thomson,	Robert	
Tod,	Oliver	
Tod,	Patrick	
Tod,	William jr.	
Trotter,	Thomas	
Trotter,	Thomas jr.	
Veitch,	Robert	
Veitch,	Robert	
Walker,	Andrew	
Wallace,	Archibald	
Wardrope,	Andrew	
Wardrope,	Mary	
Wardrope,	Miss	
Watson,	Robert jr.	
Waugh,	James	
Webster,	Elizabeth	
Wight,	Robert	
Wilkie,	James	
Williamson,	Robert	
Willson,	Alexander	
Willson,	John	
Wotherspoon,	Mrs	
Wright,	David	
Young,	James	
Young,	John	
Young,	Mrs	
Younger,	John	
Yourstone,	Miss	

MILLINERS

Including HABERDASHERS, HOSIERS, MANTUA MAKERS

Aikman,	Isobel	Ale Sellers
Aikman,	Margaret	Ale Seller
Auchenleck,	Mrs	
Baillie,	William	Hosier
Balderstone,	Misses	
Bowie,	Patrick	Haberdasher
Cheeslie,	Mrs	Mantua Maker
Geddes,	Miss	
Glass,	Helen	Mantua Maker
Johnstone,	Mrs	
Kelso,	Mrs	
McRabbie,	Miss	
Montgomery,	Mrs	
Murray,	William	Haberdasher
Mutter,	Miss	
Piper,	Mrs	
Porteous,	Mrs	Mantua Maker
Ramsay,	Misses	
Robertson,	Miss	
Robertson,	Miss	
Rutherford,	John	
Stirling,	Miss	Mantua Maker
Thomson,	Miss	Mantua Maker
Wemyss,	Miss	Mantua Maker
Willson,	Misses	

MIDWIVES	: See Doctors
MUSICAL INSTRUMENTS	: See Musicians

MUSICIANS

Bremner,	Robert	Musical Inst.
McPherson,	Mr	
Reoch,	John	
Stewart,	Alexander	
Stewart,	John	

OPTICIANS

Barclay,	William

PAINTERS

Including LIMNERS

Alexander,	John	Limner
Allan,	James	
Bonnar,	Mr & Mrs	
Boswall,	Alexander	
Campbell,	Duncan	
Guthrie,	Alexander	Limner
Medina,	John	Limner
Millar,	Alexander	
Millar,	James	
Norrie,	James	Paint & Dye Mcht.
Norrie,	Mrs	
Norrie,	Robert	
Robertson & MacFarquhar		
Rose,	Mr	
Somervail,	Nicol	
Spence,	William	
Syme,	Alexander	
Watson,	George	

PEWTERERS	: See Hammermen
POULTRYMEN	: See Fleshers
PRINTERS	: See Booksellers

SADDLERS

Anderson,	Thomas	
Boswall,	George	
Brown,	Malcolm	
Clelland,	Thomas	
Gordon,	James	
Graham,	William	
Smith,	John	Ale Seller

SEEDSMEN

Drummond,	Andrew
Drummond,	Patrick
Eagle,	Archibald
Hamilton,	Mrs
Tod, Mutter & Co.	

(Gentlemen's) SERVANTS

Anderson,	James	
Bonsie,	James	
Brown,	William	
Buchan,	Duncan	Ale Seller
Campbell,	Alexander	
Campbell,	Alexander	
Campbell,	John	
Crawford,	William	
Davidson,	William	
Dunbar,	William	
Finlayson,	James	
Fisher,	Mr	
Fraser,	William	
Grieve,	John	
Houston,	John	
Johns,	John	
Lawrie,	Thomas	
Mathie,	Thomas	
Mirrie,	Mr	
Montgomery,	David	
Montgomery,	Walter	
Morgan,	John	
Murray,	Mr	
Murray,	Robert	
Nicolson,	John	
Ormiston,	Wm.	
Philip,	John	
Pringle,	Mr	
Reid,	John	
Robertson,	Duncan	
Robertson,	William	
Stewart,	Hugh	Ale Seller
Stewart,	John	
Stewart,	Thomas	
Wright,	Hendry	

SHOEMAKERS: See Cordiners

SKINNERS

Including: FURRIERS, GLOVERS, TANNERS

Aiton,	Walter	Glover/Perfumer
Barclay,	John	
Braid,	John	Glover
Brown,	James	Glover
Brown,	Robert	Furrier
Callander,	John	Glover
Dalgleish,	John	Hangman
Donaldson,	Robt.	Glover

SKINNERS (Cont.)

Fairholm,	John	Furrier
Galloway,	James	Furrier
Givan,	Alexander	Glover
Hill,	John	
Hill,	Thomas	Tanner
Jameson,	Thomas	Furrier/Glover
Kinloch,	Robert	Furrier
Kinloch,	Robert	Glover
Lindsay,	John	
Lothian,	James	
Mitchell,	William	Furrier
Morrison,	James	Glover
Murray,	Deacon	
Murray,	Robert	
Ogilvie,	Alexander	
Ogilvie,	Malcolm	
Porteous,	Nathan	Glover
Pringle,	Deacon	
Pringle,	John	Furrier
Scotland,	John	
Scott,	David	Glover
Simpson,	Archibald	
Simpson,	Charles	
Smith,	James	Glover
Syme,	David	Furrier
Thomson,	James	Furrier
Thomson,	James	Glover
Watson,	Adam	Tanner

SMITHS

Aitken,	George	
Balfour,	William	
Begbie,	George	Locksmith
Bell,	Edward	
Donald,	Thomas	
Douglas,	John	Armourer
Erskine,	Alex.	
Herriot,	William	Gunsmith
Lethem,	Thomas	
Robertson,	David	
Robertson,	Mr	
Sibbald,	Thomas	Locksmith
Thomson,	Alex	Gunsmith
Willson,	James	

SPIRIT MERCHANTS: See Vintners

STABLERS

Including: CARRIERS, COWFEEDERS, FARRIERS, GRASS-SELLERS, HORSE HIRERS, PORTERS

Aitchison,	James	
Alstone,	James	
Barr,	Robert	Ale Seller
Begbie,	Charles	

STABLERS—Continued

Bell,	John	
Bell,	John	
Black,	William	Ale Seller
Boggie,	James	Ale Seller
Bowie,	John	
Braidwood,	John	
Brown,	Charles	
Campbell,	Charles	Horse Hirer
Clark,	Alexander	Ale Seller
Corse,	James	
Dunbar,	James	
Duncanson,	Thomas	
Elliott,	Widow	
Ferrier,	David	
Fyfe,	Patrick	
Galloway,	Alex.	Ale Seller
Gilbert,	James	Cowfeeder/ Ale Seller
Goldie,	Thomas	Carrier/ Ale Seller
Gordon,	John	
Hamilton,	Charles	
Irvine,	Thomas	
Johnstone,	Andrew	
Kennedy,	James	Horse Hirer
Linton,	John	Cowfeeder/ Ale Seller
Lithgow,	Agnes	Grass Seller
Marshall,	David	Porter
Millar,	John	Porter
Muir,	William	Ale Seller
Murray,	David	
Nicholson,	Thomas	
Old,	Mrs	
Orr,	John	
Paul,	Alexander	Ale Seller
Paxton,	John	Coachman
Ramsay,	Samuel	
Rannie,	William	
Richardson,	Wm.	Farrier
Scott,	Thomas	
Sharp,	John	
Walker,	John	
Williamson,	Alex	
Young,	John	Horse Hirer

STATIONERS: See Booksellers
SURGEONS : See Doctors
TAVERNS : See Vintners

TAYLORS

Anderson,	Robert
Anderson,	Thomas
Barclay,	Robert
Bowman,	William
Brown,	Robert
Campbell,	John
Chalmers,	William
Hamilton,	George
Harley,	Mr

McPherson,	Angus	
Moodie,	James	
Paterson,	Hugh	
Paterson,	James	
Ramsay,	Robert	
Reid,	William	
Robertson,	Thomas	
Sibbald,	William	
Sinclair,	Alexander	
Syme,	James	
Thomson,	Alex	
Warrock,	John	
Wood,	James	

TEACHERS

Anderson,	Mr	
Bartram,	Mr	
Beat,	David	Writing Master
Benazeck,	Mme.	French
Collie,	John	
Cossor,	Walter	Writing Master
Cuming,	Mrs	Boarding School
D'Effrene,	Mlle.	Dancing
Dewar,	Robert	Writing Master
Downie,	John	Dancing
Espline, (Mrs Laurence)	Mary	Boarding School
Forbes,	Mr	
Grant,	Rev. Mr	
Hamilton,	Mrs	
Hogg,	Thomas	Schoolmaster
Home,	John	
Lamotte,	Mrs	Dancing
Laurence, (Espline Mary)	Mrs	Boarding School
Lawson,	William	
LeBlanc,	Mme.	Boarding School
Lees,	John	
Lowrie,	Mr	Schoolmaster
McFarlane,	Mr	Schoolmaster
McKellar,	Patrick	Writing Master
McClure,	John	Writing Master
McQueen,	Mr	Schoolmaster
Michon & Stewart		French
Mundell,	James	
Murdoch,	John	
Paterson,	George	
Picard,	Mr.	Fencing
Quesinot,	John	French
Rae,	John	
Reid,	Mr	Schoolmaster
Richmond,	John	
Robson,	William	
Sandum,	Andrew	Fencing
Simpson,	James	
Stirling,	John	
Thomas,	Godfrey	Mathematics
Warden,	John	
Warden,	Mrs	
Young,	Sarah	

TOBACCONISTS

BELL,	Mrs	
CRAIG,	Charles	
GILLESPIE,	James	
LINDSAY,	James	
THOMSON,	James	
WILLSON,	Mrs	Vintner

TRUNK MAKERS

BLYTH,	Robert
DUNCAN,	Robert
NICOLL,	James
NICOLL,	James
WOOD,	Robert

UNIVERSITY

ALSTONE,	Dr. Chas.	Botany
GOLDIE,	Prof.	
MCFAIT,	Dr.	Mathematics
MCKENZIE,	Kenneth	Civil Law
MCKAY,	Charles	History
ROBERTSON,	Prof. Chas.	
ROBERTSON,	Jas. Prof.	Hebrew
STEUART,	Prof. John	Natural Philosophy
STEVENSON,	Prof.	
STEWART,	Prof. Matthew	Mathematics
WISHART,	Wm. D.D.	Principal

UPHOLSTERERS

Including FUNERAL UNDERTAKERS

BRUCE,	Alexander	
CADDEL,	James	Ale Seller
COUPER,	Mrs	
LAWSON,	George	
ROSS,	Daniel	
SAUNEY,	William	
SCHAW,	John	
YOUNG & TROTTER		
YOUNG, TROTTER & CADDEL		Funeral Undertakers

VINTNERS

Including: COFFEEHOUSE & TAVERN KEEPERS, SPIRIT DEALERS

ALEXANDER,	Chris.	
ARTHUR,	Patrick	British Coffee Hse.
AUCHENLECK,	David	
BALFOUR,	James	Coffee House
BLAIR,	Patrick	John's Coffee House
CLARK,	Robert	
CLELLAND,	Peter	
DICK,	Alexander	
GARDINER,	Fanny	Ale Seller
GIBB,	Robert	
GOW,	Robert	
GOW,	Gilbert	
GOW,	Mrs	
GRAY,	Mrs	
GREIG,	David	
HENDERSON,	Alex.	
HOWBOISE,	Mr	Ale Seller
HUNTER,	Archibald	
JOHNSTONE,	Richard	
LESSLIE,	Alexander	
LIVINGSTONE,	Geo.	
LOCH,	John	Hamilton's Coffee Hse.
LYON,	David	
MCCORMICK,	Samuel	New Inn
MCGREGOR,	Mrs	
MCKENZIE,	Alex.	Ale Seller
MCKENZIE,	Mrs	
MCKENZIE,	Richard	
MCPHAIL,	Hector	
MOODIE,	Alexander	
MOORE,	Thomas	
OGLE,	Mary	Exchange Coffee Hse.
OSWALD,	John	
RAMSAY,	Peter	Red Lion Inn
ROBERTSON,	John	
SANDERS,	Mrs	
SHANKS,	James	Spirit & Ale Seller
SHARP,	John	White Hart
MCCORMICK,	Samuel	New Inn
SKED,	John	
STEADMAN,	James	
STRATON,	Mrs	
SYME,	Robert	L'm kt. Coffee House
THOMSON,	Mrs	Duke's Head Tavern
THOMSON,	Walter	,,
WALKER,	John	
WALKER,	Mrs	Tavern in Advocates Close
WALKER,	Richard	
WALL,	Alexander	
WATSON,	John	
WILLSON	George	
WILLSON,	Mrs	Tobacconist
WYLIE,	David	

WATCHMAKERS

BROWN,	Mrs
BROWN,	Samuel
COWAN,	James
DALGLEISH,	James
DALGLEISH,	John
DICKIE,	Andrew

WATCHMAKERS—Continued

Geddes,	James
Nicoll,	William
Steel,	John

WAULKERS

Including: HATTERS, LINT DRESSERS

Anderson,	David	
Duncan,	Alexander	
Duncan,	Patrick	
Duncan,	Peter	
Haiggs,	Colin	Lint Dresser
McDowall,	James	
Morrison,	William	Hatter
Nimmo,	Mr	Lint Dresser
Phin,	Robert	
Smeiton,	Joseph	
Somervail,	Mr	Lint Merchant
Willson,	Andrew	

WEAVERS: See Websters

WEBSTERS

Including: WEAVERS

Bower,	Alexander	Weaver
Brown,	James	Weaver
Clark,	James	Weaver
Couper,	Mr	Weaver
Cumming,	James	Weaver
Dickson,	Robert	
Fairlie,	Patrick	
Fairlie,	Patrick jr.	
Lawson,	Patrick	Weaver
Mathie,	John	Weaver
Newton,	Hugh	
Nisbet,	Alexander	Weaver
Oliphant,	Mr	Weaver
Skeen,	Andrew	Weaver
Stark,	David	Weaver
Thomson,	Wm.	
Wotherspoon,	Jas.	Weaver

WHEELWRIGHTS: See Wrights

WIGMAKERS

Including: BARBERS & HAIR MERCHANTS

Aitken,	John	
Anderson,	Adam	
Bell,	Alexander	
Brown,	Lawrence	
Clark,	David	Ale Seller
Dale,	John	
Dick,	Mr	Hair Merchant
Dunbar,	William	Barber
Gowan,	James	
Grahame,	David	Barber
Grahame,	Mrs	
Hay,	John	
Jaffrey,	Francis	
Johnstone,	Wm.	
McFarlane,	James	
McFarquhar,	Mr	
Menzies,	Alex.	
Morrison,	John	Ale Seller
Morrison,	Robert	
Moubray,	John	Hair Merchant
Murray,	Andrew	
Noble,	Alexander	Hair Merchant
Orr,	John	
Robertson,	Colin	
Rutherford,	Wm.	Hair Merchant
Shinbow,	John	
Stewart,	James	Barber
Stewart,	John	
Thomson,	Charles	
White,	James	
White,	James	
White,	William	
Winter,	George	
Young,	James	Hair Merchant

WRIGHTS

Including: COACHMAKERS, GILDERS, GLAZIERS MASONS & WHEELWRIGHTS

Aitken,	William	
Alison,	Colin	
Allan,	James	Wright
Alstone,	David	Glazier
Angus,	James	
Anthonius,	John	
Auld,	William	
Baillie,	Thomas	
Bairnsfather,	Geo.	Plumber
Ballantyne,	James	Wheelwright
Balderstone,	Thos.	Wheelwright
Beasey,	George	Bucklemaker
Bell,	Mr	Engraver
Black,	William	
Boswall,	David	Glazier
Brodie,	Francis	Cabinet Maker
Brown,	James	
Bruce,	Charles	Glazier
Burns,	James	
Burton,	Alexander	Glazier
Butter,	Charles	
Campbell,	George	[Factor]
Clark,	John	Glazier
Clark,	Mr	Mason
Cochrane,	John	Mason
Cowan,	George	
Couden,	Robert	
Dallas,	William	
David,	Mr	
Dewar,	Robert	Glazier
Dick,	James	Mason
Dickson,	Alex.	Glazier
Douglas,	Alex.	

WRIGHTS—Continued

Dowie,	David	Mason
Finlay,	Daniel	
Finlay,	David	
Finlay,	William	Glassgrinder
Garden,	James	
Gibson,	Mr	Slater
Gill,	Baillie	Glazier
Goldman,	John	Turner
Good,	Andrew	
Good,	William	
Govan,	William	Glazier
Hardie,	James	
Hay,	Alexander	
Herriot,	James	
Home,	Robert	
Howison,	Charles	
Hue,	Michael	Gilder
Hunter,	James	
Hutton,	James	Brushmaker
Hutton,	John	Brushmaker
Inglis,	Hugh	
Inglis,	Thomas	
Innes,	Andrew	
Jameson,	Deacon	Mason
Kay,	James	
Kendall,	Mr	Slater
Lamb,	George	
Lamb,	John	
Lancashire,	Mr	Coachmaker
McVey,	William	
Mack,	John	Mason
Mein,	John	Slater
Millar,	Andrew	Wheelwright
Mitchell,	John	
Moffat,	William	Glassgrinder
Montgomery,	John	
Moodie,	Alex.	
Moubray,	John	Mason
Murray,	John	Glassgrinder
Mylne,	William	Mason
Neilsen,	John	Glassgrinder
Neilsen,	Samuel	Mason
Nicoll,	John	
Nicolson,	Alex.	Mason
Nisbet,	James	Wheelwright
Nisbet,	Mr	Manufacturer
Peacock,	John	Glazier
Peters,	Alexander	
Pringle,	Alexander	
Raeburn,	Andrew	
Reoch,	William	
Richie,	Thomas	Glazier
Riddle,	George	
Ronaldson,	James	Glazier
Scott,	John	Plumber
Scott,	Mungo	Glazier
Shore,	John	Whipmaker
Stevenson,	George	
Stewart,	Alexander	Billiard Tables
Sutor,	John	
Syme,	George	Slater
Syme,	James	Slater
Tait,	James	
Veitch,	James	Glazier
Watson,	John	Slater
Wills,	Andrew	
Wright,	James	
Wright,	James	
Yetts,	John	

WRITERS

Including: ADVOCATES, CLERKS, SECRETARIES WRITERS TO SIGNET. ACCOMPTANTS.

Alison,	Robert	
Alstone,	William	W.S.
Alves,	Andrew	W.S.
Alves,	Thomas	
Anderson,	David	W.S.
Anderson,	Mr	
Armour,	James	W.S.
Ayton,	William	
Baillie,	David	Secy. Royal Bank
Baillie,	Thomas	W.S.
Belches,	John	Clerk: Ed. Turnpike Rds.
Binning,	Charles	Advocate
Blair,	Archibald	
Boswall,	George	
Boswell,	Thomas	
Bowie,	John	Clerk
Boyes,	Thomas	
Brodie,	Thomas	W.S.
Bruce,	David	
Bruce,	Thomas	
Budge,	William	W.S.
Burnet,	Andrew	W.S.
Campbell,	Archibald	W.S.
Carmichael,	James	W.S.
Chalmers,	Alexander	
Chalmers,	Andrew	
Chalmers,	George	W.S.
Clapperton,	Alex.	Writer's Clerk
Craig,	John	Clerk to Presbytery
Craigie,	Lawrence	W.S.
Craigie,	Robert	Advocate
Crawford,	Hew	W.S.
Cunningham,	Alex.	W.S.
Davidson,	John	W.S.
Deuchar,	Andrew	
Dick,	Robert	
Dickie,	John sr.	W.S.
Douglas,	Robert	
Dow,	John	
Elliot,	William	
Ewart;	James	Accomptant
Farquharson,	Francis	Accomptant
Ferguson,	Walter	
Forbes,	William	W.S.
Fordice,	Thomas	
Forrester,	James	
Fraser,	William	W.S.
Fyfe,	John	
Gibson,	Thomas	W.S.

WRITERS—*Continued*

GLASS,	Mr	
GOLDIE,	Alex.	W.S.
GRAHAME,	Hugh	
GRAHAME,	James	W.S.
GRANT,	Ludovic	
GRANT,	Robert	W.S.
GREIG,	Mr	
GUILD,	Mr	
GUTHRIE,	Charles	
GUTHRIE,	Harry	
HALDEN,	Patrick	H.M. Solicitor
HAY,	James	W.S.
HAY,	John	
HILL,	William	Clerk
HOUSTON,	John	
HUME,	Alexander	H.M. Advocate Dep.
INNES,	Alexander	
IRVING,	Robert	W.S.
JACKSON,	Gideon	W.S.
JUSTICE & KIRPATRICK		Session Clerks
KENNEDY,	David	Advocate
KERR,	Mr	
LESSLIE,	James jr.	
LINDSAY,	David	
LOCH,	William	
MCARTHUR,	John	
MCCLELLAN,	Robt.	Clerk, Ed. Shipping Co.
MCCONACHIE,	Alex.	
MCGHIE,	William	
MCGOWAN,	John	W.S.
MCINTOSH,	Alex.	
MCINTOSH,	Mr	
MCKENZIE,	Mr	
MCLEOD,	Roderick	W.S.
MCMILLAN,	Alex.	W.S.
MANUEL,	Hugh	
MITCHELSON,	Sam.	W.S.
MOLLISON,	John	Commissary Office
MONCREIF,	David	Sec'y to Exchequer
MOSMAN,	Hugh	
MUNRO,	Albert	Treasurer Heriot's Hospital
NAPIER,	Gabriel	
ORAM,	Alexander	
ORAM,	David	
ORR,	Alexander	
PRINGLE,	John	W.S.
PURVIS,	James	W.S.
REID,	Robert	W.S.
REOCH,	James	Procurator
RICHARDSON,	Geo.	
ROBERTSON,	Alex.	W.S.
ROBERTSON,	John	
ROBERTSON,	Thomas	
ROBERTSON,	William	
ROSS,	William	Sec'y SPCK
RUSSELL,	John	W.S.
RUTHERFORD,	Edw.	
SCOTT,	James	W.S.
SCOTT,	James	
SCOTT,	Walter	W.S.
SCRYMGEOUR,	Henry	W.S.
SELLER,	William	
SIGLUR,	George	
SINCLAIR,	John	
SINCLAIR,	John	
SMITH,	James	
SMITH,	James	
SMITH,	Thomas	Clerk: London Sun & Fire Ins.
SPENCE,	James	Clerk: Bank of Scotland
STEVENSON,	Alex.	W.S.
STEWART,	Alex.	
STEWART,	Arch.	W.S.
STOBIE,	John	[Factor]
TAIT,	Alexander	
TAYLOR,	George H.	[Factor]
TAYLOR,	James	W.s.
TOD,	Thomas	
TURNBULL,	George	W.S.
TYRIE,	John	
WALKER,	john	
WALKER,	William	
WATSON,	John	W.S.
WATSON,	William	
WATSON,	William	W.S.
WHITE,	Alexander	
WHITE,	John	Dep. Clerk of Session
WILLIAMSON,	Walter	
WILLSON,	John	Admiralty Office
WILLSON,	William	W.S.
WOOD,	James	
YOUNG,	John	

(b) APPRENTICES & MASTERS

APPRENTICE		MASTER		TRADE	47	48	49	50	51	52
Aberdour,	Alexander	**Smith,**	William	Founder	×					
Adam,	Alexander	**Syme,**	George	Sclater			×			
Adniston,	James	**Lindsay,**	Patrick	Weaver					×	
Aitken,	John	**Steel,**	John	Watchmaker				×		
Allan,	James	**Campbell,**	Alexander	Brewer						×
Anderson,	David	**Haig,**	William	Baxter	×					
Anderson,	George	**Scott,**	Walter	Merchant				×		
Anderson,	James	**Learmonth,**	Alex. & John	Tanners		×				
Anderson,	William	**Anderson,**	Adam	Wigmaker		×				
Andrew,	James	**Smith,**	Gilbert	Merchant					×	
Auld,	William	**Hamilton & Balfour**		Merchant						×
Baird,	Cessford	**Kennedy,**	John	Surgeon	×					
Baird,	Thomas	**Howison,**	Charles	Wright			×			
Balderstoun,	James	**Balderston,**	Alexander	Skinner				×		
Ballantyne,	James	**Govan,**	William	Glazier				×		
Barclay,	Alexander	**Oliphant,**	Robert	Hatter	×					
Barclay,	James	**Robertson,**	David	Locksmith				×		
Bartleman,	George	**Murray,**	Adam	Baxter		×				
Bartleman,	John	**Thomson,**	Charles	Wright					×	
Bayne,	John	**Scott,**	James & Partner						×	
Bayne,	William	**Wilson,**	James	Locksmith	×					
Begbie,	Charles	**Bruce,**	Alexander	Upholsterer			×			
Bell,	John	**Hamilton,**	Hugh	Merchant		×				
Bennet,	William	**Halley,**	James	Goldsmith	×					
Binnie,	Alexander	**Dickie,**	Andrew	Watchmaker	×					
Blacklaw,	James	**Robertson,**	Patrick	Goldsmith						×
Blair,	Thomas	**Blair,**	Gilbert	Wigmaker		×				
Blane,	Archibald	**Hamilton,**	Hugh	Merchant					×	
Blenchall,	Baillie	**Brown,**	Malcolm	Saddler			×			
Blyth,	George	**Drummond,**	George	White Iron Smith						×
Bogie,	William	**Clerk,**	John	Goldsmith						×
Boog,	James	**1. Aitken,**	George	Smith				×		
		2. Dallas,	William	Wright						
Booth,	David	**Dickson,**	Robert	Weaver	×					
Booth,	Robert	**Stewart,**	John	Wigmaker	×					
Borthwick,	William	**Drummond,**	Patrick	Merchant						×
Brand,	Andrew	**Boswall,**	George	Saddler	×					
Brown,	Andrew	**1. Brown,**	Alexander							
		2. Hepburn,	Thomas	Merchants					×	
Brown,	John	**Steile,**	Hugh	Wigmaker					×	
Brown,	William	**Johnston,**	James	Merchant	×					
Brown,	William	**Paterson,**	John	Merchant			×			
Bruce,	Alexander	**Lothian,**	Edward	Goldsmith	×					
Bruce,	John	**Anderson,**	Adam	Pewterer				×		
Buchanan,	Dougall	**Duncan,**	Peter	Waulker				×		
Calder,	Walter	**Learmonth,**	Alex. & John	Hatter					×	
Caldwell,	James	**Henderson,**	Thomas	Founder					×	
Cameron,	Francis	**Miller,**	John	Hatter					×	
Carnegie,	Robert	**Dickson,**	Charles	Goldsmith	×					
Cochran,	John	**Aitchison,**	Alexander	Goldsmith						×
Cockburn,	James	**Cleghorn & Wilson**		Merchants			×			
Cockburn,	John	**Gilliland,**	James	Goldsmith	×					
Colville,	Robert	**Yair,**	John	Bookseller	×					
Corsar,	Thomas	**Porteous,**	Nathan	Skinner				×		
Coventrie,	John	**Jameson,**	John	Merchant	×					
Coverley,	William	**Monson,**	Robert	Wigmaker						×
Cowie,	Charles	**Auld,**	William	Smith						×
Craw,	James	**Bonar,**	Andrew	Merchant				×		
Crichtoun,	William	**Ged,**	Dougal	Goldsmith						×
Crombie,	Thomas	**Fairholm,**	John	Skinner	×					

102

APPRENTICE		MASTER		TRADE	47	48	49	50	51	52
Cum(m)ing,	James	Norie,	Robert & co.	Painters	X					
Cunningham,	John	Scotland,	James	Skinner		X				
Cunningham,	John	Brown,	James	Weaver			X			
Cunningham,	Walter	Currie,	Andrew	Weaver		X				
Dalgleish,	James	Grant,	James	Merchant			X			
Dalrymple,	John	Angus,	Archibald	Merchant		X				
Davie,	Adam	Davie,	William	Goldsmith						X
Dick,	Charles	Dickson,	Charles	Goldsmith			X			
Dick,	William	Thomson,	James	Merchant		X				
Dickieson,	Hector	Govan,	Stephen	Merchant					X	
Dickson,	John	Stevenson,	Alexander	Candlemaker				X		
Doak,	James	Dundas,	Ralph	Merchant				X		
Dollas,	John	Norie,	James	Painter	X					
Dorrach,	Patrick	Wilson,	William	Cordiner				X		
Douglas,	Alexander	Yourstone,	James	Cutler		X				
Douglas,	Archibald	Brown,	James	Weaver			X			
Douglas,	John	Oliphant,	Robert	Hatter				X		
Douglas,	Robert	Brown,	James	Weaver	X					
Douglas,	William	Rutherford,	James	Goldsmith		X				
Douglas,	William	Wemyss,	James	Goldsmith		X				
Drummond,	William	Richardson,	Archibald	Bookbinder		X				
Duff,	John	Reikie,	Thomas	Glazier	X					
Duncan,	Andrew	Sime,	Andrew	Cooper	X					
Duncan,	Robert									
Edmond,	John	Wemyss,	James	Goldsmith						X
Edward,	William	Hunter,	Alexander	Merchant	X					
Farquharson,	Alexander	Dalgleish,	John	Watchmaker				X		
Farquharson,	Thomas	Boswall,	George	Saddler		X				
Ferm,	James	Anderson,	Adam	Wigmaker						X
Finny,	John	Hill,	John	Skinner		X				
Finny,	Thomas	Simpson,	Charles	Skinner						X
Fleming,	William	Miller,	James	Merchant				X		
Fletcher,	Walter	Sibbald,	Thomas	Locksmith					X	
Fleucart,	William	Steel,	James	Merchant					X	
Gairdner,	George	Stirling,	James	Merchant		X				
Gairdner,	John	Paton,	Thomas	Bookbinder					X	
Gibson,	George	Burton,	James	Tanner		X				
Gilchrist,	Walter	Brown,	John	Merchant		X				
Gilchrist,	William	Scott,	David	Skinner	X					
Gloag,	John	Watson,	James	Merchant	X					
Gordon,	Lewis	Drysdale,	Alexander	Coppersmith				X		
Gordon,	Thomas	Gordon,	Patrick	Watchmaker		X				
Grant,	James	Chalmers,	George	Merchant					X	
Gray,	Andrew	Grant,	Thomas	Bowmaker					X	
Gray,	John	Williamson & Fish		Merchants				X		
Gray,	William	Daes,	William	Waulker	X					
Greig,	David	Low,	Robert	Goldsmith	X					
Greig,	John	Greig,	Andrew	Flesher						X
Greirson,	Robert	Richardson,	William	Locksmith					X	
Greive,	John	Selkirk,	Robert	Merchant				X		
Grindlay,	John	Archibald,	James	Tanner						X
Hagart,	James	Drummond,	Robert	Wigmaker					X	
Halkerston,	John	Yourstone,	James	Cutler	X					
Hally,	William	Wood,	William	Surgeon						X
Hardie,	James	Brown,	Alexander	Upholsterer						X
Hay,	Andrew	Hamilton,	John	Cordiner	X					
Hay,	John	Chalmers,	George	Merchant					X	
Hay,	Patrick	Antonius,	Henry	Wright	X					
Henderson,	John	Brown & Henderson		Merchants						X
Henderson,	Thomas	Donald,	Thomas	Smith						X

APPRENTICE		MASTER		TRADE	47	48	49	50	51	52
Henderson,	William	Doig,	David & Co.	Merchants					x	
Hepburn,	Francis	Stuart & Wallace		Merchants				x		
Hepburn,	John	Pitcairn,	George	Merchant						x
Honeyman,	James	Bonar,	Andrew	Merchant					x	
Hood,	Frederick	Murray,	James	Merchant					x	
Hunter,	George	Gilchrist,	Robert	Cooper	x					
Hunter,	James	Bowie,	Archibald	Merchant	x					
Hutton,	Robert	Cumming,	William	Merchant				x		
Jaffrey,	William	Ayton,	William	Goldsmith					x	
Jameson,	Richard	Drysdale,	John	Shoemaker				x		
Jameson,	Robert	Tod,	William jr.	Merchant					x	
Johnston,	John	1. Hamilton,	Gavin							
		2. Balfour,	John	Printers					x	
		3. McNeil,	Patrick							
Keddie,	Andrew	Kendell,	William	Slater						x
Keddie,	Thomas	Espline,	John	Tanner				x		
Kennedy,	Alexander	Syme,	Andrew	Cooper						x
Ker(r),	Archibald	Chalmers,	William	Merchant	x					
Ker(r),	William	Oliphant,	Laurence	Goldsmith					x	
Ker(r),	William	Grieve,	John	Merchant						x
Kid,	James	Lorimer,	James	Merchant	x					
Lamb,	George	Boog,	Robert	Cutler			x			
Law,	John	Eagle,	Archibald	Merchant	x					
Lawrie,	John	Hunter,	Robert	Cordiner	x					
Lawrie,	Thomas	Gairdner,	Thomas							x
Leishman,	Alexander	Tait,	James	Wright						x
Leitch,	Patrick	Robertson,	Robert	Wright	x					
Leslie,	Walter	Dale,	John	Barber	x					
Lind,	James	Fraser,	Simon	White Iron smith	x					
Lindsay,	Henry	Lindsay,	Patrick	Merchant					x	
Lindsay,	John	Blair,	James	Skinner	x					
Lindsay,	Theodore	Orr,	John	Wigmaker				x		
Logan,	Malcolm	Casson,	William	Tanner			x			
Lumsdain,	Charles	Gordon,	James	Saddler				x		
Lyon,	Andrew	Brand,	John	Merchant						x
McCall,	Duff	Scott,	Mungo	Glazier				x		
McCall,	James	Gardener,	William	Candlemaker	x					
McDonald,	Archibald	Fairbairn,	Alexander	Locksmith					x	
McDonald,	Donald	McCallister,	Mathew	Merchant		x				
McFarquhar,	John	Murray,	George	Cordiner		x				
McIlwrath,	James	Purvis,	Alexander	Merchant		x				
McKenzie,	Alexander	Moir,	John	Merchant		x				
McKenzie,	Francis	Dalgleish,	John	Watchmaker						x
McLean,	Lauchlan	McKenzie,	James	Goldsmith						x
McLeish,	John	Cleland,	Thomas	Saddler	x					
McMichan,	Murray	McMichan,	John	Merchant					x	
McQueen,	Duncan	Auchinleck,	James	White Iron Smith					x	
Malice,	Andrew	Williamson,	James	Flesher					x	
Malice,	George	Cumming,	James	Flesher				x		
Marshall,	James	Brown,	Laurence	Wigmaker					x	
Martin,	James	Milne,	John	Founder	x					
Maxwell,	William	Dalgleish,	John	Watchmaker		x				
Meikle,	George	Crawford,	Gideon	Bookseller		x				
Merrilees,	Andrew	Wilson,	James	Locksmith					x	
Miller,	James	Porteous,	Nathan	Skinner					x	
Miller,	John	Baillie & Seton		Merchants					x	
Miller,	Robert	Scott,	Robert	Merchant						x
Milne,	David	Paterson,	Robert	Merchant	x					
Milne,	Thomas	Douglas,	Andrew	Merchant						x
Mitchell,	James	Forrester,	George	White Iron Smith		x				

APPRENTICE		MASTER		TRADE	47	48	49	50	51	52
Muirhead,	Robert	More,	John	Bookbinder			X			
Murray,	James	Gifford,	Thomas	Smith	X					
Neill,	Alexander	Grant,	Alexander	Merchant						X
Neill,	John	Armstrong,	William	Coppersmith					X	
Nicolson,	Alexander	Nicolson,	Alexander	Plumber			X			
Nimmo,	Thomas	Ferguson,	James	Coppersmith					X	
Notman,	Alexander	Learmonth,	Alex. & John	Tanners	X					
Oliphant,	Charles	Davidson,	Walter	Saddler	X					
Oliphant,	James	Low,	Robert	Goldsmith					X	
Oswald,	William	Ruddiman,	Walter & Thomas	Printers	X					
Park,	John	Pollock,	Richard	Baxter			X			
Paterson,	James	Herriot,	James	Wright					X	
Paterson,	Moses	Easton,	Alexander	Cordiner	X					
Paton,	Alexander	Edmonston,	Alexander	Goldsmith					X	
Pearson,	William	Crooks,	William	Baxter				X		
Philp,	William	Thomson,	James	Wigmaker				X		
Pillans,	James	Stevenson,	Alexander	Merchant					X	
Plenderleith,	William	Eccles,	Martin	Surgeon	X					
Purdie,	James	McVey,	William	Wright	X					
Purves,	Robert	Monson,	Robert	Wigmaker				X		
Rae,	George	Le Conte,	Noel	Merchant				X		
Ramage,	Benjamin	Watkins,	Adam	H.M. Printer						X
Ramage,	John	Skowler,	William	Tanner & Currier			X			
Ramsay,	James	Andrew,	Simon	Slater	X					
Rattray,	Alexander	Henderson,	Patrick	Merchant	X					
Reddie,	Thomas	Gairdner,	William	Candlemaker					X	
Reid,	Alexander	Lothian,	Edward	Goldsmith				X		
Reid,	James	Davie,	William	Goldsmith				X		
Reid,	William	Cleugh,	Alexander	Skinner				X		
Richardson,	James	Gibson,	James	Sclater	X					
Richardson,	James	McKenzie,	Kenneth	Goldsmith						X
Richardson,	Richard	Richardson,	William	Baxter	X					
Riddell,	Thomas	Newtoun,	Andrew	Weaver						X
Ritchie,	Alexander	Mitchell,	William	Skinner						X
Robertson,	Alexander	Drysdale,	John	Cordiner	X					
Robertson,	Charles	Norrie,	James & Co.	Painters					X	
Robertson,	Ebenezer	Lumsden,	Thomas	Printer					X	
Robertson,	John	Lumsden,	Thomas	Printer						X
Robertson,	William	Cockburn,	Andrew	White Iron Smith			X			
Ross,	David	Troup,	James	Weaver	X					
Ross,	John	McKay,	James	Coppersmith					X	
Roust,	Alexander	Spence,	William	Painter					X	
Roy,	Peter	Stirling,	Alexander	Merchant	X					
Runciman,	Alexander	Norrie,	Robert & Co.	Painter					X	
Runciman,	William	Lawson,	Patrick	Weaver	X					
Ruthven,	William	Hog,	William & Son	Merchants						X
Sanders,	Archibald	Dempster,	William	Goldsmith						X
Sanderson,	Thomas	Douglas & Lindsay		Merchants			X			
Scobie,	John	Gibson,	Archibald	Cordiner					X	
Scot(t),	George	Ruddiman,	Walter & Thos.	Printers					X	
Scot(t),	James	Herriot,	John	Candlemaker				X		
Scot(t),	John	Burns & Finlayson		Merchants				X		
Scot(t),	Robert	Stephenson,	Alexander	Merchant	X					
Scot(t),	William	Douglas,	William	Merchant	X					
Scot(t),	William	Scott,	Walter	Merchant					X	
Scotland,	John	Gray,	William	Bookbinder					X	
Sheriff,	David	Dickson,	Alexander	Smith					X	
Simpson,	Robert	Inglis,	Claude	Merchant						X

APPRENTICE		MASTER		TRADE	Indenture Year					
					47	48	49	50	51	52
Sloas,	David	1. Hamilton,	Gavin							
		2. Balfour,	John	Printers					×	
		3. Neill,	Patrick							
Smith,	Thomas	Lawson,	Patrick	Weaver				×		
Smiton,	George	Baillie & Seton		Merchants				×		
Somervail,	Samuel	Allan,	Robert	Baxter						×
Spalding,	James	Caithness,	Edward	Merchant					×	
Sprot,	Thomas	Sprot,	John	Candlemaker					×	
Stark,	Alexander	Callendar & Hamilton		Merchants					×	
Steill,	Alexander	Grant,	Alexander	Merchant						×
Stevenson,	Alexander	Young,	James	Bookbinder	×					
Stewart,	James	Chalmers,	George	Merchant	×					
Stirling,	John	McKenzie,	James	Goldsmith				×		
Stod(d)art,	Adam	Stenhouse,	John	Merchant		×				
Stod(d)art,	James	Hunter,	Alexander	Merchant						×
Stod(d)art,	John	Rankin,	Andrew	Coppersmith						×
Stod(d)art,	Robert	Cargil,	Patrick	Cutler			×			
Straiton,	John	Graham,	Samuel	Bookbinder					×	
Swinton,	Robert	Gairdner,	Thos. & William	Merchants		×				
Tait,	Benjamin	Aitchison,	Alexander	Goldsmith	×					
Thomson,	Alexander	Simpson,	Thomas	Pewterer	×					
Thomson,	Alexander	Brown,	John	Merchant					×	
Thomson,	Francis	Dunsmuir,	John	Merchant	×					
Thomson,	John	Thomson,	James	Skinner						×
Thomson,	Michael	Mitchell & Douglas		Grocers				×		
Torrance,	William	Allan,	John	Baxter					×	
Vogil,	John	Dickson,	Charles	Goldsmith	×					
Walker,	Alexander	Eagle,	Archibald	Merchant						×
Wallace,	Richard	Cleghorn,	Thomas	Cooper					×	
Wardrope,	David	Wallace,	John	Surgeon	×					
Warrock,	James	Setton,	James jr.	Merchant	×					
Watson,	David	Butter,	Charles	Merchant				×		
Watson,	James	Reoch,	John	Painter	×					
Watson,	Thomas	Boswell,	David	Glazier	×					
Watt,	William	Murray,	William	Candlemaker				×		
Weir,	Alexander	Miller,	James	Painter	×					
Weir,	David	Cleghorn & Livingstone		Merchants					×	
Welsh,	John	Somervale,	John	Merchant					×	
White,	Charles	Watkine,	Charles	Wigmaker					×	
White,	John	Blyth,	John	Weaver	×					
Wight,	John	Bell,	John	Baxter					×	
Wilson,	John	Richardson,	William	Smith	×					
Wilson,	John	Robertson,	David	Locksmith						×
Wilson,	Robert	Bonar,	Andrew	Merchant	×					
Wilson,	Robert	Brown,	James	Weaver				×		
Wilson,	Thomas	Moubray,	John	Wright					×	
Wilson,	William	Peacock,	Robert	Baxter				×		
Young,	Gilbert	Campbell,	Colin	Bookbinder	×					
Young,	Thomas	Yair,	John	Bookseller					×	
Young,	Thomas	Grant,	James	Merchant					×	
Yule,	Alexander	Heriot,	William	Gunsmith					×	
Yule,	Benajmin	Smith,	Alexander	Baxter				×		
Yule,	William	Hog,	William & Thos.	Merchants	×					
Zeigler,	Alexander	Campbell,	Alexander	Goldsmith	×					

Total Indentured Apprentices

'46	'47	'48	'49	'50	'51	'53	
0*	65	45	42	49	46	39	= 286

* Following Jacobite Occupation there existed no City Council to approve indentures.

STREET GUIDE AND MAPS

STREET GUIDE AND MAPS

Street	Postion	Tax Bound	Key Map Reference	Edgar's Map 1742	Directory Page
ADAM'S LAND	Cowgate South	5	61		71
ADVOCATE'S CLOSE	High Street North	2	37	13	61
AINSLIE'S LAND	High Street North	6	51		73
ALLAN'S CLOSE	High Street North	2	44	21	63
ANCHOR CLOSE	High Street North	3	47	24	63
ANDERSON'S CLOSE	West Bow South	8	17		80&81
ANDERSON'S LAND	West Bow South	8	17		80
ANDERSON'S 2ND LAND	West Bow South	8	17		80
ANDERSON'S LAND	Fishmarket Close	7	44		75
ARGYLE SQUARE		7nw	40		79
BAILLIE FYFE'S CLOSE	High Street North	3	62	42	66
BAILLIE'S LAND	Cowgate North	8	20		81
BAIN & JOLLY'S LAND	Cowgate North	5	64		71
BAIRD'S LAND	Castlehill South	1	13		58
(NEW) BANK CLOSE	High Street North	3	51		64
BANK CLOSE	Lawnmarket South	8	25		79
BARRINGER'S	Netherbow North	4	65	45	66
BELL'S WYND	High Street South	6	52	72	73
BESS WYND	Lawnmarket	7	31	63	77
BLACK TURNPIKE	High Street South	6	53		73
BLACKFRIAR'S WYND	High Street South	5	65	83	69
BLAIR'S LAND	Castlehill South	1			58
BLYTH'S LAND	Castlehill North	1	18		59
BORTHWICK'S CLOSE	High Street South	6	45	67	74
BRAND'S LAND	Castlehill South	1	17		58
BROWNHILL'S LAND	Cowgate North	5	63		71
BROWN'S LAND	Lawnmarket North	2	33		61
+ BROWN'S LAND	Luckenbooths	7			77
BRUCE'S LAND	Grassmarket South	8	4		82
BULL'S CLOSE	High Street North	3	55	33	64
BURNETT'S CLOSE	High Street South	6	50	71	73
BURN'S LAND	Lawnmarket South	7	27		77
BYRE'S CLOSE	Lawnmarket North	2	34	12	61
CAMPBELL'S LAND	New Stairs	7	36		76
CAMPBELL'S LAND	Grassmarket South	8	1		82
CAMPBELL'S LAND	Castlehill North	1	17		59
CAMPBELL'S LAND	Bell's Wynd	6	52		73
CAMPBELL'S LAND & BREWERY	Argylle Square	7nw	40		79
CANDLEMAKER ROW		7nw	28		79&81
CANTORE CLOSE	High Street North	2	35		62
CANT'S CLOSE	High Street	5	62	81	70
CAP & FEATHER CLOSE	High Street North	3	58	36	65
CARNWATH'S COURT	Niddry's Wynd	6	59	78	71
CARRUBER'S CLOSE	High Street North	3	60	38	65
CASTLEHILL		1	9-19		58
CHALMER'S LAND	Bell's Wynd	6	52	72	73
CHALMER'S LAND	Candlemaker Row	7nw	29		79
CLAMSHELL TURNPIKE	High Street South	6	51		73
CLEGHORN'S LAND	Grassmarket South	8	2		82
CLERK'S LAND	West Bow/Castlehill	1	16		58
COCKBURN'S LAND	Lawnmarket South	7	32		77
COLLEGE	Colledge Wynd	6	54		74
COLLEDGE WYND	Cowgate South	6	47	69	74
COMISTON'S LAND	Cowgate South	7nw	40		79
CON'S CLOSE	High Street South	6	47	69	74
COVENANT CLOSE	High Street South	6	48	70	73
COWGATE NORTH			14		
SOUTH			75		

Street	Position	Tac Bound	Key Map Reference	Edgar's Map 1742	Directory Page
CRAIGLEITH COURT	Peebles Wynd	6	56	76	72
CRAIG'S CLOSE	High Street North	3	45	22	63
CRAMOND'S LAND	West Bow	1	15		58
CRAWFORD'S ROAD	Colledge Wynd	6	52		74
CRICHTON'S LAND	West Bow	1	15		58
CROCKETT'S LAND	West Bow Foot	1	10		58
CULLEN'S CLOSE	Lawnmarket South	8	24	55	80
CUMMING'S LAND	Fishmarket Close	7	44	65	75
CURRIE'S LAND	Castlehill South	1	14	52	58
CUSTOM HOUSE STAIRS	Parliament Close	7	39		76
DALRYMPLE'S LAND	Castlehill North	1	19		59
DEUCHAR'S LAND	Forrester's Wynd	7	30	61	77
DEWAR'S LAND	Grassmarket East	8	13		80
DICKSON'S CLOSE	High Street	5	61	80	70
DICKSON'S 2ND LAND	Libberton's Wynd	7	29	59	78
DON'S CLOSE	High Street North	2	39	15	62
DOUGLAS LANE	Forrester's Wynd	7	30	61	77
EASTON'S LAND	Netherbow South	5			69
ERSKINE'S LAND	Netherbow South	5	75		68
EXCHANGE STAIRS	Parliament Close	7	36		76
FAIRHOLM'S LAND	West Bow	1	14		58
FISHER'S CLOSE	Lawnmarket South	8	23	54	80
FISHMARKET CLOSE	High Street South	7	44	65	75
FLESHMARKET CLOSE	High Street North	3	54	31	64
FLINT'S LAND	Grassmarket South	8	9		82
FORRESTER'S WYND	High Street South	7	30	61	77
(NORTH) FOULIS CLOSE	High Street North	3	50	27	64
FOULIS CLOSE	Netherbow South	5	71	89	68
FOULIS' LAND	Castlehill South	1	18		58
FOULIS' LAND	Forrester's Wynd	7	30	61	77
FOUNTAIN CLOSE	Netherbow South	5	72	90	68
GAIRN'S LAND	Grassmarket South	8	11		82
GALLOWAY'S CLOSE	Lawnmarket, North	2	22		61
GAVINLOCK'S LAND	Forrester's Wynd	7	30	61	77
GEDDES CLOSE	High Street North	3	49	26	64
GLADSTONE'S LAND	Lawnmarket North	2	22		59
GOOD TOWN'S LAND	Society	7nw	30		79
GOOD'S LAND	Cowgate South	6	53		74
GOSFORD'S CLOSE	Lawnmarket South	7	26	58	78
GOUDILOCK'S LAND	Lawnmarket North	2	32	10	61
GRASSMARKET NORTH			1		
SOUTH			11		
GRAY'S CLOSE	High Street South	5	69	87	68
GRIERSON'S LAND	Cowgate North	6	45		
HALKERSTON'S WYND	High Street North	3	59	37	65
HALLYBURTON'S LAND	Cowgate South	7nw	19		81
HAMILTON'S LAND	Cowgate North	8	21		
HAMILTON'S LAND	Grassmarket South	8	5		82
HASTIE'S CLOSE	Cowgate South	6	56	95	74
HATHORN'S LAND	Cowgate North	5	62		70
HAY'S LAND	Grassmarket South	8	10		82
HELLISTOB'S LAND	Cowgate South	6	59		
HERIOT'S WARK BRIDGE	Grassmarket South	8	6		82
HERIOT'S LAND	Grassmarket South	8	8		82
HIGH SCHOOL YARDS	Cowgate South	5	65-75		71
HIGH SCHOOL WYND		5	66	97	71

Street	Position	Tax Bound	Key Map Reference	Edgar's Map 1742	Directory Page
HIGH STREET NORTH			36		
SOUTH			63		
HORSE WYND	Cowgate South	6	45		75
HYNDFORD'S CLOSE	Netherbow South	5	70	88	68
INFIRMARY	High School Yards	5	64		71
JACKSON'S CLOSE	High Street North	3	53	30	64
JAMES COURT	Lawnmarket North	1	21		59
JOLLY'S LAND	Castlehill North	1	14		59
JOLLY'S LAND	High Street South	6	49		73
KENNEDY'S LAND	Castlehill South	1	19		58
KENNEDY'S CLOSE	High Street South	6	55	75	72
KINLOCH'S CLOSE	High Street North	3	60		66
KINLOCH'S CLOSE	High Street South	5	60	79	70
LABORATORY	Colledge Wynd	6	54		74
LADY STAIR'S CLOSE	Lawnmarket North	2	23	1	60
LAWNMARKET NORTH			20		59
SOUTH			35		
LIBBERTON'S WYND	Lawnmarket	7	29	59	78
LINDSAY'S LAND	West Bow	1	19		58
LITHGOW'S LAND	Grassmarket North	1	4		57
LUCKENBOOTHS	Lawnmarket East	7	38		76
LYON'S CLOSE	High Street North	3	52	29	64
MCGOWAN'S LAND	Lawnmarket South	7	33		77
MCLENAN'S LAND	Cowgate North	8	18		81
MAGDALEN'S LAND	High Street South	6	56		73
MARLIN'S WYND	High Street South	6	58	77	72
MARY KING'S CLOSE	High Street North	2	58	77	62
MENZIE'S LAND	Castlehill North	1	12		58
MILNE SQUARE	High Street North	3	56	34	65
MILNE'S COURT	Lawnmarket North	1	20		59
MILNE'S LAND	Cowgate North	7	40		76
MIRTLE'S LAND	Cowgate South	7nw	41		79
MOFFAT'S LAND	West Bow	1	12		57
MONTEITH'S CLOSE	High Street North	4	67	47	67
MONTGOMERY'S LAND	Niddry's Wynd	6	59	78	72
MORRISON'S LAND	West Bow	1	12		57
MURDOCH'S CLOSE	High Street South	5	67	85	69
NAISMITH'S LAND	Bell's Wynd	6	52	72	73
NAIRN'S LAND	Castlehill North	1	16		59
NEW ASSEMBLY CLOSE	High Street South	6	53	73	73
NEW BANK CLOSE		3	51		64
NEW LAND	High Street North	2	36		61
NEW STAIRS	Parliament Close	7	36		76
NIDDRY'S WYND	High Street South	6	59	78	71
OGILVIE'S LAND	Cowgate South	7nw	42		79
OLD ASSEMBLY CLOSE	High Street South	6	46	68	74
OLD POST HOUSE STAIRS	Marlin's Wynd	6	58	77	72
OLD POST OFFICE CLOSE	High Street North	3	46	23	63
PARLIAMENT CLOSE		7	34-43		76
PATERSON'S COURT	Lawnmarket North	2	26	4	60
PATERSON'S LAND	Grassmarket North	1	2		57
PEARSON'S CLOSE	High Street North	2	43	20	63
PEEBLES WYND	High Street South	6	56	76	72
PENCAITLAND'S LAND	Niddry's Wynd	6	59	78	72

Street	Position	Tax Bound	Key Map Reference	Edgar's Map 1742	Directory Page
PENSTON LETTERS LAND	Lawnmarket North	2	31	9	61
PETER'S LAND	Cowgate South	6	44		75
PIPE'S CLOSE	Castlehill North	1	11		58
PLAINSTONE CLOSE	Cowgate South	5	60		71
POST OFFICE STAIRS	Parliament Close	7	37		76
PRESIDENT'S CLOSE	Cowgate South	7nw	39		79
PRESIDENT'S STAIRS	Parliament Close	7	38		76
PROVOST STEWART'S LAND	West Bow	1	17		58
RANIE'S LAND	Grassmarket East	8	14		80
RIDDEL'S LAND	Con's Close	6	47	69	74
ROBERTSON'S CLOSE	Cowgate South	5	62	96	71
ROXBURGH'S CLOSE	High Street North	2	38		62
ROYSTON'S CLOSE	Lawnmarket South	8	22	53	80
SAMUEL'S LAND	Colledge Wynd	6	54		75
SANDILAND'S CLOSE	High Street North	4	66	46	67
SANDILAND'S LAND	Forrester's Wynd	7	30	61	77
SCOTT'S CLOSE	Cowgate South	7nw	36		79
SCOTT'S LAND	Cowgate North	8	19		81
SCOTT'S LAND	Plainstone Close	5	60		71
SIDESERF'S LAND	West Bow	8	15		80
SKINNER'S CLOSE	High Street South	5	68	86	69
SKINNER'S LAND	Castlehill North	1	13		59
SMITH'S LAND	High Street North	3	63	43	66
SMITH'S LAND	Niddry's Wynd	6	59	78	71
SOCIETY		7nw	28-35		79
SOMERVAIL'S LAND	Cowgate South	7nw			79
STARK'S LAND	Cowgate North	8	16		80
STEWART'S LAND	Candlemaker Row	8	22		81
STONELAW'S CLOSE	High Street South	6	54	74	73
SURGEON'S HALL	High School Yards	5	72		71
SWAN'S CLOSE	High Street North	3	48	25	64
SWINTON'S LAND	Forrester's Wynd	7	30	61	77
SYME'S LAND	High Street South				
TAYLOR'S LAND	Cowgate South	7nw	38		79
THOM'S LAND	Libberton's Wynd	7	29	59	78
THOMSON'S LAND	Grassmarket South	8	3		82
TODD'S LAND	High Street South				
TODD'S LAND	Cowgate South				
TODD'S LAND	Castlehill North	1	15		59
TODRICK'S WYND	High Street South	5	66	84	69
TRADES HOSPITAL LAND	Grassmarket North	1	7		57
TRUNK CLOSE	Netherbow North	4	68	48	67
TWEEDDALE'S COURT	Netherbow South	4	68	48	68
UNDER BAXTER'S CLOSE	Lawnmarket North	2	28	6	60
UPPER BAXTER'S CLOSE	Lawnmarket North	2	24	2	60
VEITCH'S LAND	West Bow	1	11		57
WARDROP'S LAND	Lawnmarket South	7	28		78
WARDROP'S COURT	Lawnmarket North	2	25	3	60
WARRENDER'S COURT	Niddry's Wynd	6	59	78	71
WARRISTON'S CLOSE	High Street North	2	40	16	62
WEST BOW			10		
			21		
WIGHT'S LAND	Cowgate South	8	26		81
WORLD'S END CLOSE	Netherbow South	5	74	92	68
WRITER'S COURT	High Street North	2	41	17	62

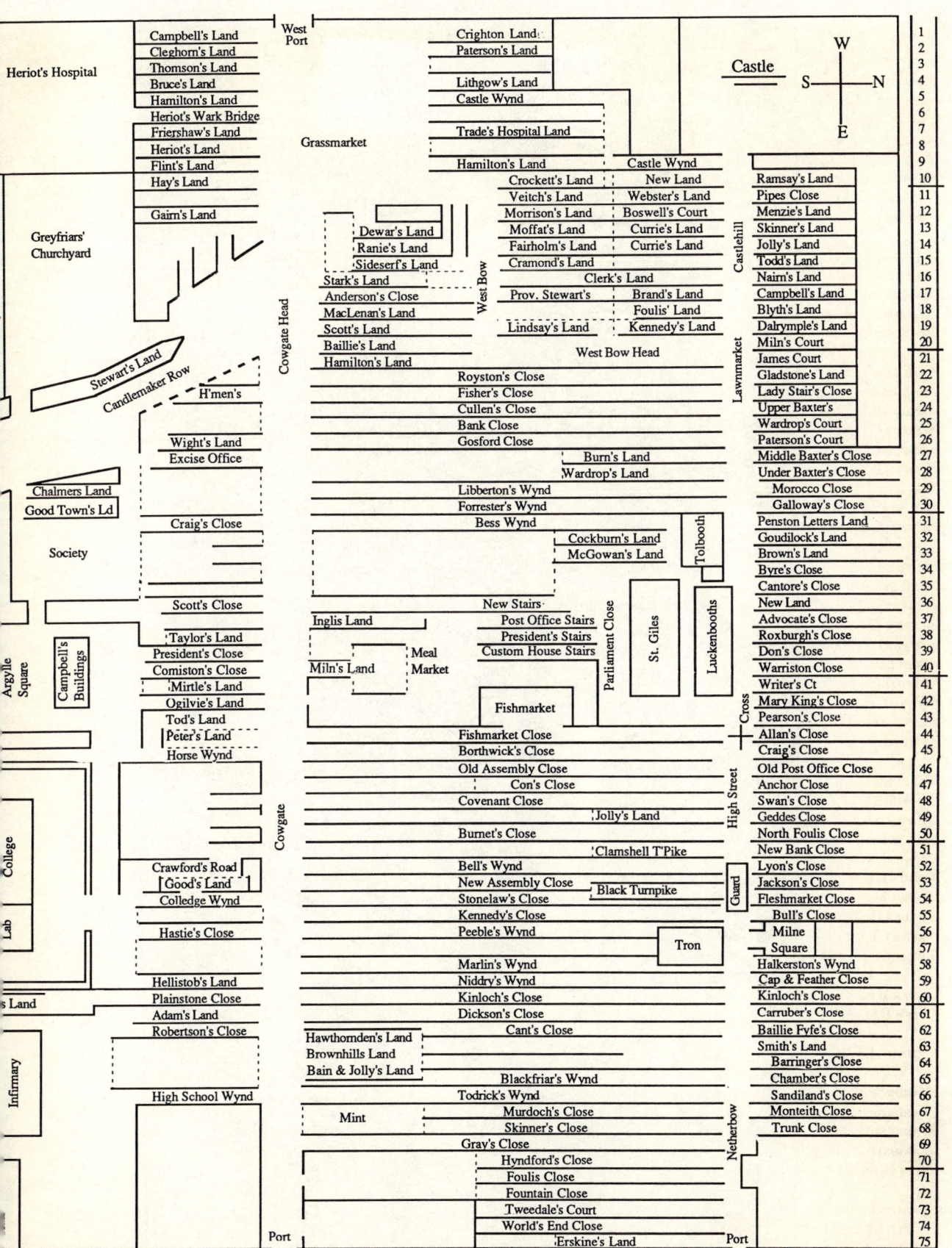

CHART OF EDINBURGH CLOSES

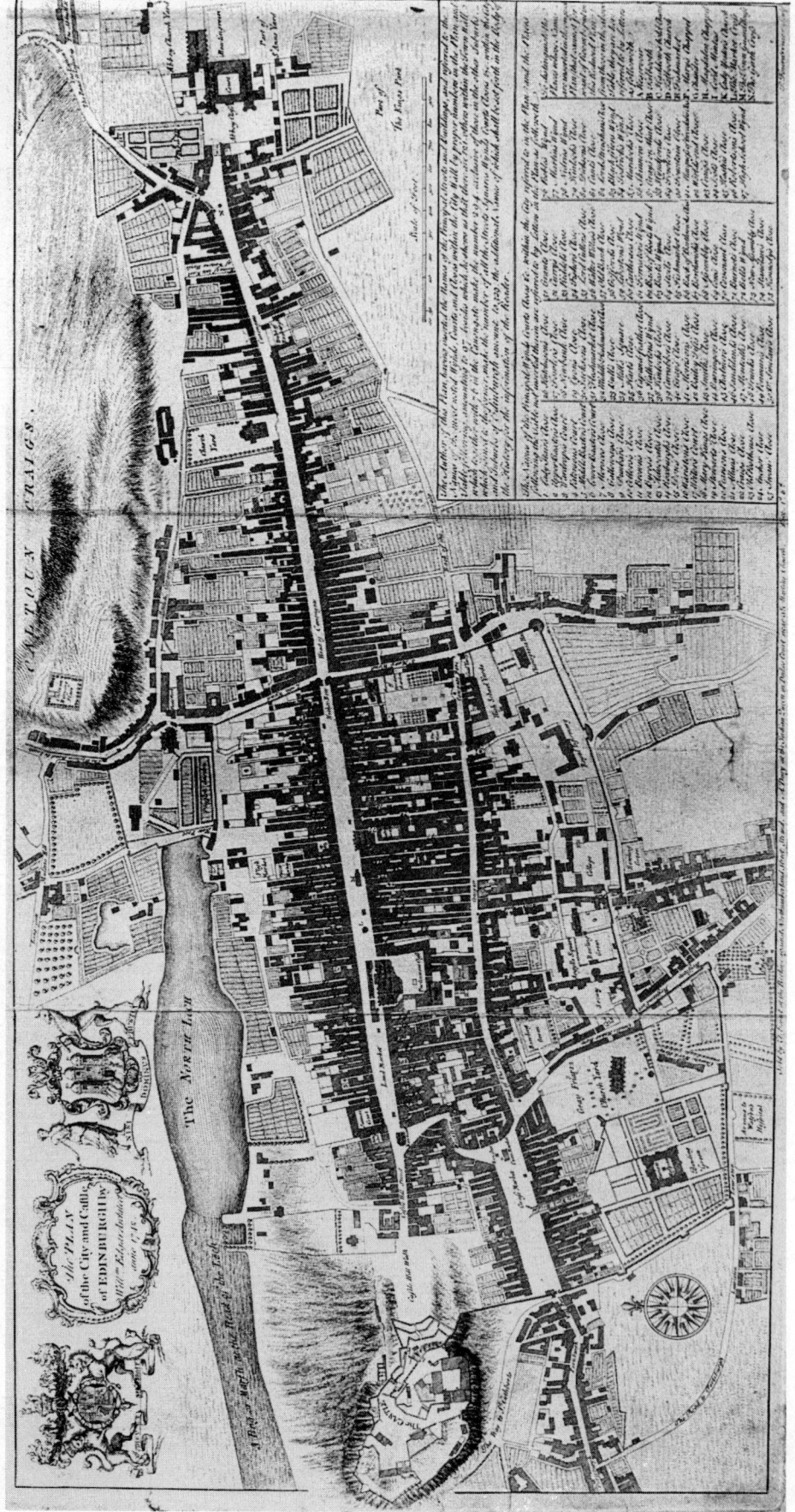

EDGAR'S MAP, 1746